Pioneering Perspectives in Cooperative Learning

Offering firsthand insights from the early originators of cooperative learning (CL), this volume documents the evolution of CL, illustrating its historical and contemporary research, and highlights the personal experiences that have helped inspire and ground this concept.

Each of the chapters in *Pioneering Perspectives in Cooperative Learning* foregrounds a key approach to CL and documents the experiences, research, and fruitful collaborations that have shaped and driven their development. Contributions are from leading scholars including Elliot Aronson, Neil Davidson, Spencer Kagan, David W. Johnson, Roger T. Johnson, Richard Schmuck, Yael Sharan, Shlomo Sharan, Robert E. Slavin, and Nancy A. Madden, as well as retrospective pieces on the work of Deutsch and Cohen. These chapters detail the historical development of cooperative learning, cooperation versus competition, and cover major approaches, including the jigsaw classroom, complex instruction, the learning together model, and several more. They include qualitative, personal, and retrospective accounts, whereby authors outline the research and theory that underpin each approach while highlighting practical strategies for classroom implementation.

This text will primarily be of interest to professors, researchers, scholars, and doctoral students with an interest in the theory of learning, educational research, and educational and social psychology more broadly. Practitioners of CL with an interest in varied forms of small-group learning and classroom practice, as well as those interested in the history and sociology of education, will also benefit from the volume.

Neil Davidson is Professor Emeritus of Teaching and Learning at the University of Maryland, USA.

Routledge Research in Education

This series aims to present the latest research from right across the field of education. It is not confined to any particular area or school of thought and seeks to provide coverage of a broad range of topics, theories and issues from around the world.

Recent titles in the series include:

Towards Rational Education
A Social Framework of Moral Values and Practices
Demetris Katsikis

Schooling and Social Change Since 1760
Creating Inequalities through Education
Roy Lowe

Pioneering Perspectives in Cooperative Learning
Theory, Research, and Classroom Practice for Diverse Approaches to CL
Edited by Neil Davidson

Activity Theory and Collaborative Intervention in Education
Expanding Learning in Japanese Schools and Communities
Edited by Katsuhiro Yamazumi

Developing Trauma-Responsive Approaches to Student Discipline
A Guide to Trauma-Informed Practice in PreK-12 Schools
Kirk Eggleston, Erinn J. Green, Shawn Abel, Stephanie Poe, and Charol Shakeshaft

Interculturality and the Political within Education
Fred Dervin and Ashley Simpson

For a complete list of titles in this series, please visit www.routledge.com/Routledge-Research-in-Education/book-series/SE0393

Pioneering Perspectives in Cooperative Learning

Theory, Research, and Classroom Practice for Diverse Approaches to CL

Edited by Neil Davidson

Routledge
Taylor & Francis Group
NEW YORK AND LONDON

First published 2021
by Routledge
52 Vanderbilt Avenue, New York, NY 10017

and by Routledge
2 Park Square, Milton Park, Abingdon, Oxon, OX14 4RN

Routledge is an imprint of the Taylor & Francis Group, an informa business

© 2021 Neil Davidson

The right of Neil Davidson to be identified as the author of the editorial material, and of the authors for their individual chapters, has been asserted in accordance with sections 77 and 78 of the Copyright, Designs and Patents Act 1988.

All rights reserved. No part of this book may be reprinted or reproduced or utilised in any form or by any electronic, mechanical, or other means, now known or hereafter invented, including photocopying and recording, or in any information storage or retrieval system, without permission in writing from the publishers.

Trademark notice: Product or corporate names may be trademarks or registered trademarks, and are used only for identification and explanation without intent to infringe.

Library of Congress Cataloging-in-Publication Data
A catalog record for this book has been requested

ISBN: 978-0-367-61835-3 (hbk)
ISBN: 978-1-003-10676-0 (ebk)
ISBN: 978-0-367-61836-0 (pbk)

Typeset in Sabon
by Apex CoVantage, LLC

I dedicate this book with love for my primary group:

My wife Jan

Our two daughters and their families:

Andrea, Charlie III, Charlie IV, and Alyssa

Megan, Bill, Ethan, and Caelan

And my brother Richard, whose motto is, "Single is a tingle!"

Contents

List of Figures	ix
List of Tables	x
Acknowledgments	xi
NEIL DAVIDSON	
About the Contributors	xii

1 Introduction to Pioneering Perspectives in Cooperative Learning — 1
NEIL DAVIDSON

2 The Legacy of Morton Deutsch: Theories of Cooperation, Conflict, and Justice — 17
LAURIE STEVAHN

3 Learning Together and Alone: The History of Our Involvement in Cooperative Learning — 44
DAVID W. JOHNSON AND ROGER T. JOHNSON

4 Complex Instruction for Diverse and Equitable Classrooms: In Loving Memory of Elizabeth G. Cohen — 63
RACHEL A. LOTAN AND NICOLE I. HOLTHUIS

5 The Structural Approach and Kagan Structures — 78
SPENCER KAGAN

6 Student Team Learning and Success for All: A Personal History and Overview — 128
ROBERT E. SLAVIN AND NANCY A. MADDEN

7	The Jigsaw Classroom: A Personal Odyssey Into A Systemic National Problem ELLIOT ARONSON	146
8	Design for Change: A Teacher Education Project for Cooperative Learning and Group Investigation in Israel YAEL SHARAN AND SHLOMO SHARAN	165
9	About Richard Schmuck's Contributions to the Study of Organization Development and Cooperation in Education RICHARD ARENDS, NEIL DAVIDSON, AND RICHARD SCHMUCK	183
10	Cooperative Learning in Mathematics and Beyond NEIL DAVIDSON	201
11	Synthesis of CL Approaches and a Multifaceted Rationale for CL—Past, Present, and Future NEIL DAVIDSON	234
	Index	256

Figures

1.1	*Mice in a Maze*	9
2.1	Deutsch's theory of cooperation and competition crosses goal interdependence (positive or negative) and actions (effective or bungling), creating different conditions (quadrants) that affect three social-psychological processes (substitutability, cathexis/attitudes, inducibility/influence)	28
2.2	Social interdependence theory posits that goal interdependence influences social interaction, which determines outcomes	30
2.3	Deutsch's theory of constructive conflict resolution posits that the relational orientation of disputants (cooperative or competitive) influences conflict processes (constructive or destructive) that affect resolution outcomes (mutual or exclusive)	34
3.1	Cycle of development of our cooperative learning procedures	48
3.2	Outcomes of cooperative learning	51
5.1	PIES: Basic principles of cooperative learning	82
5.2	Numbered Heads Together	84
5.3	Structure functions	87
5.4	Seven Keys to Success in the Structural Approach	92
5.5	Traditional versus Kagan Coaching™	103
5.6	Academic achievement gains with Kagan Structures	105
5.7	Kagan Structures yield gains	119
6.1	Integration of theoretical perspectives on cooperative learning effects on learning	135
11.1	PET scans of the brain	245
11.2	Research outcomes from using student energy and affiliative needs	246

Tables

3.1 Mean weighted effect sizes for impact of social
 interdependence on dependent variables 52
8.1 Stages of group investigation 168

Acknowledgments

Neil Davidson

I greatly acknowledge the help and inspiration of:

> David Bradford, who initiated me into small-group learning
> Donald Arnstine, who introduced me to Dewey's philosophy

The International Association for the Study of Cooperation in Education (IASCE), which had a profound influence on the research and development of cooperative learning, and on the creation of this book

Professional friends and colleagues who provided me with ideas, editorial help, and encouragement with this book:

Richard Arends, Elliot Aronson, Ron Berk, Richard Felder and Rebecca Brent, Jim Fey, Robyn Gillies, Barbara Millis, Yael Sharan, and Richard Solomon

My men's support group for the past 30 years:

Jim Greenberg, Jim Henkelman-Bahn, Herb Levitan, David Merkowitz, and me

My "Miracle Buddies," Dan Martin, Hardy Hasenfuss, and L. Darnell Williams

My wonderful Routledge editors: Elsbeth Wright and AnnaMary Goodall, for their expert guidance and enthusiastic support

Sathya Shree Kumar and the capable production team for their thorough and careful copy-editing and design

Contributors

Neil Davidson holds a doctorate combining mathematics and education from the University of Wisconsin, master's degrees in mathematics and in counseling, and an honorary doctorate in humane letters. Neil is Professor Emeritus of Teaching and Learning, University of Maryland. He did original work in developing small-group cooperative learning in mathematics in the 1960s, beginning with his dissertation on the "small-group discovery method." His publications encompass numerous articles, nine books, and half a dozen manuals or course handbooks. He has presented hundreds of seminars and workshops on various aspects of cooperative learning in mathematics and in general. He served as president of the IASCE for five years.

Richard Arends is a retired professor of educational leadership and dean emeritus of Connecticut State University, where for 13 years he served as Dean of the School of Education and Interim Provost and Vice President for Academic Affairs. The recipient of numerous awards, Arends has authored or contributed to over a dozen books on education, including Richard Schmuck and Philip Runkel's Second *Handbook of Organization Development in Schools* and *Learning to Teach*, the latter now in its tenth edition and translated in Portuguese, Spanish, Polish, Indonesian, and Chinese.

Elliot Aronson is a social psychologist and distinguished professor emeritus at the University of California Santa Cruz (UCSC). He has written or edited 22 books, including *The Social Animal* (now in its 12th edition), *The Jigsaw Classroom,* and *The Handbook of Social Psychology*. He is the only person in the 125-year history of the American Psychological Association to have received all three of its highest awards: for Distinguished Research, Distinguished Teaching, and Distinguished Writing. For his research on cooperative learning, he received the Gordon Allport prize for his "contributions to inter-racial harmony" and the Humanitarian Award from the Texas Classroom Teachers Association "for training countless teachers to use jigsaw."

Elizabeth G. Cohen (1932–2005) was Professor Emerita of Education with joint appointment in Sociology at Stanford University. In 1958, she was among the first group of women to earn a doctorate in sociology from Harvard. She was also the founding director of the Program for Complex Instruction. Her groundbreaking pedagogy applies sociological theory to promote racial, ethnic, social, and gender equity in the classroom. From the start of her career, Cohen had the conviction that theories of sociology have meaning for education. As such, she used sociological theories to champion academic success for all learners. She worked with teachers to create equitable instruction in heterogeneous classrooms by having students work cooperatively in small groups and teachers to recognize and value the different intellectual contributions that students make as they complete learning tasks. Cohen was a leader in the field of cooperative learning and the impact of her work is well-known and highly respected in the United States and internationally.

Morton Deutsch (1920–2017) is E. L. Thorndike Professor Emeritus and founder of the Morton Deutsch International Center for Cooperation and Conflict Resolution (MD-ICCCR) at Teachers College, Columbia University. An eminent social psychologist, Deutsch is one of the world's most respected scholars of conflict resolution, making monumental scientific contributions to understanding cooperation and competition, group dynamics, constructive conflict, distributive justice, and peace psychology.

Nicole I. Holthuis joined the Program for Complex Instruction at Stanford in 1990 as a graduate student and worked closely with Dr. Elizabeth G. Cohen, Dr. Rachel A. Lotan, and fellow graduate students for over 20 years. She has developed curriculum, supported teachers, conducted workshops, collected data, and published findings. She continues to work with teachers, schools, and districts as they engage in the process of understanding and implementing strategies for building equitable classroom.

David W. Johnson received his doctoral degree from Columbia University, is Emeritus Professor of Educational Psychology at the University of Minnesota, and is Co-director of the Cooperative Learning Center. He is a past editor of the *American Educational Research Journal*. He has authored over 600 research articles and book chapters and over 50 books. He has received awards from a variety of professional organizations.

Roger T. Johnson received his doctorate from the University of California in Berkeley, is Emeritus Professor of Education at the University of Minnesota, and is Co-director of the Cooperative Learning Center. He is a co-author of numerous publications with his brother David. He was a master teacher in the Harvard-Newton Intern Program, was a curriculum developer with the Elementary Science Study at Harvard University, and taught for three summers in the British Primary Schools at the University of Sussex, England.

Spencer Kagan is an internationally acclaimed researcher, presenter, and author. He has received honorary doctorates from two universities. Dr. Kagan is the principal author of the comprehensive books for educators in each of six fields: cooperative learning, brain-friendly teaching, emotion-friendly teaching, multiple intelligences, classroom discipline, and classroom energizers. His books are translated into many languages and have sold over a million copies.

Rachel A. Lotan is Professor Emerita at Stanford University's Graduate School of Education. She served as Director of the Stanford Teacher Education Program (STEP) from 1999 to 2014. Currently, she directs the Program for Complex Instruction at Stanford, where she continues to support research and dissemination of Complex Instruction. Since 2016, Dr. Lotan is Director of Theory, Practice, and Strategic Planning of Programa de Educação Docente Brasil, at the Stanford Lemann Center. In 2014, she published the third edition of *Designing Groupwork: Strategies for the Heterogeneous Classroom*, originally authored by E.G. Cohen.

Nancy A. Madden is the CEO of the Success for All Foundation, which develops, researches, and disseminates educational programs to increase achievement, particularly for disadvantaged students. She is also a professor at the Center for Research and Reform in Education at the School of Education at Johns Hopkins University.

Richard Schmuck, a social psychologist of education, is Professor Emeritus, University of Oregon, where he did research and development and taught for 32 years about cooperative educational procedures. During an active career of over 40 years, he taught hundreds of graduate students from most parts of the globe, and published 26 academic books and 199 journal articles. After he became 80 he printed a memoir, *Paths to Identity*, about his childhood and adolescence, where he described how and why he became a practical social psychologist.

Shlomo Sharan is Professor Emeritus of Educational Psychology at the School of Education, Tel Aviv University, Israel. He founded the International Association for the Study of Cooperation in Education. He has authored many books, research studies, and articles on cooperative learning, and on school organization and development.

Yael Sharan has developed, trained, and written about cooperative learning in general and in the intercultural classroom. She has conducted workshops for teachers, teacher trainers, and educational consultants in many countries, and is an expert in adapting cooperative learning to diverse groups and cultures.

Robert E. Slavin is currently Distinguished Professor and Director of the Center for Research and Reform in Education at Johns Hopkins University, and is a co-founder of the Success for All Foundation. He has authored or co-authored more than 300 articles and book chapters on such topics as cooperative learning, comprehensive school reform, ability grouping, school and classroom organization, desegregation, school-based vision care, research review, and evidence-based reform.

Laurie Stevahn holds a doctorate in educational psychology from the University of Minnesota and is Professor of Education at Seattle University. Cooperative foundations and constructive conflict ground her teaching, research, and publications on topics relevant to effective leadership, organizational learning, program evaluation, and social justice. Laurie's interactions with Morton Deutsch over the years, his publications and interviews, and stories shared by those who knew him well influenced her chapter in this volume on Mort's life and legacy.

Chapter 1

Introduction to Pioneering Perspectives in Cooperative Learning

Neil Davidson

The following famous quotations are by anthropologist Margaret Mead, who studied change processes in varied societies (in Keys, 1982, p. 79).

> *Never doubt that a small group of thoughtful, committed citizens can change the world; indeed, it's the only thing that ever has. Never believe that a few caring people can't change the world. For, indeed, that's all who ever have.*

A small group of such committed people emerged in the development of cooperative learning (CL). In this volume, we tell the stories of a dozen scholars who envisioned, introduced, and developed the notion of students learning together actively in cooperative small groups—to enjoy learning with peers, to engage in discussions of challenging and meaningful ideas, to develop skills in cooperation and teamwork, to learn more effectively, and to master not only basic facts and skills but also more complex thinking processes.

The small group of invited authors consists of those who made major contributions to the development of CL beginning in the 1960s or the early 1970s and continuing throughout their careers. Individually and collectively, these scholars have made a profound impact on the field of education in the latter half of the 20th century and continuing through the present. The living history of cooperative learning will emerge in part through the authors' reflections, and personal stories or anecdotes about their own work, starting from its beginnings and moving to the current state of the art and future impact on education.

Nature of the Book

The combined efforts in this volume provide a comprehensive description of the development of cooperative learning as viewed by its major contributors—the originators, pioneers, developers, and leaders in the field. The chapters in the book therefore consider all of the major approaches and methods of cooperative learning.

The primary purpose of this comprehensive volume is to clearly present each of these CL approaches together with their theoretical foundations, research base, and classroom procedures. The most recent comprehensive book on CL (Sharan, 1994, 1999) is now more than 20 years old, and the field has changed considerably since its publication.

A secondary purpose of this book is historical. The historical development of cooperative learning will emerge in part through the authors' reflections, and personal stories or anecdotes about their own work, starting from its beginnings and moving forward from there. There has not been any prior book on the history of cooperative learning. This volume partly fills that gap in a unique way through qualitative, personal retrospective accounts by the pioneers of CL, and it provides an opportunity for each of us to take a retrospective look at our life work with cooperative small-group learning over a period of about 50 years.

Guidelines for chapter authors were presented right at the beginning of this project. Here is a small sample of those guidelines. In reflecting on your career, a chapter can deal with your own personal journey with CL, your philosophy and motivation for beginning this work, and who or what inspired you. Additional "self-reflection" questions to consider are as follows: What ideas or concepts were foundational to you? How did you get started? How successful were your first attempts? What helped you through the rough spots? How did your work change or evolve over time?

This volume is more than historical because it offers for the first time a progression from the past to the present state-of-the art knowledge in theory, research, and practice, to building a strong case for the successful future development, implementation, and impact of CL.

This volume sets forth perspectives on the following issues in the field:

> How is cooperative learning defined?
> What are the major approaches to cooperative learning?
> What are the common elements of all the approaches?
> Which attributes distinguish one approach from another?
> What are the state-of-the art classroom practices with each approach?
> What are the theoretical foundations for each approach?
> What is the research base for each approach?
> How are cooperative learning and collaborative learning related?

The Pioneering Scholars and Their Topics (Abbreviated Titles)

The alphabetical lineup of pioneering scholars and abbreviated topic titles includes:

Elliot Aronson: Jigsaw
Elizabeth Cohen (written by Rachel A. Lotan and Nicole I. Holthuis): Building equitable classrooms via Complex Instruction
Neil Davidson: Cooperative learning in mathematics and beyond
Morton Deutsch (written by Laurie Stevahn): Theories of cooperation, conflict, and justice
David W. Johnson and Roger T. Johnson: Learning together model and constructive controversy
Spencer Kagan: Structural approach
Richard Schmuck: Small-group processes and organization development (with co-authors Richard Arends and Neil Davidson)
Yael Sharan and Shlomo Sharan: Design for change: a teacher education project for cooperative learning and group investigation
Robert E. Slavin and Nancy A. Madden: Student Team Learning and Success for All (SFA)

Rachel Hertz-Lazarowitz was also a pioneering scholar in group investigation. References to her work are included in the Sharans' chapter.

Overview of Small-Group Learning: Cooperative, Collaborative, Problem-Based, and Team-Based Learning

Let us place cooperative learning in a larger context. In the past few decades, many educators have moved toward instructional approaches in which students are active participants in the learning process. Among the most-often used approaches to stimulate active learning in the classroom is small-group work. Early efforts at group-based, active learning have led to more defined pedagogies of cooperative and collaborative learning (Barnes & Todd, 1977; Britton, 1973; Bruffee, 1993) and, more recently, problem-based learning (PBL) and team-based learning (TBL). Cooperative and collaborative learning are employed at all levels of education, whereas PBL (Barrows, 1986) and TBL (Michaelsen, Knight, & Fink, 2004) have been applied mainly in higher education. This volume is focused upon cooperative learning. The confusing relationship between cooperative and collaborative learning is clarified in this introduction. A brief discussion of the other approaches to small-group learning, PBL and TBL, will be presented later in Davidson's chapter.

Cooperative Learning

Origins

According to the *Oxford English Dictionary*, the term "cooperate" comes from the late 16th century: from Latin *cooperat*—"worked together," from the verb *cooperari*, from *co-*"together" + *operari* "to work"—to work together, jointly on an activity or project. CL, then, involves a focus on students co-laboring to accomplish a learning task, a social product, together, just as the root word suggests (Davidson & Major, 2014).

The term "cooperative learning" began to appear in the literature about 1980. Prior to that time, terms such as "small group learning" were employed. But an earlier book by Alice Miel (1952) was entitled *Cooperative Procedures in Learning*.

Definitions and Descriptions

The main definitions and descriptions of cooperative learning demonstrate the importance of students working together in small groups in a mutually supportive manner to learn academic content and, in some definitions, to construct their own knowledge. The following are several major examples (from Davidson & Major, 2014):

- "Cooperative learning will be defined as students working together in a group small enough that everyone can participate on a collective task that has been clearly assigned. Moreover, students are expected to carry out their task without direct and immediate supervision of the teacher. The study of cooperative learning should not be confused with small groups that teachers often compose for the purpose of intense, direct instruction—for example, reading groups" (Cohen, 1994, p. 3).
- "Cooperative learning refers to a set of instructional methods in which students are encouraged or required to work together on academic tasks. Cooperative learning methods may be as simple as having students sit together to discuss or help one another with classroom assignments, or may be quite complex. Cooperative learning is distinguished from peer tutoring in that all students learn the same material, that there is no tutor or tutee, and that information usually comes initially from a teacher rather than a student" (Slavin, 1987, p. 1161).
- "The structural approach to cooperative learning is based on the creation, analysis, and systematic application of structures, or content-free ways of organizing social interaction in the classroom. [Examples are Three-Step Interview, RoundRobin, RallyRobin, and RoundTable.] Structures usually involve a series of steps, with prescribed behavior at each step. An important cornerstone of the approach is the distinction between 'structures' and 'activities'" (Kagan, 1989, p. 12; Kagan & Kagan, 2009).
- "Cooperation is working together to accomplish shared goals, and cooperative learning is the instructional use of small groups so that students work together to maximize their own and each other's learning. Within cooperative learning groups, students are given two responsibilities: to learn the assigned material and make sure that all

other members of their group do likewise. Their success is measured by a fixed set of standards. Thus, a student seeks an outcome that is beneficial to himself or herself and beneficial to all other group members" (Johnson & Johnson, 1989, p. 121).

- "Cooperative learning encompasses a wide range of strategies for promoting academic learning through peer cooperation and communication. As the term 'cooperative learning' implies, students help each other learn, share ideas and resources, and plan cooperatively what and how to study. The teacher does not dictate specific instructions but rather allows students varying degrees of choice as to the substance and goals of their learning activities, thus making students active participants in the process of acquiring knowledge. . . . Cooperative learning encourages, and is in fact built upon, the contributions of group members" (Sharan & Sharan, 1987, p. 21).

Sample Procedures and Techniques

A great strength of cooperative learning is a range of specific methods/procedures to foster cooperation in learning by working together. Cooperative tasks are organized in a way that requires students to work together in order to be able to complete the assignment. Descriptions of many cooperative learning methods/procedures are given throughout the chapters in this volume. Here is a brief listing.

Simple Procedures

Think-Pair-Share (Lyman)

Three-Step Interview, Sage-N-Scribe, RallyRobin, RoundTable (Kagan)

More Complex Procedures

Formulate-listen-share-create (Johnsons)
Student Teams Achievement Divisions (STAD), Teams-Games-Tournaments (TGT), Team-Assisted Individualization (TAI), Cooperative Integrated Reading and Composition (CIRC) (Slavin and Madden)
Numbered heads together (Kagan)
Jigsaw (Aronson)
Group investigation (Sharan and Sharan)
Co-op Co-op (Kagan)
Constructive controversy (Johnsons)
Success for All, a whole school model employing CL (Slavin and Madden)
(The Tribes program, developed by Jeanne Gibbs in 1970, is an early approach to building community in cooperative learning.)

Research

Cooperative learning has shown up well in over 1,000 educational research studies designed to test its effectiveness. Research conducted in many different subject areas and various age groups of students has shown positive effects favoring cooperative learning in academic achievement, development of higher order thinking skills (both critical and creative), self-esteem and self-confidence as learners, intergroup relations including friendship across racial and ethical boundaries, social acceptance of mainstreamed students labeled as "handicapped" or "disabled," development of interpersonal skills, and the ability to take the perspective of another person.

For syntheses of cooperative learning research, see the extensive reviews by Johnson and Johnson (1989), Slavin (1990), Sharan (1980, 1990), and Newmann and Thompson (1987) at the high school level. Johnson, Johnson, and Smith (2006) have shown that cooperative learning has strong positive effects on thinking and reasoning. Additional reviews dealing with group process have focused on conditions for productive group work (Cohen, 1994) and task-related group interaction in mathematics groups (Webb, 1991).

Several authors in this volume have contributed a great deal to the research on cooperative learning. More detailed reports and references can be found in their chapters.

Much of the research has taken place at the school level, and some at the college or university level. For example, in Springer et al.'s (1999) meta-analysis, the authors found that postsecondary students participating in cooperative learning in science, technology, engineering, and math (STEM) courses *demonstrate greater achievement* than non-CL students, *express more favorable attitudes* than their non-CL counterparts, and *persist through STEM courses or programs to a greater extent* than non-CL students.

Essential Features and Elements

Several scholars have set forth the critical features and elements of cooperative learning, with some degree of agreement and some variations across the different approaches. In the following paragraphs, for example, Davidson and Worsham (1992, pp. xi–xii) describe cooperative learning and suggest:

> Cooperative learning procedures are designed to engage students actively in the learning process through inquiry and discussion with their peers in small groups. The group-work is carefully organized and structured so as to promote the participation and learning of all

group members in a cooperatively shared undertaking. Cooperative learning is more than just tossing students into a group and telling them to work together.

A class period might begin with a meeting of the entire class to provide an overall perspective. This may include a teacher presentation of new material, class discussion, posing problems or questions for group discussions, and clarifying directions for the group activities. The class is then divided into small groups, usually with four members apiece (or three in some models). Each group has its own working space, which might include a flip chart or section of the chalkboard or white board. Students work together cooperatively in each group to discuss ideas, clarify their understanding, think and reason together, solve problems, make and test conjectures, and so forth. Students actively exchange ideas with one another and help each other learn the material. The teacher takes an active role, circulating from group to group, providing assistance and encouragement, and asking thought-provoking questions as needed.

In each type of small-group learning, there are a number of leadership and management functions that must be performed. These include initiating group work, presenting guidelines for small-group operation, fostering group norms of interdependence and mutual helpfulness, forming groups, preparing and introducing new material, interacting with small groups in varied ways, using informal classroom assessments to help learning, tying ideas together, making assignments of homework or in-class work, and evaluating student performance.

Thus, the multiple facets of the teacher's role are designed to ensure that students work *together* in a mutually beneficial manner and not simply on the same project.

There is no single universal method of cooperative learning and no single guru who can speak for the entire field. There is some agreement and some variation, however, about the essential elements of cooperative learning. This can be seen in the following descriptions of critical elements.

According to Johnson, Johnson, and Smith (1998, 2006, pp. 21–23), cooperative learning has five key elements: positive interdependence, face-to-face promotive interaction, individual and group accountability, development of teamwork skills, and group processing.

Kagan and Kagan (2009) identify four critical attributes of the structural approach to cooperative learning (with acronym PIES): Positive interdependence, Individual accountability, Equal participation, and Simultaneous interaction.

Slavin (1983) identifies two key conditions—group goals/rewards and individual accountability—stemming from his research review entitled "When does cooperative learning improve student achievement?"

Synthesis of Essential Elements (Critical Attributes) of Cooperative Learning Approaches

In the previous section, it became clear that different theorists emphasized somewhat different essential elements (or critical attributes) of cooperative learning. In the 1980s, intense discussions took place about the critical attributes. Some participants took strong ideological positions, sometimes based upon the approach with which they were most familiar. For example, is use of group rewards a critical element in cooperative learning? The answer is no. Group rewards are used in Student Team Learning but not in Complex Instruction. Is use of role assignments a critical element? Again, the answer is no. Role assignments are used in the Learning Together approach but not in Student Team Learning.

These issues led me to search for commonalities across the approaches. Before stating these formally, it is useful to present an illustration.

In the top part of Figure 1.1, there are three mice facing a maze. The maze is very complex and difficult, and the mice will eventually have to run it individually.

In the middle part of Figure 1.1, the mice are cooperating; they get together for a mouse powwow, a group discussion about how to run the maze. They exchange ideas and strategize how to do the task.

In the bottom part of Figure 1.1, they build a mouse tower, a "tower of power," standing on each other's shoulders. The mouse on top draws a diagram of the maze. Then the mice all examine the diagram and discuss and plan effective routes through the maze.

Let us consider the key points of this cooperative activity, with a group problem-solving task.

1. The task is challenging and requires a group solution.
2. Individual accountability: Each mouse must eventually run the maze individually.
3. Group discussion is focused on the task, in this case planning how to run the maze.
4. Cooperative behavior: They work together cooperatively to exchange ideas and make plans, each one acting responsibly. They do not kick or bite or scratch each other; that would hurt and interfere with getting the job done.
5. Positive interdependence: They depend on each other to get the job done. The efforts of all the participants are needed. Together they accomplish more than they could achieve individually.
6. Roles: In this case, three roles were needed in the tower—top, middle, and bottom positions. However, roles are not always needed in cooperative learning. That depends on the task and on the model of CL being employed.

Introduction to Pioneering Perspectives in CL   9

Figure 1.1 *Mice in a Maze* (artist unknown)

Figure 1.1 actually illustrates the essential elements of cooperative learning. In a theoretical synthesis of varied cooperative (and collaborative) learning approaches, we have identified five attributes that are common to all these approaches. (Davidson & Worsham, 1992; Davidson, 1994, 2002; Davidson & Major, 2014). We expand on these attributes as follows:

1. A common task or learning activity suitable for group work.
2. Small-group interaction focused on the learning activity.

3. Norms for cooperative, mutually helpful behavior among students as they strive together to accomplish the learning task.
4. Individual accountability and responsibility for what students have learned and/or contributed toward the learning goal. (Some approaches also include group accountability.)
5. Positive interdependence in working together—also known as "interdependence" or "mutual interdependence."

Interdependence is the mutual reliance between two or more individuals or groups.

With positive interdependence, a student seeks an outcome that is beneficial to himself or herself and beneficial to all other group members (Johnsons).

All of the cooperative learning approaches require interdependence. This concept warrants additional attention, however, as advocates of the various methods approach it in different ways. It is at the heart of the different approaches to cooperative learning, and it includes the following alternative techniques to foster positive interdependence:

- Goals: this includes both social and academic goals.
- Tasks: a structured learning task or assignment can be designed at varying levels of intellectual challenge.
- Resources: materials may be limited, for example, two information sheets in a group of four, or with a jigsaw, where each group member has different information to share.
- Roles: students assume assigned, pre-set roles, either task roles or group maintenance roles.
- Rewards: bonus points are given for improved performance or public recognition for groups that meet criteria.
- Structure of the group affects its communication pattern and the way in which participants are interdependent.

Additional Attributes That Vary Among CL Methods

In addition to the common attributes, there are a dozen other attributes that vary among the approaches to cooperative learning (and also collaborative and PBL). Examples of these are as follows: how groups are formed, how or whether to teach interpersonal skills, the structure of the group, and the role of the teacher. Here is a full list of varying attributes.

- Grouping: teachers employ intentional heterogeneous or random grouping versus allowing students to choose their group.
- Teaching and processing social skills (group skills, communication skills, cooperative skills).
- Reflection on group process: how well did we work together and use cooperative skills?

- Community-building (aka class-building or trust-building): whole-class activities that get everyone included and interacting in a positive manner.
- Team-building: students participate in activities to become better acquainted and to build cohesiveness in their group.
- Use of structures: ways of organizing the communication pattern in the group (e.g., Celebrity Interview, Timed-Pair-Share, RoundRobin).
- Equal participation: structuring the interaction in a way that provides equal opportunities to speak.
- Simultaneous interaction: in pairs, 50% of the class members are speaking simultaneously; in quads, 25% are speaking simultaneously.
- Role of the instructor: an active democratic or friendly directive role versus a laissez-faire role.
- Classroom management options: quiet signal, timed activities, use of a timing device, assuring that everyone has a partner or group, group folders, students as materials managers, students helping with room setup, and so on.
- Status interventions: the instructor identifies a student of low status, notices a commendable performance by that student, and calls this to the attention of the entire class. (Such an intervention is named "assigning competence.")
- Perspective-taking: activities designed to foster understanding the perspective (or viewpoint) of another person, whether or not one agrees with it. This is related to empathy.

For further details, see Davidson (1994, 2002)and Davidson and Major (2014).

Unique Features of Varied Cooperative Approaches

All the cooperative approaches place value on both academic and social learning and employ the five critical attributes listed previously. However, they operate in somewhat different ways, depending on the varying attributes that are emphasized. Here is a quick capsule description of the unique features emphasized in the different approaches. Specific, detailed descriptions of these approaches are presented in the chapters that follow in this volume.

Student Team Learning: Group goals and rewards through bonus points or team recognition, with individual accountability for learning, as in the methods of STAD, TGT, TAI, and CIRC.

Learning Together: Face-to-face promotive interaction, teamwork skills, group processing, assigned roles, plus perspective-taking via creative controversy.

Complex Instruction: Multiple-ability tasks, task cards, assigned roles, random assignment to groups, status interventions by explaining multiple abilities and by "assigning competence" to students of low status.

Jigsaw: Instructional material is divided into parts, with task roles assigned to "experts" on each part. Expert groups are used to help learn one part of the lesson and prepare to teach it, and presentation of all the parts occurs in home groups.

Group investigation: The class determines subtopics and organizes into research groups. Groups plan their investigations and then carry them out. They plan and present their findings. Teacher and students evaluate their projects.

Small-group processes: Concepts from group dynamics and group development such as communication, friendships and cohesiveness, shared expectations and norms, leadership, and conflict, also applied in connection with organization development.

Structural Approach: Use of content-free structures for organizing the the interaction of students with each other, the teacher, and the curriculum (e.g., Pair Interview, Timed RoundRobin, Corners, Listen Right!).

Small-group discovery: Challenging mathematics problems, students working together at the blackboard (or whiteboard), using guidelines for cooperation, such as take turns writing, and make sure that everyone understands.

Success for All: SFA is a whole-school reform model for disadvantaged elementary and middle schools. It adds to cooperative learning elements such as tutoring for struggling readers, parent involvement approaches, social-emotional learning methods, and more.

Contrasting Cooperative and Collaborative Learning

Collaborative learning, another major approach to small-group learning, is based on the philosophy of social constructivism. It intends to create an environment that helps an individual to develop mentally, emotionally, and socially as an active participant in a supportive learning community. Students work together in small groups that are typically self-selected, self-managed, and loosely structured. The teacher offers limited guidance so that students can develop their own independence. There are very few techniques specific to collaborative learning (Barnes & Todd, 1977; Britton, 1973; Bruffee, 1993).

Additional books describing collaborative learning are by Goodsell, Maher, and Tinto (1992) and by Barkley, Major, and Cross (2014). There is considerable variability in the definitions of collaborative learning among the different books.

Cooperative learning and collaborative learning have often been confused with each other. Let us apply the varying attributes to distinguish between the two approaches. A key distinction between cooperative learning and collaborative learning is this: Cooperative learning teachers tend to structure the positive interdependence through varied means, whereas collaborative learning teachers believe that interdependence will arise naturally through the task and goal.

To be more specific, in fostering positive interdependence, *cooperative learning* teachers consider using all of the procedures introduced previously: goals, tasks, resources, roles, structures, and rewards. *Collaborative learning* teachers mainly use goal and task interdependence and occasionally limited resources, say with a jigsaw. They almost never use assigned roles and rewards or varied structures.

The role of the cooperative teacher in several models is activist—an active democratic or friendly directive style, sometimes akin to McWilliam's (2009) "meddler in the middle." In contrast, the collaborative learning teacher is more likely to be a laissez-faire leader, who designs the activities but does not intervene very often, in order to let the groups select their own members and to foster the "authority of knowledge" through self-direction and construction of their own personal knowledge. (In some discussions of leadership, we use concepts such as the sage on stage for the lecturer, or guide on the side or sage on the side in the small-group approaches.)

Collaborative learning teachers rarely or never use the following procedures among the varying attributes: heterogeneous grouping, role assignments, direct teaching of social skills, class-building and team-building activities, cooperative structures (except occasionally for jigsaw), structuring for equal participation, activist interventions by the teacher, carefully timed activities, and status treatments.

In collaborative learning, activities occur with a rather leisurely pace without pre-set time limits. Community-building might occur naturally as a result of shared successful group experiences, but it is not explicitly designed for. Similarly, students might develop group skills in the process of working together, but these skills are not explicitly taught or practiced.

In conclusion, the cooperative learning approaches employ several elements which are not used by the collaborative teachers, and which are not accepted by them. Hence, cooperative learning is not a form of collaborative learning (and vice versa). Cooperative learning and collaborative learning are distinct forms of small-group learning which have some major elements in common. However, neither of them is a special case of the other approach. See Davidson, Major, and Michaelsen (2014).

IASCE

In 1979, Shlomo Sharan and a local organizing team convened the First International Convention on Cooperation in Education, held at Tel Aviv University in Israel. At the convention, we formed a new professional association, the International Association for the Study of Cooperation in Education (IASCE). Richard Schmuck was elected as its first president.

The IASCE is the only international nonprofit organization for educators who research and practice cooperative learning in order to promote student academic improvement and democratic social processes. Since its inception, this organization has had a tremendous influence on the development of cooperative learning theory, research, classroom practice and methodology, curriculum, teacher education, and professional development. It has offered two published books, a regular newsletter, and conferences held periodically at the international or regional level. Presentations and publications by the authors in this book have been featured often in the newsletter and conferences of the IASCE.

The two edited books offered by the IASCE were *Cooperation in Education* (1979), edited by S. Sharan, A. Paul Hare, Clark Webb, and Hertz-Lazarowitz, and *Learning to Cooperate, Cooperating to Learn* (1985), edited by Slavin, S. Sharan, Kagan, Hertz-Lazarowtiz, Webb, and Schmuck.

This is a good place to acknowledge the contributions beyond these edited books of three scholars. Paul Hare also edited the *Handbook of Small Group Research*, Clark Webb organized the second international conference of the IASCE in 1982, and Rachel Hertz-Lazarowitz published a number of papers on group investigation (cited in the chapter by the Sharans).

Publications by IASCE members, independently and following IASCE conferences, have highlighted the connection between theory and practice of CL and its various methods and approaches. The following titles are examples of how the Association encouraged and gave voice to the varied and ever-growing body of research and ways of implementing research-based methods and approaches.

These books dealt with professional development for CL by Brody and Davidson (1998) and two volumes on teacher education and CL by Cohen, Brody, and Sapon-Shevin (2004) and by Baloche, Brody, and Jolliffe (2017).

The IASCE has also worked collaboratively in jointly held conferences with other organizations of similar values and goals. These include the International Association for Intercultural Education.

For many of us, the IASCE has been a wonderful source of stimulation, new learning, keeping up with the field, and collegial support. Association members get to meet and work with the early major contributors of CL, plus many more recent leaders in later years as the field has greatly expanded.

IASCE Conferences and Regional Associations

The second international convention of the IASCE was held at Brigham Young University in Utah in 1982. The third was held in Regina, Saskatchewan, in 1985. At that third conference, we recognized that the small membership of the organization consisted mainly of academics such as professors, researchers, and theorists. For cooperative learning to expand and take hold, we needed to attract many more professionals in different roles.

Hence, at the IASCE conference in 1985, we founded three regional associations to support teachers, staff developers, and administrators with professional development for cooperative learning. These were the Mid-Atlantic Association for Cooperation in Education (MAACIE), the California Association for Cooperation in Education (CACIE), and the Great Lakes Association for Cooperation in Education (GLACIE), based in Toronto. These associations offered numerous conferences, workshops, training events, and newsletters. Over the years they reached thousands of teachers, administrators, and staff developers through state and local events.

Other regional associations for cooperation in education were created later in Ohio, Northern New England, British Columbia, Australia/New Zealand, and Japan.

The IASCE was active for a period of 40 years. Then it finally closed, and the last newsletter was published in the summer of 2020 during the coronavirus pandemic. At that time, to provide ongoing communication opportunities for people interested in CL, the IASCE morphed into a network: Network of International Cooperative Learning Educators and Enthusiasts (NICLEE)—pronounced "nicely," which can be accessed at http://www.2020niclee.com.

References

Baloche, L., Brody, C., & Jolliffe, W. (Eds.) (2017). Cooperative learning: Exploring challenges, crafting innovations. *Journal of Education for Teaching: International Research and Pedagogy, Routledge, 43*(3), 273–380.

Barkley, E., Major, C., & Cross, K. P. (2005, 2014). *Collaborative learning techniques: A handbook for college faculty*. San Francisco, CA: Jossey-Bass.

Barnes, D., & Todd, F. (1977). *Communicating and learning in small groups*. London: Routledge, Kegan Paul.

Barrows, H. S. (1986). A taxonomy of problem-based learning methods. *Medical Education, 20*, 481–486.

Britton, J. (1973). *Language and learning*. Baltimore, MD: Penguin.

Brody, C., & Davidson, N. (Eds.) (1998). *Professional development for cooperative learning: Issues and approaches*. Albany, NY: SUNY Press.

Bruffee, K. (1993). *Collaborative learning: Higher education, interdependence, and the authority of knowledge*. Baltimore, MD: The Johns Hopkins University.

Cohen, E. (1994). Restructuring the classroom: Conditions for productive small groups. *Review of Educational Research, 64*(1), 1–35.

Cohen, E., Brody, C., & Sapon-Shevin, M, (Eds.) (2004). Teaching cooperative learning: The challenge for teacher educators. Albany, NY: SUNY Press.

Davidson, N. (1994, second edition 2002). Cooperative and collaborative learning: An integrative perspective. In J. Thousand, R. Villa, & A. Nevin (Eds.), *Creativity and collaborative learning: A practical guide for empowering teachers and students* (pp. 13–30). Baltimore, MD: Brookes Publishing.

Davidson, N., & Major, C. (2014). Boundary crossings: Cooperative learning, collaborative learning, and problem-based learning. In Davidson, N., Major, C., and Michaelsen, L. (Eds). (2014). Small group learning in higher education—

cooperative, collaborative, problem-based and team-based learning. *Journal on Excellence in College Teaching, 25*(3&4).

Davidson, N., Major, C., & Michaelsen, L. (Eds.). (2014). Small group learning in higher education—cooperative, collaborative, problem-based and team-based learning. *Journal on Excellence in College Teaching, 25*(3&4).

Davidson, N., & Worsham, T. (1992). *Enhancing thinking through cooperative learning.* New York, NY: Teachers College Press.

Gibbs, J. (1970, 1987, 2001, 2006). *Tribes: A new way of learning and being together.* Santa Rosa, CA: CenterSource Systems LLC.

Goodsell, A., Maher, M., & Tinto, V. (Eds.). (1992). *Collaborative learning: A sourcebook for higher education.* University Park, PA: National Center on Post-Secondary Teaching, Learning, and Assessment.

Johnson, D. W., & Johnson, R. T. (1989). *Cooperation and competition: Theory and research.* Edina, MN: Interaction Book Company.

Johnson, D. W., Johnson, R. T., & Smith, K. A. (1998, 2006). *Active learning: Cooperation in the college classroom.* Edina, MN: Interaction Book Company.

Kagan, S. (1989). The structural approach to cooperative learning. *Educational Leadership, 47,* 12–15.

Kagan, S., & Kagan, M. (2009). *Kagan cooperative learning.* San Clemente, CA: Kagan Publishing.

Keys, D. (1982). The politics of consciousness. In *Earth at Omega: Passage to planetization.* Boston, MA: Branden Press.

McWilliam, E. (2009). Teaching for creativity: From sage to guide to meddler. *Asia Pacific Journal of Education, 29*(3), 281–293.

Michaelsen, L. K., Knight, A. B., & Fink, L. D. (2004). *Team-based learning: A transformative use of small groups in higher education.* Sterling, VA: Stylus.

Newmann, F., & Thompson, J. (1987). *Effects of cooperative learning on achievement in secondary schools: A summary of research.* Madison, WI: National Center on Effective Secondary Schools.

Sharan, S. (1980). Cooperative learning in small groups: Recent methods and effects on achievement, attitudes, and ethnic relations. *Review of Educational Research, 150,* 241–271.

Sharan, S. (1990). *Cooperative learning: Theory and research.* West Port: CT: Praeger Publishers.

Sharan, S. (Ed.). (1994, 1999). *Handbook of cooperative learning methods.* Westport, CT: Praeger

Sharan, S., & Sharan, Y. (1987). Training teachers for cooperative learning. *Educational Leadership, 45*(3), 20–26.

Slavin, R. E. (1983). When does cooperative learning increase student achievement? *Psychological Bulletin, 94,* 429–445.

Slavin, R. E. (1987). Developmental and motivational perspectives on cooperative learning: A reconciliation. *Child Development, 58,* 1161–1167.

Slavin, R. E. (1990). *Cooperative learning: Theory, research and practice.* Englewood Cliffs, NJ: Prentice-Hall.

Springer, L., Stanne, M. E., & Donovan, S. (1999). Effects of small-group learning on undergraduates in science, mathematics, engineering, and technology: A meta-analysis. (Research Monograph No. 11). *Review of Educational Research, 69,* 21–51.

Webb, N. (1991). Task-related verbal interaction and mathematics learning in small groups. *Journal for Research in Mathematics Education, 22*(5), 366–389.

Chapter 2

The Legacy of Morton Deutsch
Theories of Cooperation, Conflict, and Justice

Laurie Stevahn

Introduction

> My career almost spans the existence of modern social psychology.
> (Deutsch, 2008, p. 221)

Morton Deutsch. Renowned social psychologist. Theoretical genius. Rigorous empirical researcher. Rooted in real-world universal social problems profoundly affecting humanity. Always generous. Genuinely humble. Active scholar and supportive mentor throughout his long and illustrious life. His career, largely spanning the 20th century, shaped numerous aspects of modern social psychology, influenced countless other disciplines in which interpersonal relations and group dynamics matter, and played a pivotal role in world events affecting justice and peace.

Educators may not readily recognize the name of Morton Deutsch or associate him with cooperative learning, conflict resolution, or peace education programs in school settings, yet his work provides theoretical and empirical foundations for such programs. A true leader among leaders, Mort (affectionately called by many) precedes by a generation all those highlighted in this volume. His groundbreaking conceptualizations of cooperation and competition, conflict resolution, trust and suspicion, distributive justice, oppression, and awakening a sense of injustice make him unrivaled. Many today continue to draw upon Mort's work on these topics because much of his original theorizing and research in the 20th century have been corroborated repeatedly, providing an exceptionally strong foundation.

Mort defined social situations by whether people perceived their goals as linked—positively (I need you and you need me; we succeed or fail together), negatively (I succeed if you fail; you succeed if I fail), or not at all (I am in this alone; I determine my own fate)—which essentially grounds the entire field of cooperative learning. Regardless of the different cooperative learning orientations and approaches that have been developed and applied in various contexts (especially education), and despite robust controversies among those advancing cooperative learning theory, research, and practice throughout the world, all agree that *positive interdependence* is the essential component of cooperation. Furthermore, resolving conflicts in jointly beneficial and mutually satisfying ways requires working together for win-win solutions. Positive interdependence, therefore, provides the unifying core for effective cooperation and constructive conflict, and Mort's original theoretical foundations have inspired research, theory, and practice on these topics worldwide.

Notably, David W. Johnson (Mort's doctoral student) and Roger T. Johnson (David's brother), both professors emeriti at the University of Minnesota, brought Mort's foundations into the field of education. Their numerous studies and reviews of the literature have greatly furthered our understanding of what mediates effective positive interdependence in cooperative learning groups. These include the strength of perceived mutual goals and rewards; interconnected roles, resources, and tasks; shared identities and environments; and simulated survival situations that require coordinated effort for everyone to succeed. The Johnsons' pioneering contributions to cooperative learning theory, research, and practice; constructive controversy for group decision-making; and conflict resolution training in schools (Peacemakers Program) are all firmly rooted in positive interdependence. They elaborate on these in a separate chapter of this volume.

This chapter provides insight into Morton Deutsch—the man, his life's work, and his legacy. His brilliant theorizing and ability to validate hypotheses through experimental research are gifts that enable us to better understand cooperative processes, conditions that influence the course of conflicts, and frameworks for social justice. This chapter begins by describing early influences and lived experiences that contributed to Mort's tough-minded, tender-hearted posture as a psychologist committed to understanding how various conditions affect social-psychological processes that underpin human relations and group dynamics. It continues by summarizing Mort's hallmark theories on cooperation and competition, constructive conflict resolution, and distributive justice. It concludes by suggesting how we can live Mort's legacy in our personal and professional lives.

Early Influences

> One of my earliest memories focuses on injustice. I was about three-and-a-half years old. We were all staying at a resort in the Catskills, and a counselor organized a game of softball for the older kids (the six-to-eight-year-olds). I was excluded from it because I was too young and was asked to stay on the side.... I have always had a passionate

> feeling about injustice and being excluded. I was the youngest of four sons and, having skipped grades several times, I was the youngest in my classes throughout my school years. In many situations, I was excluded or was the underdog. As a result, I developed a strong identification with and empathy for the downtrodden in the world.
>
> (Deutsch, 1995b, p. 371)

Childhood and Adolescence

Born in 1920 to Jewish parents who had immigrated to the United States from Poland in 1908, Mort was the youngest of four siblings. After skipping Grades 2, 4, and 6, then attending Townsend Harris Hall, a unique 3-year high school in New York City, Mort entered City College of New York in 1935 at age 15. As the youngest in most social situations, Mort often felt excluded. However, early exposure to a broad range of formidable theorists such as Sigmund Freud, Karl Marx, Charles Darwin, Albert Einstein, and Kurt Lewin, plus socially conscious popular writers of the day, fueled Mort's keen intellect. New York City's stimulating environment also exposed Mort to the political, economic, and social turbulence of the decade, further heightening his sensitivity to injustice. Nazis were on the rise in Europe, the Great Depression threatened life in America, labor disputes erupted, and unionizing activities intensified. So did Mort's focus on inequality and exploitation, foretelling his lifelong commitment to scientifically examining pervasive social problems to produce results useful for enhancing the human condition.

> During my adolescence, I was . . . politically radical and somewhat rebellious toward authority, helping to organize a student strike against the terrible food in the high school lunchroom and, later, a strike against the summer resort owners who were exploiting the college student waiters, of whom I was one.
>
> (Deutsch, 2008, p. 221)

Graduate Studies and World War II

By 1940 Mort had earned a master's degree in clinical psychology from the University of Pennsylvania, intending to become a psychoanalyst (eventually he did establish and maintain a private practice while also a professor of social psychology).

> I was drawn to psychoanalysis undoubtedly because it appeared to be so relevant to the personal issues with which I was struggling, and

also because it was so radical and rebellious (it seemed to be so in the early and mid-1930s).

(Deutsch, 2008, p. 221)

Shortly thereafter, he started rotating clinical internships at three New York State institutions, becoming skilled at diagnostic testing and clinical interventions with youth and adults mandated to residential facilities for what at that time was called "mental illness and delinquent behavior." These experiences furthered Mort's awareness of injustice as he realized institutions sometimes retained capable patients who performed tasks helpful to staff rather than transitioning them to society for productive living (Deutsch, 2008).

Mort's trajectory changed when the United States entered World War II. He served in the United States Air Force as a navigator and knew that he may not make it home alive.

> When Pearl Harbor was bombed in December 1941, I was still in my psychology internship. Shortly thereafter, I joined the air force. I flew in 30 bombing missions against the Germans. During combat I saw many of our planes as well as German planes shot down, and I also saw the massive damage inflicted by our bombs and those of the Royal Air Force on occupied Europe and Germany. Moreover, being stationed in England, I saw the great destruction wrecked by the German air raids and felt the common apprehensions while sitting in air-raid shelters during German bombings. Although I had no doubt about the justness of the war against the Nazis, I was appalled by its destructiveness.
>
> (Deutsch, 2008, p. 223)

Mort's witness to wartime devastation and the onset of atomic weapons influenced his doctoral pursuits upon returning home shortly before the war ended.

> When we saw what the atomic bombs had done in Japan, war seemed such a serious problem that it had to be thought about. Something had to be done to prevent it. I was preoccupied with this, not in any obsessive way but because of my social interests.
>
> (Deutsch, as cited in Frydenberg, 2005, p. 46)

In August 1945 Mort met Kurt Lewin for breakfast in midtown Manhattan. Lewin directed the newly established Research Center for Group Dynamics (RCGD) at the Massachusetts Institute of Technology (MIT), one of three possibilities Mort was considering for doctoral studies in psychology (the others were with Clark Hull at Yale University and Carl Rogers at the University of Chicago). Lewin's enthusiasm, authenticity, and charisma captivated Mort, who dates the start of his career as a social psychologist to that breakfast meeting (Deutsch, 2008). Mort joined what turned out to be a remarkable and influential group of scholars at the RCGD that provided a nurturing environment for innovative thinking and pioneering research. Lewin, widely recognized as the founder of social psychology, profoundly influenced Mort as a mentor and role model by demonstrating how to conduct rigorous *tough-minded* theoretical research on human social concerns typically deemed *soft-minded* by serious scientists. At their first meeting and thereafter, Mort noted:

> I was being treated as an equal. . . . I was being treated as a serious professional. . . . Lewin's treatment of me was, I believe, typical of his relations with his colleagues and students. He would discuss a topic with great enthusiasm and insight, he would ignite one's interest, and he would encourage one to get involved in a task that was intellectually challenging, giving complete freedom for one to work on it as one saw fit.
>
> (Deutsch, 2008, p. 224)

These same qualities characterized Mort throughout his own life and career.

Tough-Minded, Tender-Hearted

> Lewin was not only an original, tough-minded theorist and researcher with a profound interest in the philosophy and methodology of science; he was also a tender-hearted psychologist who was deeply involved with developing psychological knowledge that would be relevant to important human concerns. Lewin was both tough-minded and tender-hearted; he provided a scientific role model that I have tried to emulate. Like Lewin, I have wanted my theory and research to be relevant to important social issues but I also wanted my work to be scientifically rigorous and tough-minded.
>
> (Deutsch, as cited in Frydenberg, 2005, pp. 107–108)

Scientific Research on Social Issues

Rigorous, indeed. Mort pioneered the use of empirical experimental designs capable of capturing core dimensions of complex social phenomena, beginning with cooperation and competition. Being tough-minded meant adopting Lewin's (1951) maxim: "There is nothing so practical as a good theory" (p. 169). This involved formulating and testing well-conceptualized theories that had powerful variables (widely applicable across demographics). Such theories also were strategic (broadly applicable across disciplines and contexts), profound (useful for understanding the real world), cumulative (corrected, refined, and extended over time), and multilevel (capable of explaining many levels of human interaction, such as intrapersonal, interpersonal, intergroup, interregional, intercultural, international) (Johnson & Johnson, 2018).

Being tender-hearted meant staying close to pervasive real-world social issues. It involved formulating and validating theories dealing with universal human problems and then designing research capable of producing results for broad generalization, regardless of people's identity, role, position, stature, or culture. Like Lewin, Mort believed that science should deal with common complex problems shared across societies and produce results that people then could use to live healthy, constructive, and productive lives. Mort also demonstrated how tough-minded *hard* science could be conducted to better understand the tender-hearted *soft* social concerns always at the core of his research interests.

> What I do is try to capture some feature of everyday life which I think is important and to translate that . . . so to speak, by putting it into the enclosed box of a research design. . . . It starts off with some experience, some feeling that this process—whether it has to do with trust or suspicion, cooperation or competition, something going on in the family, something going on in the larger world that captures my interest—is also something that is universal, and then I try to think of a way of transforming it into research.
> (Deutsch, as cited in Frydenberg, 2005, p. 10)

Mort's work always began by formulating clear theoretical conceptualizations of the complex phenomena he deemed important. He then hypothesized how variable conditions would likely influence social-psychological processes capable of producing outcomes universally applicable to enhancing people's lives.

> I tell my students that there are two kinds of theorists: the *picayune* and the *grandiose*. The picayune mainly does not generalize beyond the data, so his or her generalizations are very limited; they are likely to be valid but not very useful. I identify myself as a grandiose theorist, one brashly seeking to develop ideas that apply from cave people to space people, from interpersonal to international conflict, from

the aborigines in Kakadu to the sophisticates on Park Avenue. This is grandiose indeed!

(Deutsch, 1995a, pp. 123–124, emphasis in original)

Game Theory as Rigorous Methodology

Mort's initial grandiose theory focused on what motivated or induced people to cooperate (pursue mutual interest) versus compete (pursue self-interest). He was the first to realize the usefulness of game theory as an experimental methodology to test people's behaviors in mixed-motive situations where cooperating or competing were both possible. Mort first adapted Prisoner's Dilemma, a game that essentially models trust dynamics by mathematically measuring how the choices of two players influence each other's welfare. The goal of the game is to acquire money. The game involves several rounds of play in which each player independently makes a choice anticipating that it will either result in mutual benefit (each receives $5) or self-gain/other-loss (self receives $10 and other loses $10). However, choosing self-gain/other-loss runs the risk of mutual loss because if both choose self-interest over mutual gain, both will lose money (each loses $10). After players independently make and reveal their choice, combining the choices results in one of four outcomes.

1. *Mutual Gain:* You and your opponent both risked trusting that the other would choose mutual welfare over self-interest; therefore, you both equally gain money.
2. *Self-Gain/Other-Loss:* You chose self-interest while your opponent trusted you would choose mutual welfare; betraying your opponent's trust results in you gaining money and your opponent losing money.
3. *Other-Gain/Self-Loss:* You trusted your opponent would choose mutual welfare, but your opponent chose self-interest; your opponent's betrayal of your trust results in you losing money and your opponent gaining money.
4. *Mutual Loss:* You and your opponent both chose self-interest over mutual welfare; therefore, you both equally lose money.

Throughout repeated rounds, players learn about each other's motivations as choices are revealed. This either tends to foster trust, mutual interest, and positive feelings toward each other or deepen distrust, self-interest, and ill-will.

> The Prisoner's Dilemma game . . . is a very good sort of representation of a lot of dilemmas like an arms race and disarmament. You will only choose to disarm if you think the other will cooperate and

disarm. If you disarm and the other continues to arm secretly, then you're put in a severe disadvantage. On the other hand, you could exploit the other's cooperation, if he disarms, by arming.

(Deutsch, as cited in Frydenberg, 2005, p. 71)

Mort varied the conditions of play to examine real-life circumstances that might predictably induce cooperative versus competitive interactions, outcomes, and relations. For example, sometimes players communicated their intentions prior to making choices, could change an initial choice after learning the opponent's choice, were directed to persuade opponents to cooperate by explicitly stating this expectation, or were told they were partners interested in each other's welfare. As hypothesized, when oriented toward cooperative conditions, trust increased and monetary rewards collectively were greater for both players.

Mort continued to refine and develop experimental games to study complex interpersonal dynamics throughout his career—first at Bell Laboratories, then at New York University, and finally at Teachers College, Columbia University. While at Bell Laboratories, Mort and his assistant, Robert Krauss, invented the Acme-Bolt Trucking Game designed to examine how threats influence the course of conflict in bargaining situations. The goal of this game is for two truckers working for different companies (Acme and Bolt) to maximize profit by hauling commodities from a starting location to a final destination. Each travels at the same speed and must choose between two routes: one indirect, the other direct. The indirect route is longer and slower, yielding less profit, but provides a totally unobstructed road for continuous travel. In contrast, the direct route is shorter and faster, yielding greater profit, but has a one-lane section of road over which only one truck can pass. If both truckers choose this route, they will meet head on and block each other's progress, requiring negotiations that might force an opponent to back up (reducing profit) or convince both to take turns (yielding nearly equal profit). To simulate threat, each trucker controls a gate on opposite ends of the one-way road—Acme's at the west end and Bolt's at the east end. Players can close their gates if opponents do not agree to terms, thereby denying the other access. The experiment entailed 20 rounds in each of three conditions: "bilateral threat (both players controlled gates), unilateral threat (only Acme controlled a gate), and no threat (neither player controlled a gate)" (Hunt, 1993, p. 426). Communication also varied, as sometimes players could not talk to each other to convey intentions, could talk if they wished, or were required to talk systematically. Lack of threats resulted in the greatest collective profit for both players. This game "instantly became a classic, was widely cited, and won the prestigious

AAAS [American Association for the Advancement of Science] award for social science research" (Hunt, 1993, p. 426).

Using games such as those that Mort employed in controlled experimental laboratory research placed players in dynamic situations like those in real life. As players interacted and influenced each other through choice making under various conditions, outcomes clearly validated the constructiveness of cooperative intentions, communications, and behaviors. Furthermore, this type of rigorous methodology did not involve deception common to most experimental research (Johnson & Johnson, 2018).

Under What Conditions?

> Beware of false dichotomies.
> (Morton Deutsch, speaking at the annual meeting of the American Educational Research Association, 1996)

A special session on conflict and peace education at the 1996 annual meeting of the American Educational Research Association (AERA) held in New York City featured Mort as the invited expert to share insights and wisdom on several research-based educational programs designed to enhance constructive conflict and peace studies in elementary and secondary schools. To maximize engagement, Mort suggested that those in the audience sitting theater style arrange themselves in circular fashion to further explore and consider the various programs presented. At one point, someone in the audience asked: "With so many programs, how do we know which one works best?" There it was, the question familiar to all practitioners, although sometimes phrased as "What works?" "Does it work?" "Will it work?" These questions matter to practitioners who, in nearly every professional field, tend to focus on pragmatic concerns. After all, practitioners in schools and other field-based organizations are the ones implementing the programs, strategies, or innovations and, therefore, have a personal stake in their success. Theorists in the social and behavioral sciences, on the other hand, typically strive to determine underlying principles applicable across diverse contexts, settings, or situations by articulating theoretical propositions and then devising ways to systematically test or validate each hypothesis through rigorous research. All too often, the chasm between theoretical research and practical application remains unbridged. Not for Mort.

In a caring tone that conveyed warmth and compassion, Mort replied by acknowledging the participant's concern and then firmly, yet supportively, challenged everyone to consider program effectiveness on a continuum of possibilities influenced by variable conditions. He gently invited and redirected all those present to explore new (more useful) ways to think about dynamics that influence effectiveness. Mort's point: "yes–no" and "either–or" views of effectiveness create false dichotomies that narrow perspective and cannot capture inherent complexity. Reframing the problem as one in which variable conditions influence dynamic interactions helps avoid this trap by opening a range of possibilities, some producing more positive processes and outcomes than others. A more promising question is: Under what conditions will constructive versus destructive processes and outcomes result? More specifically: What conditions lead to the constructive resolution of conflict? To what extent do applied school-based programs concretely structure and nurture those conditions?

Theorizing and researching variable conditions that predictably influence basic social-psychological processes leading to constructive (or destructive) outcomes became the hallmark of Mort's life's work. Those gathered at this 1996 AERA session got a glimpse of this unwavering focus that began early in his career when he formulated and initially tested his theory of cooperation and competition in his doctoral dissertation research. They also experienced Mort's characteristic kindness and humility, which seemed to be woven into the fabric of his DNA. Mort's brilliance in conceptualizing complex problems universal to human experience, then transforming these into methodologically rigorous research, was equally matched by his gentle demeanor, kindheartedness, and genuine respect for others.

Cooperation and Competition

> Kurt Lewin, with whom I studied as a graduate student, had a favorite question: "What is the essence of the phenomena?" This question was of central importance in the formulation of my doctoral dissertation on the effects of cooperation and competition.
>
> (Deutsch, 1973, p. 20)

World War II ended and soon thereafter the United Nations officially began operating in October 1945 "to maintain international peace and security" (Charter of the United Nations, 1945). Mort had transitioned from Air Force to civilian life in June 1945 and began doctoral studies at MIT that August, where Kurt Lewin directed the newly established RCGD. This intellectually stimulating, energetic, supportive environment at that moment in time, along with Mort's firsthand wartime encounters and society's real concerns about preventing future nuclear war, provided fertile ground for what became Deutsch's theory of cooperation and competition. Specifically, Mort wondered if the five UN

Security Council countries—France, the Republic of China, the Soviet Union, the United Kingdom, the United States—would cooperate or compete. What conditions would influence interactions and dynamics among these countries to determine whether cooperation or competition would prevail?

Deutsch's Theory of Cooperation and Competition

Deutsch's (1949a, 1949b, 2011, 2014b) theory of cooperation and competition illustrates his genius in conceptualizing problems as dynamic relationships influenced by variable conditions. The theory focuses on two ideas: (a) interpersonal interdependence defined by how people's goals are linked in any given situation and (b) actions implemented by those in the situation. Two basic types of *goal interdependence* (positive versus negative) influence how individuals perceive their relationship with each other (cooperative versus competitive), whereas two basic types of *actions* (effective versus bungling) either help (support) or harm (obstruct) goal attainment. Combining goal interdependence and actions in any situation affects three basic social-psychological processes: (a) *substitutability*—your willingness to allow the actions of others to substitute for your own to meet your needs, (b) *cathexis*—your feelings and attitudes toward others, and (c) *inducibility*—your willingness to allow others to influence you.

Mort tested this theory in his doctoral dissertation research by creating two experimental conditions (cooperative versus competitive) in a psychology course at MIT. All students were in groups working to solve identical puzzles and problems; however, their efforts and outcomes were rewarded either cooperatively or competitively. In the cooperative condition, students (cooperators) shared the same reward for mutual excellence in their contributions to completing the group task. Specifically, all group members shared the same score or had a required term paper eliminated. In the competitive condition, students (competitors) were rewarded differently for exclusive excellence in their contributions to completing the group task. Specifically, scores were ranked across group members, so each earned a different score from highest to lowest, or only the highest performer had a required term paper eliminated. Results revealed that cooperators consistently engaged in more effective discussion, greater productivity, and higher-quality problem solving compared to competitors (Deutsch, 1949b).

Essentially, people need each other to cooperate or compete. When people need each other to achieve a mutual goal, their relationship is defined by positive goal interdependence (we swim or sink together). Under this cooperative condition, *effective* actions of cooperators (a) substitute for your own, (b) stimulate positive attitudes, and (c) prompt you to accept their influence. In contrast, *bungling* actions of cooperators (a) hinder your success and therefore do not substitute for your own, (b) evoke negative attitudes, and (c) prompt you to reject their influence. However, when people need each other to compete, their relationship is defined by negative goal interdependence (I swim, you sink, and vice versa). Under this competitive condition, *effective* actions of opponents (a) do not substitute for your own, (b) stimulate negative attitudes, and (c) prompt you to reject their influence. In contrast, *bungling* actions of opponents (a) help you to succeed and therefore substitute for your own, (b) stimulate positive attitudes, and (c) prompt you to accept their influence. Accepting the influence of opponents occurs, in part, by allowing their bungling behaviors to continue, giving you a competitive advantage. Figure 2.1 illustrates these dynamics, showing the two types of goal interdependence and two types of actions at opposite ends of two intersecting

Effective Actions

Positive Goal Interdependence / Negative Goal Interdependence

Upper-left quadrant (Positive Goal Interdependence, Effective Actions):
- Your actions help our cooperative goal achievement and substitute for my effective actions.
- My attitudes toward you tend to be positive.
- I tend to accept your influence.

Upper-right quadrant (Negative Goal Interdependence, Effective Actions):
- Your actions harm my competitive goal achievement and do not substitute for my effective actions.
- My attitudes toward you tend to be negative.
- I tend to reject your influence.

Lower-left quadrant (Positive Goal Interdependence, Bungling Actions):
- Your actions harm our cooperative goal achievement and do not substitute for my effective actions.
- My attitudes toward you tend to be negative.
- I tend to reject your influence.

Lower-right quadrant (Negative Goal Interdependence, Bungling Actions):
- Your actions help my competitive goal achievement and substitute for my effective actions.
- My attitudes toward you tend to be positive.
- I tend to accept your influence.

Bungling Actions

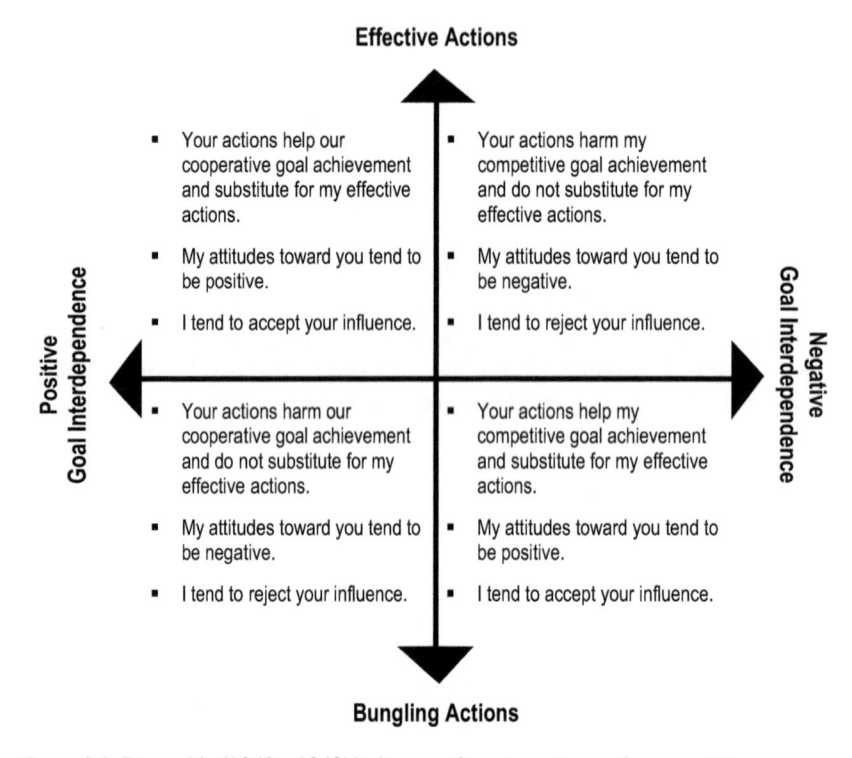

Figure 2.1 Deutsch's (1949a, 1949b) theory of cooperation and competition crosses goal interdependence (positive or negative) and actions (effective or bungling), creating different conditions (quadrants) that affect three social-psychological processes (substitutability, cathexis/attitudes, inducibility/influence).

Source: Diagram: ©2019 Laurie Stevahn.

lines (continua), respectively. Crossing these two continua creates four conditions (one per quadrant), each describing typical responses to substitutability, cathexis/attitudes, and inducibility/influence.

To illustrate, suppose a group's cooperative goal is to produce a video advocating for civil rights and each member's unique skills and contributions are needed for successful accomplishment. Necessary skills may include gathering background information, interviewing those seeking (or blocking) equal rights, fact checking, writing scripts, creating slogans, filming and editing images, identifying civil rights organizations that people may join, posting the finished product on social media, and so on. When everyone contributes in helpful ways, then teammates allow each other's actions to substitute for their own (division of labor), develop positive attitudes toward each other (appreciation and liking), and allow inducibility (accept each other's suggestions for fine-tuning work as the project progresses). However, if a group member does not contribute to the cooperative goal in helpful ways, teammates will not allow substitutability (they likely will do it themselves to compensate for the inadequate or incomplete work), will develop negative attitudes (disgust and dislike), and will not allow inducibility (will not accept suggestions from the person who is harming progress). In short, "you are willing to be helpful to another whose actions are helpful to you but not to someone whose actions are harmful" (Deutsch, 2014b, p. 6). Actions will be viewed as helpful or harmful depending on whether the goal is cooperative or competitive and whether specific actions support or obstruct successful accomplishment of that goal.

Effects of Cooperation and Competition

Deutsch's (1949a, 1949b) theory, supported by his doctoral dissertation research, predicts that people in cooperative relations (defined by positive goal interdependence) compared to competitive relations (defined by negative goal interdependence) display a consistent set of characteristics (Deutsch, 2014a, 2014b, 2014c). Specifically, cooperators (versus competitors) tend to:

- Communicate effectively (versus ineffectively).
- Interact in friendly, helpful, and trusting ways (versus unfriendly, unhelpful, and untrusting ways).
- Coordinate effort productively (versus disjointedly or ineffectively).
- Experience feelings of agreement and similar beliefs and values that increase self-confidence (versus repeated disagreement and rejection that diminish self-confidence).
- Recognize, respect, and respond to the needs of others (versus disregarding or disrespecting others).

- Enhance the power of others (versus one's own to diminish the power of others).
- View interpersonal conflicts as mutual problems to solve (versus contests to win).

Social Interdependence Theory

Deutsch's (1949a, 1949b) original theorizing and research became the foundation from which *social interdependence theory* emerged, further elaborated by David Johnson and Roger Johnson (1989, 2005, 2009, 2011). Social interdependence theory posits that perceived goal interdependence (positive/cooperative versus negative/competitive) influences social interaction (promotive/supportive versus oppositional/obstructive), which, in turn, determines outcomes (mutual versus exclusive benefits). Figure 2.2 illustrates this theory. It also shows a third individualistic option that involves no goal interdependence among people and therefore no need for interaction with others to succeed (or fail). Independent individuals determine their own fate separate and apart from the influence of others. Hundreds of studies conducted across numerous disciplines, contexts, countries, and cultures broadly confirm that cooperative goal

GOAL	INTERACTION	OUTCOME
Cooperative — Positive Interdependence	**Promotive** — Supportive	**Mutual** — Joint/Shared Outcome
Competitive — Negative Interdependence	**Oppositional** — Obstructive	**Exclusive** — Win-Lose Outcome
Individualistic — No Interdependence	None	**Individual** — Self-Determined Outcome

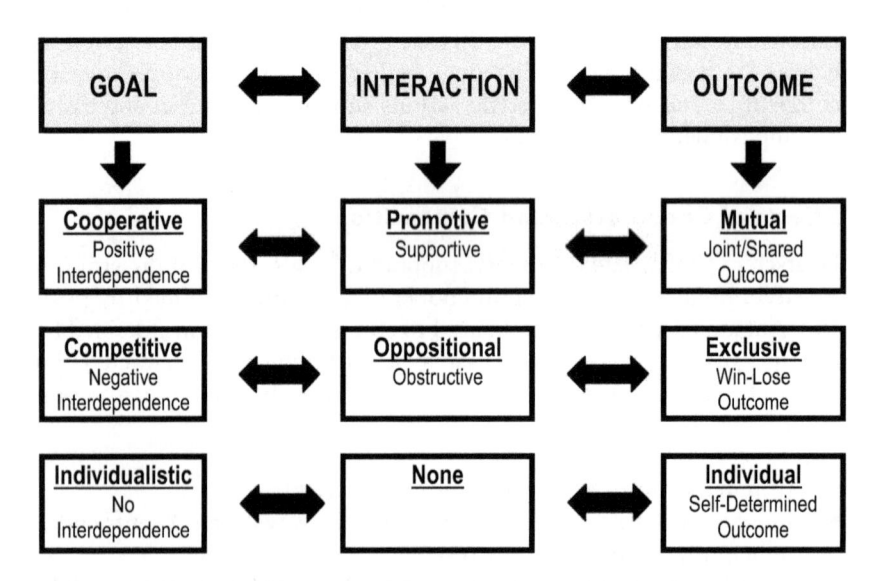

Figure 2.2 Social interdependence theory posits that goal interdependence influences social interaction, which determines outcomes (Deutsch, 2011, 2014b; Johnson & Johnson, 1989, 2005, 2009, 2011). Bidirectional arrows indicate that perceived interdependence, interactions, and outcomes induce and are induced by each other.

Source: Diagram: ©2019 Laurie Stevahn.

structures (compared to competitive or individualistic) enhance (a) productivity and achievement; (b) positive interpersonal relations; and (c) psychological health, well-being, and social competence (Johnson & Johnson, 2017).

Despite the elegance of social interdependence theory, Mort (as well as the Johnsons) recognized that few interdependent situations (if any) are purely positive or negative. Instead, people typically bring mixed motives to social situations, so people's perceived strength of positive or negative interdependence may vary. Mort also reminded us of the numerous and complex ways that people may experience interdependence.

> People's goals may be linked for various reasons. Thus, positive interdependence can result from people liking one another, being rewarded in terms of their joint achievement, needing to share a resource or overcome an obstacle together, holding common membership or identification with a group whose fate is important to them, being unable to achieve their task goals unless they divide up the work, being influenced by personality and cultural orientation, being bound together because they are treated this way by a common enemy or an authority, and so on. Similarly, with regard to negative interdependence, it can result from people disliking one another or from their being rewarded in such a way that the more the other gets of the reward, the less one gets, and so on.
>
> (Deutsch, 2014b, pp. 4–5)

Nonetheless, even given the complex motives that people bring to social situations, abundant research consistently demonstrates that social interdependence theory tends to hold true across different disciplines, contexts, cultures, and countries around the world (Johnson & Johnson, 2017). This is instructive for educators working to create welcoming, safe, inclusive school environments that optimize learning and support student success.

Constructive Conflict Resolution

> Whether the participants in a conflict have a cooperative orientation or a competitive one is decisive in determining its course and outcomes.
> (Deutsch, 2014b, p. 3)

Mort's distinction as a social psychologist particularly derives from his groundbreaking theorizing and research that essentially established the field of conflict resolution in the modern era. Ranked the 63rd most eminent psychologist of the 20th century (Haggbloom et al., 2002), much of Mort's work continues to define key aspects of that field today. His numerous publications (readily available from various repositories) and interviews (many available on the Internet) explicate his ingenious adaptations of game theory (described previously) to experimentally study people's conflict behaviors in cooperative or competitive situations. Although details of Mort's research go beyond the scope of this chapter, the following short list of contributions points to core aspects of constructive conflict that should be considered in training programs and when trying to resolve "conflicts of all sorts—interpersonal, intergroup, and international" (Deutsch, 2014a, p. xxiv).

- "No one has to face the prospect of a conflict-free existence. Conflict can neither be eliminated nor even suppressed for long" (Deutsch, 1973, p. 10). Mort recognized that conflict inherently exists in human relationships, making it pervasive in people's lives and, therefore, profoundly universal.
- "Conflict is potentially of personal and social value. Conflict has many positive functions" (Deutsch, 1973, p. 8). Mort emphasized that the goal is not to eliminate conflict, which is impossible, but rather to engage in conflict constructively to experience its benefits. In fact, conflict can stimulate interest, direct attention to concerns, illuminate issues and injustices, shift power structures for inclusion and equality, adjust social or working norms to enhance people's lived experiences, deepen trust when constructive outcomes result, and test personal capabilities for growth and development. In addition, people often seek or participate in competitive athletic contests for fun or value the suspense that arises from reading novels, watching films, or attending the theater, all driven by plots, protagonists, and conflicts (Deutsch, 1973).
- "A *conflict* exists whenever *incompatible* activities occur. . . . An action that is incompatible with another action prevents, obstructs, interferes, injures, or in some way makes the latter less likely or less effective" (Deutsch, 1973, p. 10, emphasis in original). Mort's definition of conflict reveals its complex manifestations, clarifies its confusion with competition, and paves the way for observational empirical measures. He particularly emphasizes that conflict and competition are not necessarily interchangeable. "Conflict can occur in a cooperative or competitive context, and the processes of conflict resolution that are likely to be displayed will be strongly influenced by the context within which the conflict occurs" (Deutsch, 1973, pp. 10–11). Conflict, therefore, is not exclusive to competitive situations; it often occurs among people pursuing cooperative goals. For example, consider educators who are mutually committed to enhancing the literacy skills of all learners in an elementary school yet disagree over which

curricular materials or instructional programs will best achieve that shared goal.
- "Competition can vary from destructive to constructive: unfair, unregulated competition at the destructive end; fair, regulated competition in between; and constructive competition at the positive end. In constructive competition, the losers as well as the winners gain" (Deutsch, 2014b, pp. 9–10). Again, Mort reminds us that although competition is a form of conflict, it has redeeming qualities under certain conditions. Sporting contests, for example, can be enjoyable and motivate athletes to further develop their skills when comparable abilities make it possible for anyone to win, everyone knows and abides by fair rules, referees monitor accountability, and rewards are not high-stake. Similarly, people can benefit from playing competitive games for fun, personal improvement, or individual assessment, as when trying to decide whether to continue to invest time, energy, or resources in that endeavor. Despite these and other potential benefits, Mort issues this warning: "Nevertheless, serious problems are associated with competition when it does not occur in a cooperative context and if it is not effectively regulated by fair rules" (Deutsch, 2014b, p. 10).
- *"What conditions give rise to a constructive or destructive process of conflict resolution?"* (Deutsch, 2014a, p. xxxiv, emphasis in original). This became the essential question guiding Mort's theorizing and research, summarized in the section that follows.

Deutsch's Theory of Constructive Conflict Resolution

Conceptualizing conflict as a relational process that holds possibility for either constructive or destructive interactions and outcomes made Mort's previous theorizing and research on cooperation and competition particularly relevant to investigating conflict resolution. Specifically, in situations of conflict, the question became: "What initiates or gives rise to one or the other process?" (Deutsch, 2014b, p. 12). Prior studies demonstrated that interdependence (positive or negative) and actions (effective or bungling) influence social-psychological processes (substitutability, attitudes, inducibility). These, in turn, produce characteristic effects (helpful or harmful) on communication, behaviors, power, attitudes, relations, and so on. Mort theorized that interdependence, actions, and social-psychological processes would similarly influence human dynamics in conflict situations. Deutsch's theory posits that constructive conflict resolution results from cooperative versus competitive processes: "constructive processes of conflict resolution are similar to cooperative processes of problem solving, and destructive processes of conflict resolution are similar to competitive processes" (Deutsch, 2014b, p. 9). Figure 2.3 visually depicts

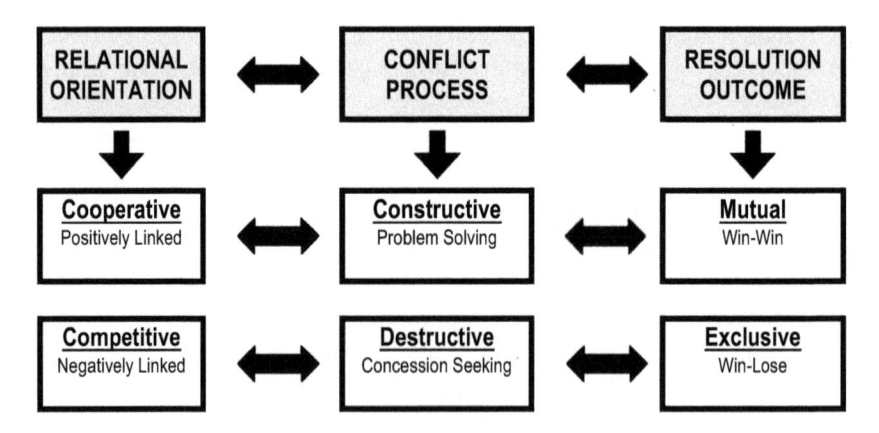

```
RELATIONAL           CONFLICT            RESOLUTION
ORIENTATION  ⬌       PROCESS     ⬌       OUTCOME
     ⬇                   ⬇                   ⬇
Cooperative          Constructive        Mutual
Positively Linked ⬌  Problem Solving ⬌   Win-Win

Competitive          Destructive         Exclusive
Negatively Linked ⬌  Concession Seeking ⬌ Win-Lose
```

Figure 2.3 Deutsch's (1973) theory of constructive conflict resolution posits that the relational orientation of disputants (cooperative or competitive) influences conflict processes (constructive or destructive) that affect resolution outcomes (mutual or exclusive). Bidirectional arrows indicate that conflict orientations, processes, and outcomes induce and are induced by each other.

Source: Diagram: ©2019 Laurie Stevahn.

these dynamics. Importantly, this theory implies that cooperative orientations, norms, values, and contexts encourage and support constructive conflict processes capable of producing mutually satisfying win-win resolution. In contrast, competitive orientations, norms, values, and contexts discourage and obstruct shared problem solving, instead fostering and reinforcing destructive processes likely to end in win-lose resolution (or sometimes lose-lose resolution, in which all disputants are dissatisfied). The theory also implies that conflict processes and outcomes likely will be more constructive when disputants reframe their issues as mutual problems to be solved.

The many studies that Mort and his students systematically conducted to confirm his theorizing on conflict resolution began to reveal a basic pattern that came to be known as Deutsch's Crude Law of Social Relations: "The characteristic processes and effects elicited by a given type of social relationship also tend to elicit that type of social relationship, and a typical effect tends to induce the other typical effects of that relationship" (Deutsch, 2014b, p. 12). This means:

> Cooperation induces and is induced by perceived similarity in beliefs and attitudes, readiness to be helpful, openness in communication, trusting and friendly attitudes, sensitivity to common interests and deemphasis of opposed interests, orientation toward enhancing mutual power rather than power differences, and so on.

Similarly, competition induces and is induced by the use of the tactics of coercion, threat, or deception; attempts to enhance the power differences between oneself and the other; poor communication; minimization of the awareness of similarities in values and increased sensitivity to opposed interests; suspicious and hostile attitudes; the importance, rigidity, and size of issues in conflict; and so on.

(Deutsch, 2014b, p. 12)

Because cooperative learning induces, cultivates, and nurtures the very characteristics conducive to constructive conflict resolution, it becomes more than solely an instructional strategy to promote student achievement. It also helps establish the types of supportive relationships, respectful norms, and democratic values in schools and classrooms that underpin constructive conflict.

Social Justice and Peace Psychology

"That's not fair" expresses a feeling that frequently leads to conflict. . . . Conflict can lead to changes that reduce injustice, or it can increase injustice if it takes a destructive form, as in war.

(Deutsch, 2014c, p. 29)

Mort's theories of cooperation and competition and constructive conflict resolution naturally led to examining relational dynamics in situations of oppression and injustice. In fact, Mort's experiences of injustice (exclusion) as a child focused his attention on justice (fairness) at an early age, and he maintained this focus in his theorizing and research throughout his life. Early in his career, Mort co-conducted a study on interracial housing (Deutsch & Collins, 1951) that influenced the Newark Public Housing Authority to rethink its policies toward eliminating (reducing) racial prejudice and discrimination. Near the end of his life, Mort and colleagues were conducting studies to investigate conditions mediating people's willingness to participate in a global community dedicated to tackling worldwide problems that interdependently affect us all (Marcus, Deutsch, & Liu, 2017). He anticipated that, if not resolved, such issues would threaten sustained peace. Examples include,

global climate change; weapons of mass destruction; global economic disruptions; disease pandemics; gross inequalities within and among nations; the enormous cost of militarism, wars, and the disastrous consequences of war; the enormous costs of sexism, racism, and other forms of social injustice to the world community; the inadequate education of children to be capable and responsible world citizens; etc. These problems will require effective global cooperation if they are to be managed well.

(Deutsch, Marcus, & Brazaitis, 2015, pp. 329–330)

Concern for peace through constructive conflict also grounded Mort's work in the 1980s when he turned his attention to the social psychology of distributive justice, defined as *"fairness of the distribution* of the conditions and goods that affect individual well-being" (Deutsch, 1985, p. 1, emphasis in original). He recognized that his prior research on cooperation and conflict

> could be labeled as "justice" research quite properly. . . . [It] focused on the important question: Under what conditions are people with conflicting interests able to work out an agreement (that is, a system of justice defining what each shall give and receive in the transaction between them) that is stable and mutually satisfying?
>
> (Deutsch, 1985, p. 6)

This produced the *equality principle* (equal distribution, such as every person having one vote) and the *need principle* (preferential distribution, such as early access or unobstructed seating for people using wheelchairs). Both of these principles were applicable to determining fair distributions beyond the prevailing *equity principle* (proportional distribution, such as financial reward according to productivity or merit), which was the primary principle prior to Mort's research (Deutsch, 1985).

Eventually, Mort developed a framework for more comprehensively considering injustice/oppression, what keeps it in place, and how to overcome it. He presents the framework and its complexities in various publications (e.g., see Deutsch, 2006, 2014c) and suggests actions capable of producing positive change. Essentially, the framework identifies types of justice/injustice, including:

- *Distributive Justice*—fairness in outcomes from applying equity, equality, or need principles, such as believing that the final allocation of a resource is fair.
- *Procedural Justice*—fairness in the processes used to determine outcomes, such as believing that reaching consensus is a fair process for deciding an outcome.
- *Sense of Justice*—whether people experience injustice (or not), such as whether parents or guardians perceive an unequal division of labor in providing childcare when inequality actually exists.

- *Retributive and Reparative Justice*—responding to a violation of moral norms and repairing the moral community, such as responding to race-based discrimination in housing, financing, or employment in ways that produce accountability and restoration.
- *Scope of Justice*—who is (or is not) entitled to fair treatment and outcomes demonstrated by moral inclusion (or exclusion) in the community, such as deeming people worthy of human safety, dignity, respect, access, and opportunities (versus unworthy, sometimes to the extreme as in apartheid, genocide, and the Holocaust).

Mort further suggests research-informed actions for working against injustice and oppression. These include awakening a sense of injustice, using power appropriately, increasing bargaining power, appealing to moral values, cultivating allies, and using nonviolent strategies (Deutsch, 2006, 2014c). He also notes that constructive conflict resolution training plays an important role in developing a justice orientation. For example, in addition to integrative negotiation and other constructive conflict skills, training should teach participants to (a) recognize systemic forms of injustice, (b) cultivate an expansive sense of moral community and fair treatment for all, (c) increase human empathy through social perspective-taking, (d) acquire insight on forgiveness and reconciliation, and (e) develop skill in inventing alternative solutions capable of addressing varied conflicting interests in ways that go beyond win-lose solutions (Deutsch, 2014c). Ultimately, Mort emphasizes:

> The relationship between conflict and justice is bidirectional: injustice breeds conflict, and destructive conflict gives rise to injustice. Preventing destructive conflict requires more than training in constructive conflict resolution. It also necessitates reducing the gross injustices that characterize much of our social world at the interpersonal, intergroup, and international levels.
>
> (Deutsch, 2014c, pp. 53–54)

Living Mort's Legacy

> Throughout my career in social psychology, I have been concerned with the interrelations among experimental research, theory, and social policy. I started my graduate study not long after Hiroshima and Nagasaki, and my work in social psychology has been shadowed by the atomic cloud ever since. . . . My continuing interest [is] in contributing to the understanding of how to prevent destructive conflict and initiate cooperation.
>
> (Deutsch, 1973, p. ix)

Mort learned from the past, lived in the present, and looked to the future. He would invite us to do the same. The Morton Deutsch International Center for Cooperation and Conflict Resolution (MD-ICCCR) at Teachers College, Columbia University (founded by Mort in 1986, his name later added to honor his legacy), intentionally bridges theory, research, and practice to advance collaboration among scholars, practitioners, and activists. The center offers numerous graduate degrees relevant to cooperation, conflict, and justice; produces research studies and publications on those topics; sponsors training programs and outreach projects; hosts conferences and research awards; and provides real-world consultations with local, national, and international leaders, organizations, and community members toward strategically advancing constructive conflict.[1] Those who regularly explore the center's website know that it offers a wealth of resources useful for learning, reinforcing, and expanding our understanding of cooperation, conflict, and justice from a social-psychological perspective. The website also stimulates thinking about future possibilities for advancing theory, research, and practice by pointing to issues, actions, and questions that scholars, practitioners, and activists can further develop, implement, and investigate. Routinely visiting the website provides current information, inspiration, guidance, updates, and opportunities to connect with others devoted to advancing cooperation, constructive conflict, and justice throughout the world.

Lessons Learned for Future Action

It's challenging to succinctly articulate lessons learned from Mort because there are so many. His legacy looms large. Mort died in March 2017 at age 97 leaving us with an established discipline of conflict resolution significantly shaped by his life's work. In tribute, a collection of articles in the *Negotiation Journal* (2018, January) by colleagues who knew him well provides reflections and perspectives on "Mort the scientist" and "Mort the man," capturing the theoretically complex brilliance of his research and his personal warmth, humility, and kindness (Coleman, 2018; Druckman, 2018; Johnson & Johnson, 2018; Opotow, 2018; Pruitt, 2018).

Perhaps the most central lessons are those most closely connected to the two enduring themes that defined Mort's long career. The first was his attention to understanding conditions that affect interpersonal, intergroup, and international dynamics of cooperation and competition, conflict processes, and distributive justice. As he indicates, "I have continued to believe that these foci are central to understanding social life and also that a 'social' social psychology rather than an 'individual' social psychology would have these as its fundamental concerns" (Deutsch, 2008, pp. 238–239). The second was Mort's unwavering social conscience and commitment to framing his work for real-world application. He strategically positioned his theorizing and research for "social relevance to key social problems" (Deutsch, 2008, p. 239). Sometimes, real-life experiences or observations inspired his work; other times, he pursued theoretical research to illuminate universal social issues and suggest how results could ground and guide pragmatic action for constructive change. Regardless of the starting point, justice and peace steadfastly motivated Mort's pursuits.

> Sometimes images, derived from such social problems as war and peace, prejudice, marital conflict, and injustice, would be the starting point for the development of a theoretical analysis or an experimental study. At other times I would use theory and research . . . to shed light on important social issues.
> (Deutsch, 2008, p. 239)

What would Mort want us to learn from his work, make real in our lives, and carry to the future? Here's a short list, each echoing the two intertwined themes that grounded Mort's life and career, providing us direction for living his legacy.

Theory, research, and practice go hand in hand; focus on all three. Pursue research to confirm, refine, and expand theory; use validated theory to formulate concrete actions likely to foster success in real-world settings; and confirm and refine the effectiveness of practical applications by conducting evaluation studies in the field. Mort reminds us: "There are many kinds of research, all with merit. They have differing purposes and often require varying types of skill" (Deutsch, Goldman-Wetzler, & Chung, 2014, p. 1061). This holds researchers, practitioners, and activists alike to a higher standard in dealing with each other than often occurs. Mort would encourage us to recognize and uphold the value of each other's contributions toward collectively furthering understanding of effective cooperation, conflict, and justice. This means that educators should develop theory-based programs and/or inspect curricula prior to adoption to determine the extent to which each embodies validated theory. It also challenges researchers to find ways to rigorously study theory in the field where messy social situations complicate theory-based implementations. In short, we need each other to advance progress.

Pay attention to conditions; enact structures that promote constructive interpersonal dynamics for social well-being. Whether focused on cooperation, conflict, or justice, Mort persistently asked, "Under what conditions?" We should do the same. This orientation keeps us focused on the uniqueness of every situation, challenging us to develop tangible applications that will make the theoretical conditions come to life in any particular setting. This helps avoid the one-size-fits-all, cookbook-recipe, paint-by-number approaches that cannot effectively deal with the nuances, circumstances, and complexities across different contexts. Our job is to make theoretical conditions tangible by structuring shared goals; arranging tasks in ways that require interconnected contributions; modeling and expecting social perspective-taking; framing conflicts as mutual problems to be solved; deepening commitment to humanity through inclusive practices; and teaching, developing, and refining communication skills that promote and support effective processes and outcomes. Simply put, we must determine whether effective conditions exist in our environments by examining expectations, roles, rules, rewards, policies, norms, systems, interactions, and so on that influence constructive interpersonal processes and outcomes. Then it's our job to enact and strengthen those conditions that cultivate and sustain cooperation and constructive conflict for a just and humane world. We should stop asking "What works?" and start asking "Under what conditions will it work?" and then take action to implement those conditions.

Connect across contexts; gather researchers, practitioners, and activists together to listen and learn from and with each other. Advancing theory, research, and practice likely will be more successful when researchers, practitioners, and activists join together to share goals, concerns, values, perspectives, and experiences rather than staying separate and apart. If working to make the world more just and humane truly matters, then we must find ways to interact across contexts, seriously listen to each other, and respect each other's challenges and concerns. Mort would advise us to form respectful diverse partnerships capable of opening creative and effective pathways forward for everyone.

Walk the talk and stay the course; people's actions do change the world. Despite the numerous and serious afflictions in the world, change happens when people care enough to act, putting knowledge and skill to use, no matter our roles or contexts. Mort would encourage us all to live with hope and optimism. He also would challenge each of us to know what we stand for and stand steady, using science to inform our practice, knowing that large-scale progress happens over the arc of time as people together persevere in tackling serious social issues.

> There is still a lot to learn so it's important to have an open mind about the possibility of new developments in the field. . . . I think it is important to maintain hope despite the cynicism that exists throughout most of our world. You can bring about positive change, and you can help bring improvement to the world. . . . I was lucky enough to be a student of Kurt Lewin. He did not have the view that scientists should live away from the world; their ideas should have impact on the world. . . . My hope is that even as one is concerned with abstract ideas, one is also concerned with improving the world.
>
> (Deutsch, as cited in Smith, 2015, para. 11 & 13)

Enduring Qualities to Emulate

Those who knew Mort well—especially colleagues and students—frequently note an additional lesson they learned from the enduring personal qualities that so consistently defined Mort's human interactions. These included his warmth and caring, graciousness and lack of ego, respect for and belief in people's capabilities, generosity with time and attention, supportive mentoring, and welcoming tone. Mort constantly exhibited these personal virtues as he invited people into mutual exploration of possibilities. Gratitude looms large, particularly among Mort's students, for the safe yet challenging environment he intentionally created. His students often express how grateful they are for the creative tension interwoven with interpersonal support that they experienced under Mort's leadership, enabling them to pursue their professional interests by developing their own ideas to advance theory, research, and practice relevant to cooperation, conflict, and justice. As a leader, Mort treated people as his equal, including students. In his presence, you knew you mattered. Regardless of one's role or stature, Mort always showed sincere respect as he inclusively brought people together from different contexts, listened to concerns, championed mutual problem-solving, and encouraged future action. These are the personal values and principles that grounded Mort's life. These are the enduring qualities that impacted so many, including nearly 70 former doctoral students who traveled from far and near to New York City to celebrate his 95th birthday in 2015 (see tributes on YouTube: Celebrating Mort Deutsch's 95th Birthday, Life and Work).

Ultimately, Mort's contributions to social science and social well-being call each of us to action. We can answer the call by adopting his attitudes, living his values, and applying his theoretical foundations in our personal and professional contexts. This means advancing the study and practice of cooperative learning, conflict resolution, and peace education in schools, organizations, and institutions at interpersonal, intergroup, and international levels. It also means emulating Mort's integrity, kindness, humility, and fortitude, remembering that his theoretical brilliance never overshadowed his humble demeanor and the world's social afflictions never deterred his hopeful spirit. Tackling social issues, whether locally or globally, starts by enacting cooperative conditions capable of supporting and sustaining socially just and inclusive communities where peaceful problem solving becomes the norm. Mort's theoretical foundations provide substantial guidance for advancing these efforts now and in the future. His ever-optimistic orientation also inspires courage for the journey: "Let us maintain hope that we can improve the world and let us act to fulfill that hope" (Deutsch et al., 2015, p. 349). Through us, the legacy of Morton Deutsch lives on.

Note

1. see https://icccr.tc.columbia.edu

References

Charter of the United Nations. (1945). *Chapter I: Purposes and principles.* Retrieved from www.un.org/en/sections/un-charter/chapter-i/index.html

Coleman, P. T. (2018). Ten major scientific contributions that promote a more just, peaceful, and sustainable world. *Negotiation Journal, 34*(1), 105–116.

Deutsch, M. (1949a). A theory of cooperation and competition. *Human Relations, 2*, 129–151.

Deutsch, M. (1949b). An experimental study of the effects of cooperation and competition upon group process. *Human Relations, 2*, 199–231.

Deutsch, M. (1973). *The resolution of conflict: Constructive and destructive processes.* New Haven, CT: Yale University Press.

Deutsch, M. (1985). *Distributive justice: A social-psychological perspective.* New Haven, CT: Yale University Press.

Deutsch, M. (1995a). The constructive management of conflict: Developing the knowledge and crafting the practice. In B. B. Bunker & J. B. Rubin (Eds.), *Conflict, cooperation, and justice: Essays inspired by the work of Morton Deutsch* (pp. 123–129). San Francisco, CA: Jossey-Bass.

Deutsch, M. (1995b). Justice: Why we need a new moral philosophy. In B. B. Bunker & J. B. Rubin (Eds.), *Conflict, cooperation, and justice: Essays inspired by the work of Morton Deutsch* (pp. 371–379). San Francisco, CA: Jossey-Bass.

Deutsch, M. (2006). A framework for thinking about oppression and its change. *Social Justice Research, 19*(1), 7–41.

Deutsch, M. (2008). A career that spans the history of modern social psychology. In R. Levine, A. Rodrigues, & L. Zelezny (Eds.), *Journeys in social psychology: Looking back to inspire the future* (pp. 221–240). New York, NY: Psychology Press.

Deutsch, M. (2011). Cooperation and competition. In P. T. Coleman (Ed.), *Conflict, interdependence, and justice: The intellectual legacy of Morton Deutsch* (pp. 23–40). New York, NY: Springer.

Deutsch, M. (2014a). Introduction. In P. T. Coleman, M. Deutsch, & E. C. Marcus (Eds.), *The handbook of conflict resolution: Theory and research* (3rd ed., pp. xvii–xxxviii). San Francisco, CA: Jossey-Bass.

Deutsch, M. (2014b). Cooperation, competition, and conflict. In P. T. Coleman, M. Deutsch, & E. C. Marcus (Eds.), *The handbook of conflict resolution: Theory and research* (3rd ed., pp. 3–28). San Francisco, CA: Jossey-Bass.

Deutsch, M. (2014c). Justice and conflict. In P. T. Coleman, M. Deutsch, & E. C. Marcus (Eds.), *The handbook of conflict resolution: Theory and research* (3rd ed., pp. 29–55). San Francisco, CA: Jossey-Bass.

Deutsch, M., & Collins, M. E. (1951). *Interracial housing: A psychological evaluation of a social experiment.* Minneapolis, MN: University of Minnesota Press.

Deutsch, M., Goldman-Wetzler, J., & Chung, C. T. (2014). A framework for thinking about research on conflict resolution initiatives. In P. T. Coleman, M. Deutsch, & E. C. Marcus (Eds.), *The handbook of conflict resolution: Theory and research* (3rd ed., pp. 1061–1086). San Francisco, CA: Jossey-Bass.

Deutsch, M., Marcus, E. C., & Brazaitis, S. J. (2015). Developing a global community: A social psychological perspective. In M. Galluccio (Ed.), *Handbook of international negotiation: Interpersonal, intercultural, and diplomatic perspectives* (pp. 329–351). Switzerland: Springer International. https://doi.org/10.1007/978-3-319-10687-8_24

Druckman, D. (2018). A pioneer's legacy: The influence of Morton Deutsch. *Negotiation Journal, 34*(1), 121–125.

Frydenberg, E. (2005). *Morton Deutsch: A life and legacy of mediation and conflict resolution.* Brisbane, Australia: Australian Academic Press.

Haggbloom, S. J., Warnick, R., Warnick, J. E., Jones, V. K., Yarbrough, G. L., Russell, T. M., . . . & Monte, E. (2002). The 100 most eminent psychologists of the 20th century. *Review of General Psychology, 6*(2), 139–152.

Hunt, M. (1993). *The story of psychology.* New York, NY: Doubleday.

Johnson, D. W., & Johnson, F. P. (2017). *Joining together: Group theory and group skills* (12th ed.). New York, NY: Pearson.

Johnson, D. W., & Johnson, R. T. (1989). *Cooperation and competition: Theory and research.* Edina, MN: Interaction Book Company.

Johnson, D. W., & Johnson, R. T. (2005). New developments in social interdependence theory. *Genetic, Social, and General Psychology Monographs, 131*(4), 285–358.

Johnson, D. W., & Johnson, R. T. (2009). An educational psychology success story: Social interdependence theory and cooperative learning. *Educational Researcher, 38*(5), 365–379.

Johnson, D. W., & Johnson, R. T. (2011). Intellectual legacy: Cooperation and competition. In P. T. Coleman (Ed.), *Conflict, interdependence, and justice: The intellectual legacy of Morton Deutsch* (pp. 41–64). New York, NY: Springer.

Johnson, D. W., & Johnson, R. T. (2018). Morton Deutsch's tough-minded, tender-hearted, and creative theories and research. *Negotiation Journal, 34*(1), 97–104.

Lewin. K. (1951). *Field theory in social science.* New York, NY: Harper.

Marcus, E. C., Deutsch, M., & Liu, Y. (2017). A study of willingness to participate in the development of a global human community. *Peace and Conflict: Journal of Peace Psychology, 23*(1), 89–92.

Opotow, S. (2018). Morton Deutsch: Scholar, mentor, visionary. *Negotiation Journal, 34*(1), 89–96.

Pruitt, D. G. (2018). Remembering the father of experimental research on conflict. *Negotiation Journal, 34*(1), 117–120.

Smith, M. (2015). *Interview with Morton Deutsch, Ph.D., Professor Emeritus and founder of the International Center for Cooperation and Conflict Resolution (MD-ICCCR).* Retrieved from http://ac4.ei.columbia.edu/2015/01/28/interview-with-morton-deutsch-ph-d-professor-emeritus-and-founder-of-the-international-center-for-cooperation-and-conflict-resolution-md-icccr/

Chapter 3

Learning Together and Alone
The History of Our Involvement in Cooperative Learning

David W. Johnson and Roger T. Johnson

The origin of our approach to cooperative learning has two quite distinct roots. David's commitment to cooperative learning came from his involvement in the civil rights movement of the early 1960s, while Roger's interest in cooperative learning came from his involvement in the science education revolution of the early 1960s and his involvement in the development of the ESS Science Inquiry Curriculum.

Civil Rights' Roots

In 1961 David was fortunate enough to meet the students from Greensboro, North Carolina, who were conducting sit-ins at the local businesses that refused to serve Black-Americans. This inspired David to form a civil rights group at Ball State University to integrate student housing and ensure that all students were served at local restaurants. He discovered that the campus housing was segregated and restaurants near the campus would serve mixed groups of students but not groups of all black students. As David was the past editor of the Ball State News and Director of Internal Affairs in the student government, he had the political power (with the help of dedicated black and white students) to ensure that all discriminatory practices were ended. As a result of these efforts, he was awarded the Russell Bull Scholarship by the United Packinghouse, Food, and Allied Workers (national award given annually for the most outstanding work in civil rights on university campuses; Martin Luther King chaired the Award Committee). These experiences convinced David that he should get a doctorate in social psychology to learn how to eliminate racism and resolve racial conflicts constructively. Wanting to live in New York City, he entered graduate school at Teachers College, Columbia University, to study with Goodwin Watson, who was then one of the premiere social action professors in the United States. Unfortunately for David, Goodwin Watson retired in 1962, the year David began his graduate work. Fortunately for David, Morton Deutsch was hired to replace Watson in 1963 and graciously agreed to be David's advisor.

At that time, David was active in several civil rights and peace groups, such as the Student Nonviolent Coordinating Committee (SNCC), Congress on Racial Equality (CORE), the Northern Student Movement (NSM), and the Society Against Nuclear Energy (SANE). His first two research studies were on the impact of teaching Black history to Black children and teenagers as part of the Harlem Parents' Committee Freedom School (Johnson, 1966a, 1966b). David both taught the Black history classes and evaluated their impact on the students.

At that time, the psychological literature on reducing prejudice was dominated by contact theory (Allport, 1954; Watson, 1947; Williams, 1947). It posits that four conditions are needed to reduce prejudice: cooperation, equal status, personal conversations, and support from authorities. David concluded that cooperative interaction was the key factor. While schools were being desegregated, it seemed that many if not most teachers had no idea how to organize integrated classes to reduce racism and conflict between white and minority students. David, therefore, decided to develop a clear procedure for doing so based on having white and minority students work together cooperatively.

At Columbia University, David also studied with Kenneth Herrold and Matthew Miles in applied group dynamics. In 1964 Miles published a book on innovation in education. In considering how to ensure schools adopted cooperative learning, David considered Miles' findings. As a result of the training in applied group dynamics, in the summer of 1966, David was awarded an internship by the National Training Laboratory in Applied Behavioral Science (NTL). He spent the summer of 1966 in Bethel, Maine, training participants in applied group dynamics (i.e., leadership, communication, trust-building, decision-making). NTL emphasized experiential learning. The heart of experiential learning is participants engaging in an experience, reflecting on it (incorporating relevant theory and research), and then deriving conclusions about what they have learned. Eventually, two books resulted from David's interest in experiential learning (Johnson, 1972/1999; Johnson & F. Johnson, 1975/2017).

David focused on education as the setting for interventions aimed at reducing racism. He believed that racism would be most effectively ended through intervening in the socialization of children, adolescents, and young adults. In the fall of 1966 David accepted a position at the University of Minnesota in the Psychological Foundations Area of the Educational Psychology Department and began training teachers in the use of cooperative learning. He continued his research on negotiations and perspective-taking, experiential learning, and aspects of engaging in social action. In the late 1960s, he met David DeVries and Keith Edwards, who were doing outstanding work at Johns Hopkins University on cooperative learning. The three of them agreed to submit a symposium to the

American Psychological Association Convention each year, alternating who submitted and chaired the session. Participants in the symposiums included Stuart Cook, Slomo and Yael Sharan, David Buckholdt, Carole and Russel Ames, Patrick Laughlin, David Thomas, and eventually Elliot Aronson and Robert Slavin. While David DeVries and Keith Edwards moved on to other interests (leaving one of their graduate students, Robert Slavin, in charge of their Center), we have always missed them and appreciated their pioneering work on cooperation and games.

Inquiry Learning

Roger's involvement in cooperative learning began with the revolution in science teaching in the late 1950s. It resulted from "Sputnik," the first satellite launched into space, not by the United States, but by the Soviet Union in 1957. President Eisenhower then funded a revolution in science education that emphasized an inquiry, materials-based approach to teaching elementary science (as opposed to a textbook and worksheet approach). A group of professors at Harvard and MIT recruited outstanding science teachers to help them develop the curriculum. Roger was recruited after a nationwide search to both help in developing the curriculum and be a master teacher demonstrating the curriculum to other teachers. He spent several summers at Harvard University doing so. The result was the Elementary Science Study (ESS), in which students were assigned to small groups, given a set of materials, and expected to use inquiry methods in completing assignments. It was assumed that students knew how to work together in small groups. Roger's work on the ESS science curriculum was influenced by the writings of Piaget (1950), Vygotsky (1978), and Bruner (1960). As part of the implementation of the ESS science curriculum, Roger demonstrated lessons in districts throughout the United States and got to know the staff development personnel and science teachers in numerous districts.

Since David was in New York City and Roger was then in Colorado, when Roger drove to and from Boston each summer, he would stop by and visit David. In their conversations, David would point out that the groups needed to be structured cooperatively and students needed to be trained in the small-group skills required to work cooperatively with each other. When Roger accepted a position at the University of Minnesota in 1969, their conversations took a more serious turn, and while Roger was training elementary science teachers to use inquiry methods in their classes, he added that inquiry lessons needed to be structured cooperatively. He and David also organized the Cooperative Learning Center in 1969 to combine Roger's interests in science education and inquiry learning with David's interests in reducing racism and violence in American society and experiential learning. They then began forming a national and international network of school districts implementing cooperative learning.

Unique Partnership

The two of us (David and Roger) represent a unique partnership. David thinks in a linear fashion, while Roger thinks in a more random fashion. While we both followed the scientific method, David worked in a clear theory–research–practice progression, while Roger observed what worked in classrooms and then built conclusions from effective practice. David was convinced that the long-term institutionalization of cooperative learning in schools depended on publishing theory and research articles and ensuring that any literature review on pedagogical methods would include cooperative learning. Roger was convinced that demonstrating that cooperative learning worked in real classes and schools would ensure its further implementation. The two quite opposite approaches complemented each other and resulted in considerable creativity in deriving and implementing our cooperative learning methods. Even in training, we are opposites. Roger is an extrovert with a spontaneous sense of humor. David is an introvert who learns jokes as a way to cover it up. People who know us often comment on how opposite we are in our thinking and priorities, but we have always sensed that the combination of the two of us was much more productive than each of us separately. Professionally, we have disagreed almost every day and our conflict has greatly contributed to our productivity. We are truly a gestalt, the combination of the two of us making a creative whole.

Creating the "Learning Together and Alone" Method

Our method of cooperative learning is known as the "Learning Together and Alone" method, based on the title of our first book (Johnson & Johnson, 1975/1999) and the fact that we believe that all three ways of structuring learning situations (e.g., cooperative, competitive, and individualistic) are appropriate under certain conditions. We developed our method following four principles: (a) practical procedures should be derived from theory, (b) the theory must be validated by research, (c) operational procedures should be formulated from the validated theory, and (d) the implementation of the operational procedures will reveal shortcomings in the theory, which results in revisions in the theory, a new round of validating research studies, modified procedures, and more fruitful implementation, which illuminates new shortcomings in the theory and so forth (see Figure 3.1).

First, David used Deutsch's (1949, 1962) theory of cooperation and competition and Watson's structure–process–outcome theory (Watson,

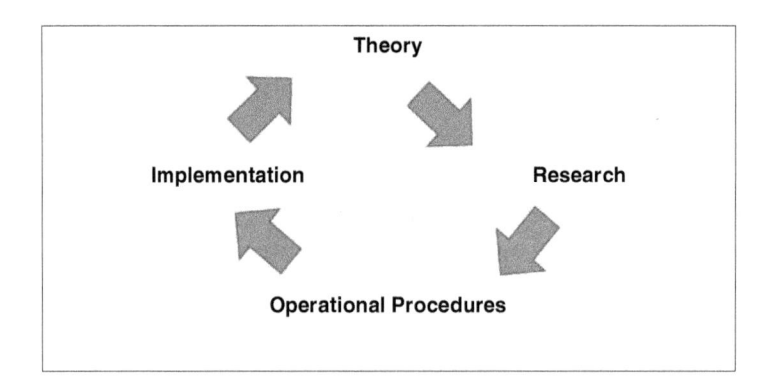

Figure 3.1 Cycle of development of our cooperative learning procedures

Source: Reprinted with permission from: Johnson, D. W., & Johnson, R. T. (1989). *Cooperation and competition: Theory and research*. Edina, MN: Interaction Book Company.

1966; Watson & Johnson, 1972) to explain the impact of interaction among students on outcomes of interest. Second, beginning in 1970, David and Roger published reviews of the research on cooperative, competitive, and individualistic efforts (e.g., Johnson, 1970; Johnson & Johnson, 1974, 1975/1999, 1978, 1989) in order to ascertain the relative efficacy of cooperation. In addition, David and Roger (with our students and colleagues) have conducted and published over 115 research studies on cooperative, competitive, and individualistic efforts. Third, from the research and validated theory David and Roger derived operational procedures for implementing cooperative learning for educators and others (see Johnson & Johnson, 1975/1999; Johnson, Johnson, & Holubec, 1984/2013). Fourth, the operational procedures were implemented in a wide variety of schools and other settings. From the implementation, insights into how the theory could be improved were derived, which led to revisions of the theory, new research, improved operational procedures, and improved implementations. This cycle of theory, research, operational procedures, implementation, guided David and Roger's development of our cooperative learning methods.

Theory-Based Approach to Cooperative Learning

Many cooperative learning practices were and are atheoretical. The links with the scientific literature on learning and attitude change seem to be lacking. In order for the practices to be institutionalized, and incorporated into ongoing educational practice, there should be clear links to a social science theory that is validated by research. Thus, a principle that guided our development of cooperative learning procedures was that they should be clearly derived from a theory that has been validated by research. In his planning to reduce racism in North America, David focused his attention on contact theory (Allport, 1954; Watson, 1947, Williams, 1947). Contact theory states that there are four conditions that must be met to eliminate prejudice: cooperation, equal power, personal conversations, and support by authorities. Of the four, David concluded that cooperative experiences are the most important. There were several theories of cooperation, including Deutsch's (1949) theory, Thibaut and Kelley's (1959) theory, Skinner's (1968) theory of group contingencies, and others. For a number of reasons, David chose Deutsch's theory as the base for his operationalizing cooperative learning procedures. From Deutsch's (1949) theory of cooperation and competition and from Goodwin Watson's theory of structure–process–outcomes (Watson, 1966; Watson & Johnson, 1972), David proposed that the way teachers structure learning goals determines how students interact with each other, which in turn determines outcomes. Deutsch (1949, 1962) posited that positive goal interdependence leads to promotive interaction, negative goal interdependence leads to obstructive or oppositional interaction, and no interdependence leads to no interaction.

Validating Research

In order for a theory to be the foundation for practical procedures, it should be validated by research. While there were studies providing basic validation of Deutsch's theory of cooperation and competition (Deutsch, 1949), there were many aspects of the theory that were unproven or uncertain, and interesting implications that had not been explored. The operationalization of the theory into practical procedures also revealed questions that needed to be answered. For example, Deutsch's theory was focused on positive goal interdependence and assumed that the goals had intrinsic value. But the use of cooperative learning procedures in actual classrooms, where the goals are externally imposed, revealed that often students did not intrinsically value the school's goals and, therefore, the motivation to achieve the goals was lacking. We identified eight other types of positive interdependence (reward, resource, role, task, identity, fantasy, environmental, outside-enemy) (Johnson & Johnson, 1992) and conducted a series of studies to investigate the impact of various types of positive interdependence on student–student interaction and learning outcomes.

Beginning in 1970, to determine the extent to which theories of cooperation and competition were validated, we published a series of reviews of the research on cooperative, competitive, and individualistic efforts (e.g., Johnson, 1970; Johnson & Johnson, 1974, 1975/1999, 1978, 1979,

1989, 2009). In addition, we edited an issue of the *Journal of Research and Development in Education*, having major researchers contribute articles on cooperative learning to the issue (Johnson & Johnson, 1978). Our intent was to clarify the current knowledge about the relative efficacy of cooperative, competitive, and individualistic learning. After our 1974 review in which we reviewed over 40 studies and concluded that cooperation produced higher achievement than did competitive or individualistic efforts, however, Michaels (1977) followed with a review of ten studies that indicated competition produced higher achievement than did cooperative or individualistic efforts and Slavin (1977) published a review of about 24 studies that indicated individualistic efforts produced higher achievement than did competitive or cooperative efforts.

Wanting to end such conflicting reviews, we decided to do a meta-analysis of all the available research on cooperative, competitive, and individualistic efforts and published two of the earliest meta-analyses in education (Johnson, Maruyama, Johnson, Nelson, & Skon, 1981; Johnson, Johnson, & Maruyama, 1983) and one of the earliest books featuring meta-analysis (Johnson & Johnson, 1989). We conducted a series of meta-analyses on the impact of cooperation on a wide range of variables, including achievement and related variables (Johnson, Maruyama, Johnson, Nelson, & Skon, 1981), interpersonal attraction (including cross-ethnic and cross-handicapped relationships) (Johnson et al., 1983), individual versus group measures of achievement (Johnson, Druckman, & Dansereau, 1994), problem-solving (Qin, Johnson, & Johnson, 1995), university students (Johnson, Johnson, & Smith, 1998), motor performance (Stanne, Johnson, & Johnson, 1999), the various methods of cooperative learning (Johnson & Johnson, 1989, 2002b), our Learning and Alone method (Johnson & Johnson, 2002a), adult teams (Johnson & Johnson, 2003), the relationship between interpersonal attraction and achievement (Roseth, Johnson, & Johnson, 2008), relationship between motivation and achievement (Johnson, Johnson, Roseth, & Shin, 2014), as well as on two related aspects of cooperative learning, constructive controversy (Johnson & Johnson, 1987/2015) and conflicts of interests (Johnson & Johnson, 1987/2007). In our book on theory and research, even more variables, such as social support and self-esteem, were subjected to meta-analyses (Johnson & Johnson, 1989). These reviews established beyond a reasonable doubt that cooperation had more powerful effects than competitive and individualistic efforts on many different variables. We believed (and still believe) that this is important for the institutionalization of cooperative learning in education.

In our research reviews, we organized the results of the available studies into three categories (see Figure 3.2): effort to achieve, interpersonal relationships, and psychological health (Johnson & Johnson, 1989). Within each of these categories we organized the dozens and dozens of dependent variables researchers had studied over the past 120 years. So many studies have been conducted that the results are well established. We now have over 1,200 research studies from which we can calculate effect sizes and hundreds more that have been conducted but do not report enough data to calculate effect sizes. This is one of the largest bodies of work in the history of the social sciences. While prior to 1960, most of the studies had been conducted in North America, now there are studies from all parts of the world and from many, many different countries and cultures. The fact that their findings are consistent provides considerable generalizability to cooperative learning. Some of the effect sizes may be seen in Table 3.1.

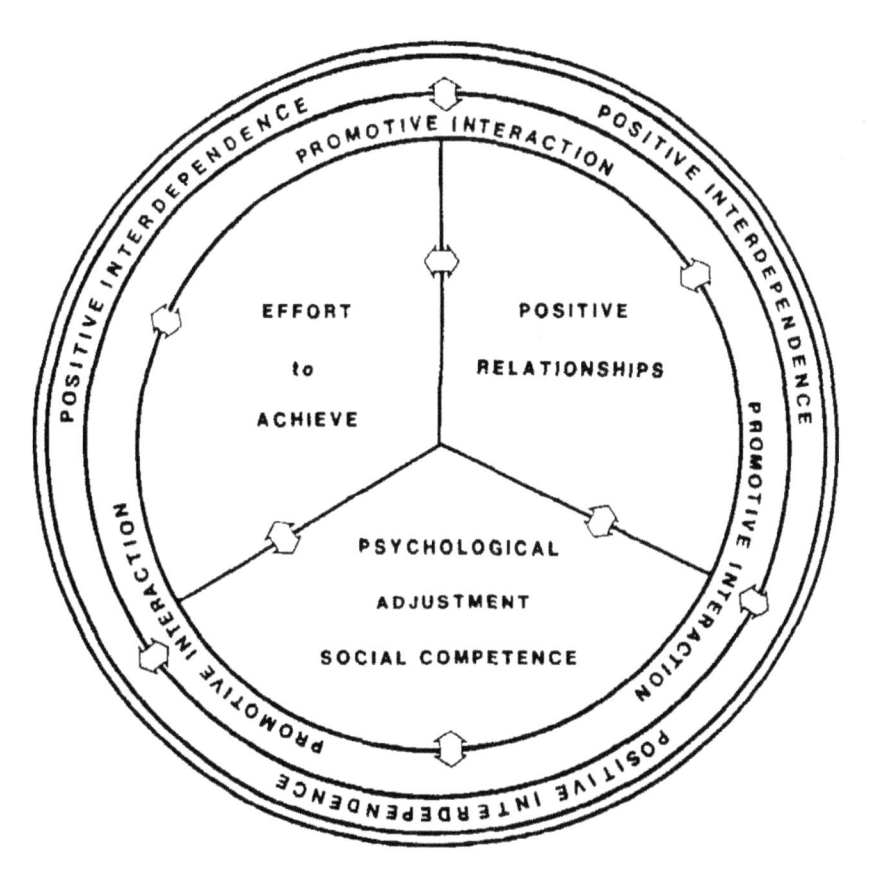

Figure 3.2 Outcomes of cooperative learning

Source: Reprinted by permission from: Johnson, D. W. & Johnson, R. (1989). *Cooperation and Competition: Theory and Research.* Edina, MN: Interaction Book Company

Table 3.1 Mean weighted effect sizes for impact of social interdependence on dependent variables

Variable	Cooperation vs. competition	Cooperation vs. individualistic
Achievement	0.54	0.51
Interpersonal attraction	0.68	0.55
Social support	0.60	0.51
Self-esteem	0.47	0.29
Positive attitudes	0.37	0.42

Reprinted by permission from: Johnson, D. W. & Johnson, R. (1989). *Cooperation and Competition: Theory and Research*. Edina, MN: Interaction Book Company

In addition to our research reviews, we conducted a systematic program of research on various aspects of cooperative learning to further validate the underlying theory and provide further guidance for the development of practical procedures for the use of cooperative learning. Overall, we published more than 115 studies on various aspects of cooperative efforts, including achievement, positive relationships, social support, self-esteem, positive interdependence, individual accountability, social skills, group processing, a variety of positive attitudes, cross-ethnic relationships, cross-handicapped relationships, perspective-taking, psychological health, conflict among ideas, and communication. In addition, we clarified the conditions under which competitive efforts are constructive. These studies expanded the scope of social interdependence theory, clarified and modified some of its assumptions, and provided considerable further validation of its basic premises. Needless to say, it is the largest body of work so far on social interdependence theory and cooperative learning.

Finally, it should be recognized that the use of cooperative learning groups creates certain opportunities that do not exist when students work competitively or individually. In cooperative groups discussions can take place in which students can construct and extend conceptual understanding of what is being learned and develop shared mental models of complex phenomena. Group members can hold each other accountable to learn, provide feedback on how well groupmates are doing, and give support and encouragement for further attempts to learn. Students can observe the most outstanding group members as behavioral models to be emulated. It is through discussions in small groups that students acquire attitudes and values. Finally, it is within cooperative groups that students establish a shared identity as members of the school or university. Cooperative efforts create opportunities for students that are lacking in noncooperative classrooms.

Operational Procedures

Practical procedures for using cooperative learning have a long history, dating back tens of thousands of years (Johnson et al., 2013). Two of the most recent in the United States were the teaching procedures in the late 1800s advocated by Colonel Francis Parker and in the early to mid-1900s by John Dewey. While their teaching procedures were highly respected and imitated, once these individuals died, the use of their cooperative learning methods seemed to fade quickly. The reason may have been that there were no clear operational procedures for implementing their methods of cooperative learning. Parker and Dewey trained teachers primarily by saying, "Watch me teach, and do likewise." They did not leave behind a clear operational procedure for planning and conducting cooperative learning. In the mid-1930s, competition began to dominate American education, and in the 1960s, individualistic learning rose to dominance. David concluded that a problem with Parker's and Dewey's approach was that they never spelled out in detail the teaching procedures for planning and conducting a cooperative lesson. The first principal that guided our development of cooperative learning procedures, therefore, was that a clear operationalization of the teacher's role in planning and conducting a cooperative learning lesson was needed.

Our second principle was derived from the shortcomings of the "make and take" teacher training procedures. Although teachers often like learning simple procedures they can directly use in their classes, the literature on innovation indicates that to be successful, teachers need to become more involved in planning and conducting lessons for which they can take personal ownership. Thus, they needed a conceptual procedure that is specific enough to be readily applied but not so simple that they did not take some effort on the part of the teacher to apply and implement them. What resulted was our description of the teacher's role in cooperative learning that could be used to replan any existing lesson to make it cooperative. We (David and Roger) decided, therefore, that the heart of cooperative learning had to be a conceptual framework with which teachers could take any lesson for any age student in any subject area and replan it to include cooperative learning. Once utilized for a period of months or years, the procedure hopefully will be integrated into the teacher's professional identity.

Instructor's Role

We developed four types of cooperative learning: formal, informal, base groups, and constructive controversy (Johnson et al., 1984/2013). *Formal cooperative learning groups* last from one class period to several weeks. Students work together to ensure that they and their groupmates have successfully completed the learning task assigned. The teacher's role in formal cooperative learning consisted of four parts:

1. *Make a number of preinstructional decisions.* Instructors specify the objectives for the lesson (both academic and social skills) and decide

on the size of groups, the method of assigning students to groups, the roles students will be assigned, the materials needed to conduct the lesson, and the way the room will be arranged.
2. *Explain the task and the positive interdependence.* An instructor clearly defines the assignment, teaches the required concepts and strategies, specifies the positive interdependence and individual accountability, gives the criteria for success, and explains the expected social skills to be used.
3. *Monitor students' learning and intervene within the groups to provide task assistance or to increase students' interpersonal and group skills.* An instructor systematically observes and collects data on each group as it works. When needed, the instructor intervenes to assist students in completing the task accurately and in working together effectively.
4. *Assess students' learning and helping students process how well their groups functioned.* Students' learning is carefully assessed and their performances are periodically evaluated. Members of the learning groups then discuss how effectively they worked together and how they can improve in the future.

Informal cooperative learning lasts from a few minutes to one class period. There are three parts of using informal cooperative learning: a *preinstructional pair discussion* to serve as an advanced organizer and to set expectations as to what will be covered in the class session, *intermittent pair discussions* every 10–15 minutes in which students review what was just covered and integrate it into existing conceptual frameworks, and *closure pair discussions* in which what was taught is reviewed and closure (or nonclosure) is provided.

Cooperative base groups are long-term groups with stable membership in which members give each other the support, encouragement, and assistance each needs to make academic progress and develop cognitively and socially in healthy ways. Base groups also hold members accountable for striving to learn. Typically, cooperative base groups last for a semester or year. Base groups meet at the beginning and end of each class session (or week) to complete academic tasks (such as checking each members' homework), routine tasks (such as taking attendance), and personal support tasks (such as providing guidance for completing an assignment).

Constructive controversy is a form of cooperation when ideas and opinions clash but must be reconciled (Johnson & Johnson, 1987/2007). The teacher's role consists of assigning students to groups of four, dividing the groups into pro and con pairs, having each pair (a) prepare the best case possible for their assigned position, (b) present their position as persuasively as they can, (c) engage in an open discussion in which they critically analyze each other's positions and give them a "trial by fire," (d) reverse perspectives and present the opposing position as best they can, and, (e) dropping all advocacy, come to an agreement reflecting their best reasoned judgment about the issue.

Together, these types of cooperative learning provide an integrated system for instructional organization and design (as well as classroom management). The class may begin with a base-group meeting, informal cooperative learning can be used while the teacher explains what the students are to do during the class session, a formal cooperative learning lesson or controversy can be conducted, followed by a brief teacher summary using informal cooperative learning, and a closing base group meeting.

Finally, long-term implementation of cooperative learning depends on teachers mastering a conceptual system that allows them to replan their existing lessons to include cooperative learning. The conceptual system includes not only the teacher's role in each type of cooperative learning but also the inclusion of the five basic elements of cooperation: positive interdependence, individual accountability, promotive interaction, appropriate use of social skills, and group processing. The conceptual structures of the teacher's role and the five basic elements provide teachers the tools they need to take their existing lessons and replan them to be cooperative.

Basic Elements That Make Cooperation Work

Not all groups are cooperative (Johnson & F. Johnson, 2017). Simply assigning students to groups and telling them to work together does not in and of itself result in cooperative efforts. It is only when teachers carefully structure five basic elements into a lesson that students truly cooperate with each other and the full potential of the group will be reached. Through the use of the five basic elements, teachers become instructional engineers/designers who can take their existing lessons, curricula, subject areas, courses, and students and structure any lesson cooperatively. Mastering the five basic elements enables teachers to (Johnson & Johnson, 1989, 1987/2007):

1. Take existing lessons, curricula, and courses and structure them cooperatively.
2. Tailor cooperative learning lessons to unique instructional needs, circumstances, curricula, subject areas, and students.
3. Diagnose the problems some students may have in working together and intervene to increase the effectiveness of the student learning groups.

The five essential elements are (Johnson & Johnson, 1989, 1987/2007):

1. *Positive Interdependence:* Positive interdependence is the perception that you are linked with others in a way so that you cannot succeed

unless they do (and vice versa), that is, their work benefits you and your work benefits them. In order to supplement positive interdependence, *joint rewards* (if all members of your group score 90% correct or better on the test, each will receive five bonus points), *divided resources* (giving each group member a part of the total information required to complete an assignment), *complementary roles* (reader, checker, encourager, elaborator), and other means of creating positive interdependence may also be used.

2. *Individual and Group Accountability:* Individual accountability exists when the performance of each individual student is assessed and the results given back to the group and the individual. The purpose of cooperative learning groups is to make each member a stronger individual in his or her right. Students learn together so that they can subsequently perform higher as individuals. To ensure that each member is strengthened, students are held individually accountable to do their share of the work. Common ways to structure individual accountability include (a) giving an individual test to each student, (b) randomly selecting one student's product to represent the entire group, or (c) having each student explain what they have learned to a classmate.

3. *Promotive Interaction:* Positive interdependence results in students promoting each other's success by sharing resources and helping, assisting, supporting, encouraging, and praising each other's efforts to learn. Cooperative learning groups are both an academic support system (every student has someone who is committed to helping him or her learn) and a personal support system (every student has someone who is committed to him or her as a person). There are important cognitive activities and interpersonal dynamics that can only occur when students promote each other's learning. This includes orally explaining how to solve problems, discussing the nature of the concepts being learned, teaching one's knowledge to classmates, and connecting present with past learning. It is through promoting each other's learning face to face that members become personally committed to each other as well as to their mutual goals.

4. *Social Skills:* In cooperative learning groups students are required to learn academic subject matter (taskwork) and also to learn the interpersonal and small group skills required to function as part of a group (teamwork). Cooperative learning is inherently more complex than competitive or individualistic learning because students have to engage simultaneously in taskwork and teamwork. Group members must know how to provide effective leadership, decision-making, trust-building, communication, and

conflict-management, and be motivated to use the prerequisite skills. Teachers have to teach teamwork skills just as purposefully and precisely as teachers do academic skills. Because cooperation and conflict are inherently related, the procedures and skills for managing conflicts constructively are especially important for the long-term success of learning groups. Procedures and strategies for teaching students social skills may be found in Johnson (2014) and Johnson and F. Johnson (2017). Contributing to the success of a cooperative effort requires interpersonal and small group skills such as leadership, decision-making, trust-building, communication, and conflict-management skills. Students have to be taught the social skills required for high-quality cooperation just as purposefully and precisely as academic skills.
5. *Group Processing:* Group processing exists when group members discuss how well they are achieving their goals and maintaining effective working relationships. Groups need to describe what member actions are helpful and unhelpful and make decisions about what behaviors to continue or change.

These five elements are essential to all cooperative systems, no matter what their size. Understanding what positive interdependence, promotive interaction, individual accountability, social skills, and group processing are, and developing competencies in structuring them, allows teachers to replan any lesson to make it cooperative, adapt cooperative learning to their unique circumstances, and fine-tune their use of cooperative learning to solve problems students are having in working together.

Competitive and Individualistic Efforts

Social interdependence theory includes the conditions under which competition and individualistic efforts may be constructive (Johnson & Johnson, 1999b). Competition tends to be more constructive when winning is relatively unimportant, all participants have a reasonable chance to win, and there are clear, specific, and fair rules, procedures, and criteria for winning.

Individualistic efforts may be the most appropriate when cooperation is too costly, the goal is perceived to be unimportant, participants expect to be successful, the task is unitary and nondivisible, directions for completing the task are simple and clear, there is adequate space and resources for each student, and what is accomplished will be used subsequently in a cooperative effort.

Implementation

Our three-year implementation program consists of the following. In the first year, a three-hour introduction to cooperative learning is given to all teachers in a school or school district and a 30-hour training in the foundations of cooperative learning is given for the best teachers who were interested in cooperative learning. Follow-up assistance is provided to the trained teachers during the school year. In the second year, the participating teachers are given a 30-hour training in advanced cooperative learning and follow-up assistance is provided as they continue to use cooperative learning. In the third year the best teachers are trained to conduct the foundations course (e.g., leadership training). In addition, 30-hour courses are offered on constructive conflict resolution ("creative controversy" and "teaching students to be peacemakers") (Johnson & Johnson, 2002c, 2007, 1987/2015), leading the cooperative school (for administrators and staff development personnel) (Johnson & Johnson, 1991/1994), assessment of cooperative efforts (Johnson & Johnson, 2002d), and managing diversity in the classroom and school (Johnson & Johnson, 2002e). This three-year cycle is eventually turned over to the leadership personnel in the district, and Roger and David's involvement is phased out. The intent is to leave the district with an autonomous training program in cooperative learning.

Roger had contacts in school districts throughout the United States who had pioneered the implementation of inquiry learning in their science programs. In the early 1970s, many of these districts agreed to support teacher training in cooperative learning. Our implementation efforts then spread across the country and into Canada and Mexico. We became early members of the National Staff Development Council. To assist in our implementation of cooperative learning, we established an international network of the educators we have trained and we published a newsletter to stay in touch with them. We have now trained teachers and professors throughout North America, Western and Eastern Europe, the Middle East, and much of Africa, Asia, and South America. Affiliated Cooperative Learning Centers have been established in China, Japan, Saudi Arabia, Spain, Norway, and other countries. Our writings on cooperative learning have been translated into at least 21 languages (i.e., Chinese, Japanese, Korean, Thai, Arabic, Greek, Italian, Spanish, Catalonian, French, Russian, Ukrainian, Polish, German, Norwegian, Danish, Finnish, Dutch, Bahasa Indonesian, Portuguese, Turkish). More than one of our books and articles have been translated into many of these languages. Our training materials have been translated into even more languages. The writings of other scholars of cooperative learning have been translated into other languages. We have a web page (www.co-operation.org). David has a regular blog for *Psychology Today*. We helped found the International Association for the Study of Cooperation in Education (IASCE), and David was one of the early members of the International Association for Conflict Management.

Future of Cooperative Learning

There are countless programs and procedures that have been proposed for educators that have been adopted for a while and then disappear. Of the many instructional practices that have been recommended during the past 75 years, the vast majority were never widely adopted, and most of those were abandoned after a few years. Among teaching procedures in formal education, lecturing has dominated for over a thousand years or perhaps several thousand years. It will not be easy to change this habit and establish cooperative learning as the new status quo.

So far, the success of cooperative learning is remarkable and unusual. What makes cooperative learning different from most educational innovations is that it is based on theory validated by considerable research. In the early 1980s, when President Reagan asked the Department of Education what was the result of all the money they had spent on research, they replied that the main thing they knew for sure was that cooperative learning resulted in higher achievement than did competitive or individualistic learning. Thus, an emphasis on research-based practices was initiated. Whenever educators are asked what is proven to work, cooperative learning has to be mentioned. Our reviews of research, and our systematic program of research, contributed to the conclusion of all scholars that cooperative learning was an effective instructional procedure. It is on this foundation that the future of cooperative learning rests. Because of the scholarly foundation, cooperative learning is discussed in almost all texts on instructional methods and in almost all teacher training programs throughout the world. What is now needed are a group of young scholars who will continue to produce research studies and research reviews supporting the use of cooperative learning and a continuing supply of young teachers who view cooperative learning as part of their professional identity and something they will use for the entirety of their career.

The worldwide implementation of cooperative learning in all its forms provides an ongoing demonstration of its effectiveness and desirability. But that was also true for Frances Parker and John Dewey. Having the practical procedures for cooperative learning is necessary but not sufficient to ensure that cooperative learning will continue as an instructional procedure. It is the combination of theory, research, operational procedures (i.e., teacher's role), and systematic implementation in schools and universities that gives cooperative learning the opportunity to become an institutionalized instructional practice.

References

Allport, G. (1954). *The nature of prejudice*. Cambridge, MA: Addison-Wesley.
Bruner, J. (1960). *The process of education*. Cambridge, MA: Harvard University Press.
Deutsch, M. (1949). A theory of cooperation and competition. *Human Relations*, 2, 129–152.
Deutsch, M. (1962). Cooperation and trust: Some theoretical notes. In M. Jones (Ed.), *Nebraska symposium on motivation* (pp. 275–319). Lincoln, NE: University of Nebraska Press.
Johnson, D. W. (1966a). Freedom school effectiveness: Changes in attitudes of Negro children. *Journal of Applied Behavioral Science*, 2, 325–331.
Johnson, D. W. (1966b). Racial attitudes of Negro Freedom School participants and Negro and white civil rights participants. *Social Forces*, 45, 266-274.
Johnson, D. W. (1970). *The social psychology of education*. New York, NY: Holt, Rinehart, & Winston.
Johnson, D. W. (1972/2014). *Reaching out: Interpersonal effectiveness and self-actualization* (11th ed., 2014). Boston, MA: Allyn & Bacon.
Johnson, D. W., & Johnson, F. (1975/2017). *Joining together: Group theory and group skills* (12th ed., 2017). Boston, MA: Allyn & Bacon.
Johnson, D. W., & Johnson, R. T. (1974). Instructional goal structure: Cooperative, competitive, or individualistic. *Review of Educational Research*, 44, 213–240.
Johnson, D. W., & Johnson, R. T. (1975/1999). *Learning together and alone* (5th ed.). Boston, MA: Allyn & Bacon.
Johnson, D. W., & Johnson, R. T. (1978). Cooperative, competitive, and individualistic learning. *Journal of Research and Development in Education*, 12, 3–15.
Johnson, D. W., & Johnson, R. T. (1979). Conflict in the classroom: Controversy and learning. *Review of Educational Research*, 49, 51–70.
Johnson, D. W., & Johnson, R. T. (1987/2007). *Teaching students to be peacemakers* (4th ed.). Edina, MN: Interaction Book Company.
Johnson, D. W., & Johnson, R. T. (1987/2015). *Creative controversy: Intellectual challenge in the classroom* (5th ed.). Edina, MN: Interaction Book Company.
Johnson, D. W., & Johnson, R. T. (1989). *Cooperation and competition: Theory and research*. Edina, MN: Interaction Book Company.
Johnson, D. W., & Johnson, R. T. (1991/1994). *Leading the cooperative school* (2nd ed.). Edina, MN: Interaction Book Company.
Johnson, D. W., & Johnson, R. T. (1992). *Positive interdependence: Activity manual and guide*. Edina, MN: Interaction Book Company.
Johnson, D. W., Druckman, D., & Dansereau, D. (1994). Training in teams. In D. Druckman, R. Bjork et al. (Eds.), *Learning, remembering, believing: Enhancing human performance* (pp. 140–170). Washington, DC: National Academy Press.

Johnson, D. W., & Johnson, R. T. (2002a). Learning together and alone: An overview and meta-analysis. In H. Shachar, S. Sharan, & G. Jacobs (Guest Editors). *Asia Pacific Journal of Education, 22*(1), 95–105.

Johnson, D. W., & Johnson, R. T. (2002b). Cooperative learning methods: A meta-analysis. *Journal of Research in Education, 12*(1), 5–24.

Johnson, D. W., & Johnson, R. T. (2002c). Teaching students to be peacemakers: A meta-analysis. *Journal of Research in Education, 12*(1), 25–39.

Johnson, D. W., & Johnson, R. T. (2002d). *Meaningful assessment: A manageable and cooperative process* (2th ed.). Edina, MN: Interaction Book Company.

Johnson, D. W., & Johnson, R. T. (2002e). *Multicultural education and human relations: Valuing diversity* (2th ed.). Edina, MN: Interaction Book Company.

Johnson, D. W., & Johnson, R. T. (2003). Training for cooperative group work. In M. West, D. Tjosvold, & K. Smith (Eds.), *International handbook of organizational teamwork and cooperative working* (pp. 167–183). London: John Wiley.

Johnson, D. W., & Johnson, R. T. (2009). An educational psychology success story: Social interdependence theory and cooperative learning. *Educational Researcher, 38*(5), 365–379.

Johnson, D. W., Johnson, R. T., & Holubec, E. J. (1984/2013). *Cooperation in the classroom* (9th ed., 2013). Edina, MN: Interaction Book Company.

Johnson, D. W., Johnson, R. T., & Maruyama, G. (1983). Interdependence and interpersonal attraction among heterogeneous and homogeneous individuals: A theoretical formulation and a meta-analysis of the research. *Review of Educational Research, 53*(1), 5–54.

Johnson, D. W., Johnson, R. T., Roseth, C. J., & Shin, T. S. (2014). The relationship between motivation and achievement in interdependent situations. *Journal of Applied Social Psychology, 44*, 622–633.

Johnson, D. W., Johnson, R. T., & Smith, K. (1998). Cooperative learning returns to college: What evidence is there that it works? *Change, 30*(4), 26–35.

Johnson, D. W., Maruyama, G., Johnson, R., Nelson, D., & Skon, L. (1981). Effects of cooperative, competitive, and individualistic goal structures on achievement: A meta-analysis. *Psychological Bulletin, 89*, 47–62.

Michaels, J. (1977). Classroom reward structures and academic performance. *Review of Educational Research, 47*, 87–99.

Miles, M. B. (1964). *Innovation in education*. New York, NY: Teachers College Press.

Piaget, J. (1950). *The psychology of intelligence*. New York, NY: Harcourt.

Qin, Z., Johnson, D. W., & Johnson, R. T. (1995). Cooperative versus competitive efforts and problem solving: A meta-analysis. *Review of Educational Research, 65*(2), 129–143.

Roseth, C. J., Johnson, D. W., & Johnson, R. T. (2008). The relationship between interpersonal relationships and achievement within cooperative, competitive, and individualistic conditions: A meta-analysis. *Psychological Bulletin, 134*(2), 223–246.

Skinner, B. (1968). *The technology of teaching*. New York, NY: Appleton-Century-Crofts.

Slavin, R. (1977). Classroom reward structure: An analytical and practical review. *Review of Educational Research, 47*, 633–650.

Stanne, M., Johnson, D. W., & Johnson, R. T. (1999). Social interdependence and motor performance: A meta-analysis. *Psychological Bulletin, 125*(1), 133–154.

Thibaut, J., & Kelley, H. (1959). *The social psychology of groups*. New York, NY: Wiley.

Vygotsky, L. (1978). *Mind and society*. Cambridge, MA: Harvard University Press.

Watson, G. (1947). *Action for unity*. New York, NY: Harper & Bros.

Watson, G. (1966). *Social psychology: Issues and insights*. Philadelphia, PA: Lippincott.

Watson, G., & Johnson, D. W. (1972). *Social psychology: Issues and insights* (2nd ed.). Philadelphia, PA: Lippincott.

Williams, R. (1947). *The reduction of intergroup tensions*. New York, NY: Social Science Research Council.

Chapter 4

Complex Instruction for Diverse and Equitable Classrooms
In Loving Memory of Elizabeth G. Cohen

Rachel A. Lotan and Nicole I. Holthuis

> Most teachers want to offer children equal chances to succeed in school, regardless of race, gender, or socioeconomic background. They also hope that the classroom will be a place where children who have different societal statuses will meet each other and learn that stereotypical and prejudicial beliefs held by society are not true.
> (Elizabeth G. Cohen, 1986, p. 31)

From the 1950s on, considerable legislative and judicial progress was made to remedy racism through desegregation at both the societal and classroom levels. After *Brown* v. the *Board of Education*, the landmark decision of the US Supreme Court, educational innovations were directed toward raising academic achievement of students of color, improving intergroup relations in desegregated schools, and reducing or eliminating racist attitudes and behavior. Social scientists documented and researched the complexities and frequently contradictory results of some of these educational interventions. Many concluded that to realize the benefits of school desegregation—increased learning opportunities and preparing children to live in a democratic and integrated society—certain conditions needed to be met: equitable interactions in multiracial contact, interdependence and pursuit of common goals, and organizational and institutional support (Allport, 1954; Cohen, 1972; Katz & Taylor, 1988).

Led by Professor Elizabeth Cohen and for over five decades, scholars at Stanford, other universities, and research institutes designed and evaluated interventions to promote equitable and just environments to realize the academic, social, and civic benefits of diverse classrooms for all learners. One outcome of these efforts is Complex Instruction (CI), a well-known pedagogical approach based on robust sociological frameworks, sociocultural theories of cognitive development and learning, and solid empirical evidence. Designed to create equitable learning opportunities and outcomes for all students by supporting equitable interactions in academically, racially, ethnically, and linguistically diverse classrooms, CI is well-known in the field of education in the United States and in other countries. For a partial list of publications, see https://complexinstruction.stanford.edu/library.

A pioneer in a new approach to applied research in sociology, Elizabeth Cohen conducted experimental tests of Status Characteristics Theory (Berger, Cohen, & Zelditch, 1966, 1972), later known as Expectation States Theory (Berger, Rosenholtz, & Zelditch, 1980). She found that in four-member, mixed-race groups of adolescent boys engaged in an interactive task, race was associated with differences in rates of participation and measures of influence. These findings supported explanations and predictions of the theory regarding the process by which race, a status characteristic, affects participation and influence, indicators of the power and prestige order in the group. In laboratory studies, white adolescents, perceived to be high status, had higher rates of interaction and greater influence on the group's decisions than their African-American or Mexican-American counterparts, who were considered low status (Cohen, 1972, 1982).

Moving from the laboratory to the field, a Stanford team led by Cohen started and operated the Center for Interracial Cooperation at a desegregated middle school in Oakland, CA in the summer of 1972 (Cohen, Lockheed, & Lohman, 1976). The team developed interventions designed to reduce the discrepancies in participation and levels of influence and produce equal-status interactions among white and African-American students. The two interventions introduced were "expectation training" (Cohen & Roper, 1972) and role modeling (Cohen et al., 1976). While these interventions were successful, the researchers also concluded that they were necessary, albeit insufficient conditions for extended equal-status interactions. Structural and curricular changes such as the introduction of norms for working in small cooperative groups and the "multiple-abilities curriculum" (Rosenholtz, 1977) followed. Researchers continued to document the effects of diffuse status characteristics, such as gender (Lockheed, Harris, & Nemceff, 1983) and specific status characteristics, such as reading ability (Rosenholtz & Wilson, 1980; Rosenholtz & Simpson, 1984) among mixed-status groups of school-aged children engaged in a collective task in more complex settings.

Concurrently, from the mid-1970s and early 1980s, cooperative learning and small-group work methods emerged to address the pedagogical and technical challenges of teaching in desegregated classrooms. Educational researchers offered a variety of cooperative learning methods to increase levels of trust, interdependence, and friendliness, improve attitudes and racial and ethnic relations, and, ultimately, to reduce the gap in learning outcomes among students from diverse demographic backgrounds

(Aronson, Blaney, Sikes, & Snapp, 1978; Slavin, 1980; Johnson, Johnson, & Maruyama, 1983; Sharan & Sharan, 1976; Sharan, 1980).

At Stanford, the Multicultural Improvement of Cognitive Abilities (MICA) project, with the collaboration of Dr. Ed DeAvila, a learning theorist, and Dr. Cecilia Navarrete, an experienced bi-lingual teacher, offered the first significant entry into multiple classrooms in multiple schools in 1979. Teachers used Finding Out/Descubrimiento, a bilingual, Spanish-English elementary math and science curriculum developed by Navarrete and DeAvila (DeAvila, Duncan, & Navarrete, 1987; Cohen & DeAvila, 1983). As school administrators, teachers, and educational researchers became increasingly interested in the work of the Stanford group and its documented positive outcomes, the project expanded to secondary schools and to different subject areas. This is when it became known as *Complex Instruction*. Thus, both CI and Finding Out/Descubrimiento, its programmatic precursor, grew out of groundbreaking, practice-based research in schools and classrooms, principles of curriculum construction, and professional learning and development of teachers.

Complex Instruction: A Pedagogical Approach

As we walk into Ms. Abram's third-grade classroom, we hear a productive buzz. Jay, one of the students wearing a *Materials Manager* badge, had put a box containing batteries, wires, tape, bulbs, string, toilet-paper rolls, and scissors on the table. Members of his group are excited as they check out the materials.

Energy transfer is the topic of the day. Students need to figure out how to design and build a working flashlight. Ruby, the *Reporter*, is trying to attach a piece of wire to a battery. Carlos and Nancy are busy emptying the box. Michael seems frustrated:

> "How are we supposed to build a flashlight? We don't have a case to put the battery in! We don't have the right bulb! We can't make it work! Nothing works here! Call the teacher!"

Nancy, the Facilitator, raises her hand, and Ms. A. approaches the group.

> "We don't have the right materials. We can't make it light up," says Nancy.
> "Does everyone in the group agree with Nancy?" asks Ms. A.
> "I am not sure," says Ruby, "I got it to light up a couple of times, but it won't stay on."
> "That's a good first step, Ruby," says Ms. A. "Please describe to the group what you tried so far. Then, group, see what you can do to take your project to the next step. I will check back in a few."

When Ms. A. returns to the group a few minutes later, the flashlight is working! She says,

> I noticed that Ruby was able to think through how to connect the battery and the bulb. She didn't give up even though the light didn't stay on. Then as a group, you figured out how to connect all the components of the flashlight and you even added an on/off switch. You made it work! And now, get ready to explain to me how the energy travels from the switch to the bulb! I will be back.

***

CI is a pedagogical approach that supports and promotes equitable student learning in academically, linguistically, racially, ethnically, and socially heterogeneous classrooms. In many such classrooms, students have a wide range of previous academic achievement and different life experiences, and some might still be developing their proficiency in the language of instruction. In CI classrooms, all students have access to intellectually challenging, multidimensional, language-rich learning tasks, provided to the groups on activity cards and additional resource materials. All students have multiple opportunities to demonstrate what they know and are able to do using different media and modes of expression. The conceptual framework and the empirical findings that underlie CI address the way the teacher manages the classroom for small-group instruction, specifies the learning tasks, and addresses the connection between the student's academic and social status on the one hand, and participation on the other.

To enhance learning and to maximize student interactions, teachers delegate authority to groups of students who are randomly assigned. By using cooperative norms and specific student roles, students become responsible for their own and their peers' learning. They are held accountable by producing group as well as individual products. Teachers address potentially unequal participation among members of the group by using two interventions: (1) by redefining and explaining that multiple intellectual, cognitive, and social abilities and skills are needed to complete the task, so that all students are able to make important contributions, and (2) after observing students as they work in groups, teachers notice and make public individual students' contributions to the group task, thereby acknowledging and assigning competence to most if not all students in the classrooms. More detailed explanation of the conceptual framework and references to empirical findings follow.

CI rests on four underlying propositions. First, rather than a collection of any number of individual students and a teacher, the classroom is a social system described and analyzed in sociological terms such as authority, roles and responsibilities, norms of behavior, equal/unequal status, legitimacy, power, and influence. Second, learning is a social activity. Constructivist theorists agree that cognitive, social, and affective growth and development happen through social interactions among the learners and their more knowledgeable peers or adults (Vygotsky,1978). Intellectual conflict is essential for cognitive growth (Piaget, 1963) and constructive, structured controversy energizes learning and can have positive outcomes on student learning and well-being (Johnson & Johnson, 2009a). Third, when working with CI in heterogeneous classrooms, teachers purposefully and unceasingly plan for range and heterogeneity a priori rather than adapting, modifying, or adjusting their curriculum and instruction, to "accommodate or deal with" diversity post hoc. Finally, to implement a non-routine pedagogical technology like CI, teachers learn by engaging in collegial interactions, develop their practice with adequate mentoring and feedback, and benefit from appropriate administrative and institutional support.

Research in CI classrooms documented a significant positive relationship between the overall level of peer interaction in small groups—as measured by the proportion of students talking and working together—and average learning gains on a variety of measures. Some of these outcome measures were standardized tests (Cohen, Lotan, & Leechor, 1989; Cohen et al., 1997), end-of-unit multiple choice items (Lotan, 2008), final unit essays (Scarloss, 2001; Lotan, 2008), performance assessments (Schultz, 1999), and indicators of language development (Bunch, 2006) and of cognitive development (DeAvila, Cohen, & Intili, 1982; Ben-Ari, 1997; Ben-Ari & Kedem-Friedrich. 2000). All students, particularly those who had previously been reading below grade level, benefitted from interacting with their peers on challenging learning tasks (Leechor, 1988; Schultz, 1999).

Several scholars of CI researched the classroom conditions that support the quality of students' disciplinary discourse during groupwork. For example, Holthuis (1999) found that in CI classrooms the overall level and quality of science talk was considerable, and while it didn't vary by gender, it did vary by the type of activity in which the students engaged. Scarloss (2001) found that in CI classrooms student interactions in small groups contributed to students' enhanced sense-making of social studies topics. Cossey (1997) investigated the quality of mathematical communication in CI classrooms. She found that students who were members of groups with higher-quality mathematical discourse developed further proficiency in mathematical communication. Over the years, researchers documented other significant, positive outcomes of the implementation of CI in heterogeneous mathematics classrooms (e.g., Boaler & Staples, 2008; Nasir, Cabana, Shreve, Woodbury, & Louie, 2014).

The implementation of CI can be particularly useful in multilingual classrooms. In such classrooms, students who are still learning English benefit from interaction with their peers who are native or near-native speakers of English and who serve as linguistic resources and language models (Bunch, Abram, Lotan, & Valdes, 2001). In the language-rich CI classrooms, students have multiple opportunities to produce oral and written language using different text types, genres, and linguistic repertoires. This increased production of both oral and written language leads to growth and development of students' use of academic discourse (Bunch, 2006, 2009; Bunch et al., 2001; Bunch & Willett, 2013; Lotan, 2008).

In CI classrooms, teachers use two crucial interventions to counteract the status generalization process that leads to status problems. First, appreciating the intellectual heterogeneity in the classroom, in a "multiple-abilities orientation" that precedes the group task, teachers demonstrate to students that in addition to the traditionally recognized academic abilities of reading, writing and calculating quickly, many different intellectual abilities are needed to complete the task successfully. Intellectual abilities such as analyzing, asking good questions, explaining, interpreting complex texts, drawing diagrams and graphs, making plans, designing an experiment with multiple variables, synthesizing information, organizing a group, facilitating adeptly, and many more kinds of "smarts" are demonstrated by members of the group.

Teachers emphasize that while no one person is good at all these intellectual abilities and is able to demonstrate them all convincingly and consistently, everyone is good at some of these abilities and can demonstrate intellectual strengths. By stating that different students will make different intellectual contributions, the teacher creates a mixed set, rather than a uniformly high or low set of expectations for students' competence and performance.

This intervention fosters more equal participation. In Tammivaara (1982) laboratory study and in Rosenholtz's (1985) and Bower's (1997) classroom experiments, the multiple-abilities orientation weakened status effects. In a regular classroom setting, Cohen, Lotan, and Catanzarite (1988) showed that teachers' use of multiple-abilities orientation reduced but did not eliminate the relationship between status and interaction. Thus, in addition to the use of a multiple-abilities intervention, a second, more targeted and precise intervention was necessary.

Assigning competence to low-status students is the second intervention. By using a curriculum that is multidimensional and requires many different intellectual abilities, and by closely observing students who exhibit low-status behavior, the teacher will be able to notice those students' successful contributions to the group effort and to the successful completion of the task. The teacher then describes specifically and publicly how the low-status student's contribution becomes relevant to the success of the group.

The use of these two status interventions by the teacher was associated with higher rates of participation of students who were previously perceived as low status by their peers. At the same time, rates of participation of students perceived as high status were not diminished. In a classroom-level analysis, the more frequent use of the two status interventions was associated with more equal-status interactions among the students (Cohen & Lotan, 1995).

Learning to practice these status interventions successfully takes time and effort. It requires that teachers understand their benefits in weakening the relationship between status and interaction and consequently achievement outcomes (Cohen & Lotan, 1995). They also need to demonstrate consistently and persuasively how all their students' intellectual strengths and life experiences become relevant in the classroom. Outside sources that often contradict these messages are difficult to combat.

Necessary Conditions for Successful Implementation of Complex Instruction

Two conditions are necessary for the successful implementation of CI: (1) the design of the learning tasks and (2) the availability of professional and organizational support for teachers who are ready to expand their instructional repertoire to include a complex pedagogical approach.

Groupworthy Tasks

The findings reported previously were conditional on the nature of the learning tasks in which students engaged while working in small groups. The group tasks in CI make for tighter connection between the content to be learned and the teacher's teaching practices. To generate high levels of problem-solving talk and to set the stage for status interventions by the teacher, learning tasks are to be "groupworthy" (Lotan, 2003, 2014).

Unlike tightly defined, recipe-like tasks with predictable outcomes, groupworthy tasks are open-ended, productively uncertain, and require authentic problem-solving and critical thinking. In working on such tasks, students have opportunities to propose new approaches to solve problems, discuss moral dilemmas or different interpretations of complex texts, share perspectives based on their own experiences, develop explanations for scientific or social phenomena, summarize what they had learned, and prepare presentations. Through authentic, meaningful, content-based talk, students are able to integrate increasingly advanced disciplinary content and discourse.

While working on groupworthy tasks, students use different media (visuals, videos, recordings, manipulatives) and resources that provide multiple, diverse entry points for students to understand what they are to do, and what is expected of them. Tasks are organized around compelling ideas, essential questions, and important disciplinary content. They promote problem-solving conversation and conceptual discussions.

The requirement for a group product increases positive interdependence (Johnson & Johnson, 2009b), and the requirement for an individual report at the conclusion of groupwork ensures individual accountability. Completing individual reports ensures that all students have opportunities to summarize their experiences and thinking in their own words.

Instructions to the task (i.e., the task cards) and individual reports include criteria for the evaluation of the group's product and for the individual report, respectively. Because evaluation criteria are included in the instruction to the task, students can assess the quality of their own and their peers' group products during the group reports. Clearly articulated evaluation criteria increase group interactions, produce higher-quality group products, and stronger individual outcomes (Abram et al., 2001; Scarloss, 2001).

When working on groupworthy tasks, students assume greater control over their learning process and its outcomes. More often than not, teachers expect no single outcome or no uniform way to approach a question or a problem. The intellectual heterogeneity of the group and opportunities for students to use each other as resources greatly contribute to the development of deep, nuanced, and critical thinking. When teachers assign tasks that are open-ended in their process and in their product, they delegate intellectual authority to the students (Lotan, 1997, 2014). Furthermore, when students engage in tasks that require varied and multiple, intellectual contributions, teachers have increased opportunities to implement status interventions.

Teacher Learning and Organizational Support

The introduction of instructional innovations is incomplete without systematic and reliable opportunities for teacher learning. To organize the classroom for equitable interactions among students, the teacher's task becomes increasingly complex, non-routine, and uncertain. Organizational sociologists (March & Simon, 1958; Cohen, Deal, Meyer, & Scott, 1979) argue that in such work environments, supportive feedback, collegial collaboration, and availability of material resources are essential. At Stanford, scholars documented the relationship between the quality of CI implementation on the one hand, and opportunities for teacher learning, sustained and sound feedback from mentors and coaches, and support from school administrators on the other (Ellis & Lotan, 1997; Lotan, Cohen, & Morphew, 1998).

Complex Instruction: A Maturing Educational Innovation

At Stanford, with Elizabeth's rigorous focus, incessant direction, and mentorship, scholars continued to explore aspects of the implementation of CI in over 30 doctoral dissertations, numerous journal articles, and technical reports. What aspects of the interactions among members of a group are more or less productive? What are the features of the learning task and how are they related to the content and the quality of the interaction? What are the pedagogical moves in which the teacher engages to support the interaction? The CI team continued to address one of the most vexing issues of students working in small groups: the reproduction of societal inequities in the unequal distribution of power and participation in small cooperative groups. The potential of fostering academic and social integration in desegregated and untracked schools and classrooms is one of the major contributions of CI to the field. Specifying the conditions that support equal-status, task-related talk among students from diverse demographic backgrounds, varied levels of previous academic preparation and achievement, social attractiveness, and language proficiency in the language of instruction is its core.

The importance of such talk for learning is evident in the current context. The pressure for increased academic rigor through ambitious, standards-based, subject-specific teaching and learning, and the accompanying assessments is evident in the Common Core State Standards, for example. The standards also demand that classrooms provide equitable opportunities for success to students who have traditionally been underserved: students from low-income communities, English language learners, and students with specific learning needs. Numerous studies support the proposition that student engagement in meaningful discussions that build on student thinking lead to disciplinary literacy and higher achievement in the different subject areas.

From the late 1980s, the Program for Complex Instruction at Stanford collaborated with universities, colleges, schools and departments of education in the United States and other countries. Based on her extensive experience in building bridges between research and practice at WestEd's regional laboratory, Filby (1997) identified several factors that contributed to the growth and recognition of CI among practitioners and its generative influence for scholarly research:

- constant dedication to theory development and application to practice;
- finding responses to the challenge of producing equal-status interactions in heterogeneous classrooms through a process of "engineering" by
    - designing and constructing curricula,
    - restructuring the classroom,
    - developing status interventions,
    - preparing teachers;

- constantly checking and testing proposed responses against theoretical claims;
- the documented quality of CI and its profound appeal to teachers.

Looking Forward

Many scholars and teacher-researchers not affiliated with the Program for Complex Instruction at Stanford have published journal articles, book chapters, and doctoral dissertations describing observations and data in the context of CI classrooms. Published articles in a range of journals include theoretical contributions as well as practical recommendations. Several articles report about the implementation of CI in settings with increased racial, ethnic, social and linguistic heterogeneity among students. A partial list of titles can be found at https://complexinstruction.stanford.edu/library.

Designing groupwork: Strategies for the heterogeneous classroom, third edition (Cohen & Lotan, 2014), is a practical resource reaching many teachers who are interested in groupwork in general and CI in particular. It is widely used in courses of university-based teacher education programs and in professional development courses in districts and counties across the United States and in other countries. In addition, audiences have appreciated the text and the videos in *"Heterogenius" classrooms: Detracking math and science—A look at groupwork in action* (Watanabe, 2012). Two books published by the National Council of Teachers of Mathematics (Featherstone et al., 2011; Horn, 2012) recognize that CI is a useful approach to build equitable mathematics classrooms.

Since 2009, the San Francisco Unified School District has been sponsoring a wide-reaching and serious implementation of CI. The district made considerable and consistent investments preparing and supporting teachers for the implementation of CI in mathematics and science in its schools with positive outcomes (see www.sfusdmath.org). More recently, CI was described in several far-reaching publications (National Research Council, 2000; Oakes, Lipton, Anderson, & Stillman, 2018; Darling-Hammond & Oakes, 2019).

The wide reach of the body of knowledge about educational innovations might have mixed results. Given the extensive and well-formulated knowledge base of CI, its important goal, principles, and practices are explicit. Its implementation in different contexts and settings added much knowledge. It also exemplifies the benefits and challenges of what McLaughlin (2008) calls "mutual adaptation." The pull between large-scale dissemination and maintaining program integrity is a delicate balance, that is, at times, difficult or even impossible to achieve.

Many potentially promising educational innovations are in danger of backfiring, particularly when they are simplified, reduced to narrow techniques, and quickly reproducible checklists. Indeed, we have seen teachers and administrators take up the more-easily understood and more-readily implemented components of CI, such as the use of cooperative norms and student roles. These seem to have become commonplaces in small-group instruction. However, CI will only keep its promise when teachers are able to implement the status interventions and benefit from the supports and resources provided by school administrators and peers. An important, central message cannot be lost: Recognizing and actively addressing status problems and their consequences are indispensable as we strive to create equal-status interactions, which in turn, enhance all students' learning experiences and outcomes.

We would be remiss if we neglected to imagine the ways that teachers, administrators, and researchers will continue to learn and build on the theoretical and practical aspects of CI. For example, with significant growth in the cognitive and neurological sciences, researchers leverage innovative medical technologies to explore what happens in the brain when we feel excluded or threatened. In one such study, researchers used functional magnetic resonance imaging (fMRI) to see what parts of the brain were most active when a person feels threatened (Eisenberger, Lieberman, & Williams, 2003). The authors found that social pain is analogous in its neurocognitive function to physical pain and—perhaps more interestingly—may allow restorative measures to be taken. Such a more nuanced understanding of how, when, and why we feel threatened and how social pain might be ameliorated might have implications for schooling.

Tribute to a Visionary

Complex Instruction is an actualization of Elizabeth G. Cohen's vision to support teachers as they aim and work to create a just, equitable, and democratic society. Her standing as a "grande dame" in the field of cooperative learning is uncontested. Her seminal articles and reviews of research as well as her book *Designing Groupwork. Strategies for Heterogeneous Classroom* have influenced and inspired the field of learning in small groups from its earliest days to the present.

Complex Instruction embodies the principles of cooperative learning and is the product of a large group of individuals for whom equity and equal status interactions in classrooms was at the forefront of their commitment and their common goal. Over the years, a bounty of interested students, researchers, visiting scholars, and professors participated in various capacities to learn from and contribute to the work of Complex Instruction. In doing so, we were able to see its power across different subject matters, grade levels, and various cultural and national contexts.

Elizabeth Cohen led this joint endeavor until her death in 2005. She continues to inspire those of us who have been standing on her shoulders.

Because none of us is as smart as all of us together. It's what CI is about.

References

Abram, P. L., Cohen, E. G., Holthuis, N. I., Scarloss, B. A., Lotan, R. A., & Schultz, S. E. (2001). The use of evaluation criteria to improve student talk in cooperative groups. *Asian Pacific Journal of Education*, 22(1), 16–27.

Allport, G. W. (1954). *The nature of prejudice*. Oxford: Addison-Wesley.

Aronson, E., Blaney, N., Sikes, J., & Snapp, M. (1978). *The jigsaw classroom*. Beverly Hills, CA: Sage.

Ben-Ari, R. (1997). Complex instruction and cognitive development. In E. G. Cohen & R. A. Lotan (Eds.), *Working for equity in heterogeneous classrooms: Sociological theory in practice* (pp. 193–208). New York, NY: Teachers College Press.

Ben-Ari, R., & Friedrich, K. (2000). Restructuring heterogeneous classes for cognitive development: Social interactive perspective. *Instructional Science*, 28(2), 153–167.

Berger, J. B., Cohen, B. P., & Zelditch, M. Jr. (1966). Status characteristics and expectation states. In J. Berger & M. Zelditch, Jr. (Eds.), *Sociological theories in progress 1* (pp. 29–46). Boston, MA: Houghton Mifflin.

Berger, J. B., Cohen, B. P., & Zelditch, M. Jr. (1972). Status characteristics and social interaction. *American Sociological Review*, 37, 241–255.

Berger, J. B., Rosenholtz, S. J., & Zelditch, M. Jr. (1980). Status organizing processes. *Annual Review of Sociology*, 6, 479–508.

Boaler, J., & Staples, M. (2008). Creating mathematical futures through an equitable mathematics approach: The case of Railside School. *Teachers College Record*, 110(3), 608–645.

Bower, B. (1997). Effects of the multiple-ability curriculum in secondary social studies classrooms. In E. G. Cohen & R. A. Lotan (Eds.), *Working for equity in heterogeneous classrooms: Sociological theory in practice* (pp. 117–136). New York, NY: Teachers College Press.

Bunch, G. C. (2006). "Academic English" in the 7th grade: Broadening the lens, expanding access. *Journal of English for Academic Purposes*, 5(4), 284–301.

Bunch, G. C. (2009). "Going up there:" Challenges and opportunities for language minority students during a mainstream classroom speech event. *Linguistics and Education*, 20(2), 81–108.

Bunch, G. C., Abram, P. L., Lotan, R. A., & Valdes, G. (2001). Beyond sheltered instruction: Rethinking conditions for academic language development. *TESOL Journal*, 10(2–3), 28–33.

Bunch, G. C., & Willett, K. (2013). Writing to mean in middle school: Understanding how second language writers negotiate textually-rich content-area instruction. *Journal of Second Language Writing*, 22(2), 141–160.

Cohen, E. G. (1972). Interracial interaction disability. *Human Relations*, 25, 9–24.

Cohen, E. G. (1982). Expectation states and interracial interaction in school settings. *Annual Review of Sociology, 8*, 109–235.
Cohen, E. G. (1986). *Designing groupwork: Strategies for the heterogeneous classroom.* New York, NY: Teachers College Press.
Cohen, E. G., Bianchini, J. A., Cossey, R., Holthuis, N. C., Morphew, C. C., & Whitcomb, J. A. (1997). What did students learn: 1982–1994. In E. G. Cohen & R. A. Lotan (Eds.), *Working for equity in heterogeneous classrooms: Sociological theory in practice* (pp. 137–165). New York, NY: Teachers College Press.
Cohen, E. G., Deal, T. E., Meyer, J. W., & Scott, W. R. (1979). Technology and teaming in the elementary school. *Sociology of Education, 52*, 20–33.
Cohen, E. G., & DeAvila, E. A. (1983). *Learning to think in math and science: Improving local education for minority children* (Final Report to the Johnson Foundation). Stanford University School of Education.
Cohen, E. G., Lockheed, M. E., & Lohman, M. R. (1976). The center for interracial cooperation: A field experiment. Sociology of Education, 49(1), 47–58.
Cohen, E. G., & Lotan, R. A. (1995). Producing equal status interaction in heterogeneous classrooms. *American Educational Research Journal, 32*(1), 99–120.
Cohen, E. G., & Lotan, R. A. (2014). *Designing groupwork: Strategies for the heterogeneous classroom* (3rd ed.). New York, NY: Teachers College Press.
Cohen, E. G., Lotan, R. A., & Catanzarite, L. (1988). Can expectations for competence be treated in the classroom? In M. Webster Jr. & M. Foschi (Eds.), *Status generalization: New theory and research* (pp. 27–54). Stanford, CA: Stanford University Press.
Cohen, E. G., Lotan, R. A., & Leechor, C. (1989). Can classrooms learn? *Sociology of Education, 62*, 75–94.
Cohen, E. G., & Roper, S. S. (1972). Modification of interracial interaction disability: An application of status characteristic theory. American Sociological Review, 37(6), 643–657.
Cossey, R. (1997). *Mathematical communication: Issues of access and equity.* Unpublished Doctoral Dissertation, Stanford University, Stanford, CA.
Darling-Hammond, L., & Oakes, J. (2019). *Preparing teacher for deeper learning.* Cambridge, MA: Harvard Education Press.
DeAvila, E. A., Cohen, E. G., & Intili, J. K. (1982). Improving cognition: A multicultural approach. In S. S. Seidner (Ed.), *Issues of language assessment and research.* Springfield, IL: Illinois State Board of Education.
DeAvila, E. A., Duncan, S. E., & Navarrete, C. (1987). *Finding out descubriemento.* Miami, FL: Santillana Publishing Co. Inc.
Eisenberger, N., Lieberman, M., & Williams, K. (2003). Does rejection hurt? An fMRI study for social exclusion. *Science, 302*, 290–292.
Ellis, N. E., & Lotan, R. A. (1997). Teachers as learners: Feedback, conceptual understanding, and implementation. In E. G. Cohen & R. A. Lotan (Eds.), *Working for equity in heterogeneous classrooms: Sociological theory in practice* (pp. 209–222). New York, NY: Teachers College Press.
Featherstone, H., Crespo, S., Jilk, L., Oslund, J., Parks, A., & Wood, M. (2011). *Smarter together: Collaboration and equity in the elementary math classroom.* Reston, VA: National Council of Teachers of Mathematics.

Filby, N. N. (1997). A viewpoint on dissemination. In E. G. Cohen & R. A. Lotan (Eds.), *Working for equity in heterogeneous classrooms: Sociological theory in practice* (pp. 277–285). New York, NY: Teachers College Press.

Holthuis, N. (1999). *Scientifically speaking: Identifying, analyzing, and promoting science talk in small groups*. Unpublished Doctoral Dissertation, Stanford University, Stanford, CA.

Horn, I. (2012). *Strength in numbers: Collaborative learning in secondary mathematics*. Reston, VA: National Council of Teachers of Mathematics.

Johnson, D. W., & Johnson, R. T. (2009a). Energizing learning: The instructional power of conflict. *Educational Researcher, 38*(1), 37–51.

Johnson, D. W., & Johnson, R. T. (2009b). An educational psychology success story: Social interdependence theory and cooperative learning. *Educational Researcher, 38*(5), 365–379.

Johnson, D. W., Johnson, R. T., & Maruyama, G. (1983). Interdependence and interpersonal attraction among heterogeneous and homogeneous individuals. A theoretical formulation and a meta-analysis of research. *Review of Educational Research, 53*, 5–54.

Katz, P. H., & Taylor, D. A. (Eds.). (1988). *Eliminating racism*. New York, NY: Springer.

Leechor, C. (1988). *How high and low achieving students differentially benefit from working together in cooperative small groups*. Unpublished Doctoral Dissertation, Stanford University, Stanford, CA.

Lockheed, M. E., Harris, A. M., & Nemceff, W. P. (1983). Sex and social influence: Does sex function as a status characteristic in mixed-sex groups of children? *Journal of Educational Psychology, 75*(6), 877–888.

Lotan, R. A. (1997). Principles of a principled curriculum. In E. G. Cohen & R. A. Lotan (Eds.), *Working for equity in heterogeneous classrooms: Sociological theory in practice* (pp. 105-116). New York, NY: Teachers College Press.

Lotan, R. A. (2003). Group-worthy tasks. *Educational Leadership, 6*(6), 72–75.

Lotan, R. A. (2008). Developing language and content knowledge in heterogeneous classrooms. In R. Gillies (Ed.), *The teacher's role in implementing cooperative learning in the classroom* (pp. 187–203). New York, NY: Springer.

Lotan, R. A. (2014). Crafting groupworthy learning tasks. In E. G. Cohen & R. A. Lotan (Eds.), *Designing groupwork: Strategies of the heterogeneous classroom* (3rd ed., pp. 85–96). New York, NY: Teachers College Press.

Lotan, R. A., Cohen, E. G., & Morphew, C. C. (1998). Beyond the workshop: Evidence from complex instruction. In C. Brody & N. Davidson (Eds.), *Professional development for cooperative learning issues and approaches* (pp. 122–145). Albany, NY: State University of New York Press.

March, J. G., & Simon, H. A. (1958). *Organizations*. New York, NY: Wiley.

McLaughlin, M. W. (2008). Implementation as mutual adaptation: Change in classroom organization. In D. J. Flinders & S. J. Thornton (Eds.), *The curriculum studies reader*. New York, NY: Routledge.

Nasir, N. S., Cabana, C., Shreve, B., Woodbury, E., & Louie, N. (Eds.). (2014). *Mathematics for equity: A framework for successful practice*. New York, NY: Teachers College Press.

National Research Council. (2000). *How people learn: Brain, mind, experience, and school: expanded edition*. Washington, DC: The National Academies Press. https://doi.org/10.17226/9853

Oakes, J., Lipton, A., Anderson, L., & Stillman, J. (2018). *Teaching to save the world*. New York, NY: Routledge.

Piaget, J. (1963). *The origins of intelligence in children*. New York, NY: W.W. Norton & Company, Inc.

Rosenholtz, S. J. (1977). *The multiple abilities curriculum: An intervention against the self-fulfilling prophecy*. Unpublished Doctoral Dissertation. Stanford University, Stanford, CA.

Rosenholtz, S. J. (1985). Treating problems of academic status. In J. Berger & M. Zelditch, Jr. (Eds.), *Status, rewards, and influence*. San Francisco, CA: Jossey-Bass.

Rosenholtz, S. J., & Simpson, C. (1984). The formation of ability conception: Developmental trend or social construction. *Review of Educational Research, 54*, 31–63.

Rosenholtz, S. J., & Wilson, B. (1980). The effect of classroom structure on shared perceptions of ability. *American Educational Research Journal, 17*, 175–182.

Scarloss, B. A. (2001). *Sensemaking, interaction, and learning in student groups*. Unpublished Doctoral Dissertation, Stanford University, Stanford, CA.

Schultz, S. E. (1999). *To group of not to group: Effects of groupwork on students' declarative and procedural knowledge in science*. Unpublished Doctoral Dissertation, Stanford University, Stanford, CA.

Sharan, S. (1980). Cooperative learning in small groups: Recent methods and effects on achievement, attitudes, and ethnic relations. *Review of Educational Research, 50*, 241–271.

Sharan, S., & Sharan, Y. (1976). *Small-group teaching*. Englewood Cliffs, NJ: Educational Technology Publications.

Slavin, R. E. (1980). Cooperative learning. *Review of Educational Research, 50*(2), 315–342.

Tammivaara, J. S. (1982). The effects of task structure on beliefs about competence and participation in small groups. *Sociology of Education, 55*, 212–222.

Vygotsky, L. (1978). *Mind and society* (M. Cole, V. John-Steiner, S. Scribner, & E. Soublmerman, Eds.). Cambridge, MA: Harvard University Press.

Watanabe, M. (Eds.). (2012). *"Heterogenius" classrooms—Detracking math & science: A look at groupwork in action*. New York, NY: Teachers College Press.

Chapter 5

The Structural Approach and Kagan Structures

Spencer Kagan

The Structural Approach to cooperative learning, also known as Kagan Cooperative Learning, is an approach to cooperative learning based on the use of structures. Kagan Structures are step-by-step, content-free instructional strategies that structure the interaction of students with each other, the curriculum, and the teacher to ensure the implementation of four basic principles of cooperative learning, to be explained in this chapter. To understand the theoretical underpinnings and practical implementation of the Structural Approach to cooperative learning, first we will examine three empowering theoretical concepts: Situationism; the Seven Keys to Success; and Teacher A, B, C. After presenting these theoretical constructs, we overview the unique approach to teacher training used in the Structural Approach and review research demonstrating a range of positive outcomes when teachers implement Kagan Cooperative Learning Structures. We interpret why Kagan Structures produce a wide range of positive outcomes and how structures can be the basis of an instructional revolution that reverses the negative effects of a massive, unintended training in competitive and individualistic social orientation.

Situationism

The Structural Approach to cooperative learning is applied situationism. Situationism is a way of explaining human behavior. There has been a great deal of debate among psychologists about what determines a person's behavior: Is it their personality or their current situation? Personality psychologists explain behavior based on individual needs, motives, and values; how a person was brought up; their culture; their experiences and education. Social psychologists instead look to the situation a person is in, claiming situations determine behavior.

As a research psychologist for 19 years I studied what determines cooperative versus competitive behavior. My research and that of my colleagues demonstrated that by manipulating situational variables, regardless of personality, we can make anyone either very cooperative or very competitive (Kagan & Madsen, 1971, 1975; Nelson & Kagan, 1974). When children are placed in situations in which cooperation is necessary to obtain rewards, they become extremely cooperative. If competition is necessary for reward attainment, children become very competitive. Situations overpower personality.

We can easily grasp how situations are more powerful than personality in determining cooperative versus competitive behavior by engaging in a simple thought experiment I call "The Basket of Gold Coins."

The Basket of Gold Coins

In our thought experiment, we imagine two different situations.

Situation 1: Imagine a room with 200 people seated before a stage. On the stage is a tall woman holding a large basket containing about 200 gold coins. Each coin is worth $1000. The woman announces:

> *I am going to toss all these coins out into the room. I have a timer. After 3 minutes, any coin you are holding is yours to keep.*

The woman then tosses out the coins.

Now imagine what the room would look like! There would be a big scramble to gather coins. In the process, there would be some pushing, shoving, grabbing, and perhaps even some scuffles for coins.

Situation 2: The woman comes back the next day. Her basket contains the same number of gold coins. This time she announces:

> *I am going to toss all these coins out into the room. I have a timer. I am going to place my basket on the stage. After 3 minutes, all the coins that are back in the basket will be shared equally among us. No one can keep any other coins.*

The woman then tosses out the coins.

Now imagine what the room would look like. Someone farther from the basket might hand a coin to someone closer to the basket to more quickly get the coin in the basket. Those gathering coins might hand them to runners to get the coins in the basket more quickly. Participants in our experiment might even form something like a bucket brigade, handing coins from one to another to more quickly deposit coins into the basket.

What changed? The personality of the people in the room did not change. The number of gold coins did not change. People were given the same three minutes. Why were the people competitive in the first situation and cooperative in the second? What changed is the situation. When it comes to cooperation versus competition, situations are far more powerful than personality. Structures are situations that cause positive classroom behaviors. The Structural Approach to cooperative learning relies on structures, carefully sequenced instructional strategies, to create situations in the classroom that promote student cooperation and learning.

The Seven Keys to Success

At the heart of the Structural Approach to cooperative learning are Kagan Structures. The frequent use of simple Kagan Structures results in greater cooperation, more active engagement, and academic gains. However, in working with thousands of teachers and schools, we find that educators experience the greatest positive impact when Kagan Structures are not just used in isolation. The full power of the Structural Approach is released when Kagan Structures are implemented in a classroom that maintains several contextual elements. Combined with structures, we call all these elements the Seven Keys to Success. The Seven Keys to Success are (1) Basic Principles (PIES); (2) Structures; (3) Teams; (4) Management; (5) Teambuilding; (6) Classbuilding; and (7) Social Skills. Let's look at these Seven Keys and how each unlocks the door to more successful cooperative learning.

Key 1. Basic Principles (PIES)

When I realized the power of situations to determine cooperative interaction, I began developing a program of applied situationism for the classroom. In the process, together with my colleagues, we discovered four principles that must be in place to have all students engaged in productive cooperative learning. We define true cooperative learning as occurring when all four principles are in place. If any principle is not in place, the students may be working together, but gains for all are not assured. We say if a principle is left out, the students are doing group work, not cooperative learning.

The four principles that define cooperative learning in the Structural Approach are Positive Interdependence, Individual Accountability, Equal (or Equitable) Participation, and Simultaneous Interaction (Kagan & Kagan, 2009). The four principles are symbolized by the acronym PIES. For each of the four PIES principles there are critical questions. A positive answer to the critical question indicates the principle is in place. For example, the E of PIES is equal or at least equitable participation. The critical question is simply, "Is participation approximately equal?" If we create a situation in which equal or equitable participation is not assured, then we are not doing cooperative learning as defined by the Structural Approach. All four principles must be in place for true cooperative learning in the structural approach. The P of PIES has two components and so has two critical questions. The four principles, their critical questions, and the consequence of putting each principle in place are summarized in Figure 5.1.

The PIES critical questions are very helpful in distinguishing true cooperative learning, which is almost always successful, from group work, which often is not successful. For example, teachers frequently use a structure called Turn-N-Talk. With Turn-N-Talk the teacher has students turn to a partner and discuss a topic. Teachers think the structure is good cooperative learning because there is a great deal of interaction and students are working together. Translation: The P and S of PIES are in place. A PIES analysis reveals it is not good cooperative learning because both the I and the E are not in place: If a highly motivated student is paired with an unmotivated student, the high achiever might well do most or even all of the talking. Thus, equal participation is not assured by the structure. Further, an unmotivated student can choose not to perform at all! So there is no individual accountability. Without PIES in place, there is no guarantee of positive outcomes for all students. Some students may experience gains, while others do not. Without PIES in place students are doing group work, not true cooperative learning, and group work often does not outperform traditional teaching methods.

In contrast to the teacher doing Turn-N-Talk, a teacher familiar with Kagan Structures might do a Timed Pair Share. In Timed Pair Share, in turn, each student in the pair talks for an equal amount of time while their partner listens. Thus, there is equal participation and each student is accountable for performing. To the untrained eye, Turn-N-Talk and Timed Pair Share may look equivalent; when we look at those structures through the lens of PIES, Turn-N-Talk is group work and Timed Pair Share is true cooperative leaning.

Key 2. Cooperative Learning Structures

At the heart of the Structural Approach to cooperative learning are structures that have PIES in place—true cooperative learning structures. The nickname for structures that implement all four of the PIES principles is "Kagan Structures."

Over time, Kagan Structures have undergone repeated revisions to better implement PIES. When I developed the first Kagan Structure, Numbered Heads Together, it had only four steps. Students sit in teams of four and students each have a number—1, 2, 3, or 4. Originally the four steps of Numbered Heads Together were as follows:

1. Teacher asks a question.
2. Students put their heads together to determine their best answer.
3. Teacher calls a student number.
4. A student with that number responds.

PIES: Basic Principles of Cooperative Learning

Acronym	Principle	Critical Question	Key Words/Phrases	Students Feel	Students Do
P	**Positive Interdependence:** Outcomes positively correlated	*Does one doing well help others?*	Positive Correlation Shared Goal	On the same side	Encourage each other; tutor; coach
	Positive Interdependence: Outcomes depend on all	*Does task completion depend on others?*	Interdependence	Need each other Part of a team	Cooperate
I	**Individual accountability**	*Is an individual performance (oral or written) required?*	Accountable Responsible Visible	Can't hide "On the hook"	Contribute; perform
E	**Equal participation**	*Is participation approximately equal?*	Equitable Fair No hogs or logs	Equal status Included	Participate equally
S	**Simultaneous interaction**	*Are at least 25% writing or talking at any one moment?*	Engagement	Engaged	Participate maximally

Figure 5.1 PIES: Basic principles of cooperative learning

As we used Numbered Heads Together over the years, we discovered it could better implement PIES by modifying the steps. To better implement the simultaneity principle(s), we developed simultaneous response modes so that all the students with the called number could respond rather than just one. For example, in one of many simultaneous response modes, students have response boards so all of the students whose number is called can respond at the same time. To better implement individual accountability, we inserted a step between the teacher asking the question and students putting their heads together: We inserted an individual write. That is, students secretly write their best answer before sharing with their teammates. That way each student is individually accountable for performing. Without that step, students could take a free ride by not thinking, just waiting to hear the answer from their teammates. To further improve the simultaneity principle, we created a variation of Numbered Heads Together: Paired Heads Together. In Paired Heads Together when we call for a response, half the class is called upon (one student per pair), not a quarter of the class (one student per team). With pairs, we double the overt active participation, better implementing the simultaneity principle.

Over time many of the structures have been modified not only to better implement PIES but also to more fully align with brain research (Kagan, 2014). For example, the principle of retrograde memory enhancement is a well-established principle of brain science (McGaugh, 2003). Retrograde memory enhancement simply means that anything associated with emotion is better remembered. To align Numbered Heads Together with that finding, we inserted applause or team cheers following correct responses. Brain research also indicates students perform better when there is frequent movement in the class. Movement results in increased nourishment to the brain. Thus, we developed variations of Numbered Heads Together that allow students to move and interact with others in the class while going through the basic steps of Numbered Heads Together. In Traveling Heads Together students whose number is called "travel" to a new team to share their answer. Stir-the-Class is more complex. Teams stand around the perimeter of the room. They huddle to consult during the heads-together step, *unhuddle* (a word we invented, meaning to get out of the huddle and stand in a line) when done. When the teacher calls a number, the teacher states how many teams ahead the called-upon student is to rotate to share his or her answer.

Following these improvements, Numbered Heads Together now has seven steps, rather than four, and includes variations. Our handout to teachers for Numbered Heads Together is presented in Figure 5.2.

Numbered Heads Together

Teammates put their "heads together" to reach consensus on the team's answer. Everyone keeps on their toes because their number may be called to share the team's answer.

Steps

Setup: Teacher prepares questions or problems to ask teams.

1 Students **number off**.

2 Teacher poses a problem and gives **think time**. (Example: *How are rainbows formed? Think about your best answer.*)

3 Students privately **write** their answers.

4 Students stand up and "put their **heads together**," showing answers, discussing, and teaching each other.

5 Students sit down when **everyone** knows the answer or has something to share.

6 Teacher calls a **number**. Students with that number answer **simultaneously** using:
  • AnswerBoard Share
  • Chalkboard Responses
  • Choral Practice
  • Response Cards
  • Finger Responses
  • Manipulatives

7 Classmates **applaud** students who responded.

Variations:
Paired Heads Together: Students are in shoulder partner pairs. After teacher asks a question, pairs huddle to improve the answers they have each written. Teacher then calls for either A or B to share their best answer with their face partner.

Traveling Heads Together: Traveling Heads starts the same as Numbered Heads, but when the teacher calls a number, the students with that number on each team stand, then "travel" to a new team to share their answers. For fun, seated students beckon for a standing student to join their team.

Stir-the-Class: Teams stand around the outside of the class with spaces between teams. Teammates stand shoulder-to-shoulder. The teacher poses a question, then students write their own answers on an AnswerBoard or slip of paper. Teammates huddle to reach consensus, then unhuddle when done. The teacher selects a number and tells students with that number how many teams to rotate forward to share their answer.

08/09

Kagan Structures are copyright © Kagan Publishing & Professional Development. All Rights Reserved. Do not duplicate or distribute without permission.

Kagan

Publishing: 1 (800) 933-2667 • Professional Development: 1 (800) 266-7576
www.KaganOnline.com

It's All About Engagement!

Figure 5.2 Numbered Heads Together

What Is a Structure?

We have been describing structures as ways to implement PIES, but we have not to this point offered a formal definition of structures. What are the essential elements of a structure? *Structures are repeatable, content-free instructional strategies that produce predicable outcomes by creating situations that determine how students interact with their academic content, each other, and the teacher.* We have already focused on one part of that definition: Structures are situations. When we did the thought experiment with the basket of gold coins, we saw how situations create predictable behavior. Now let's focus on another part of what defines structures: Structures are repeatable and content-free.

Repeatable, Content-Free

Perhaps the most important thing that distinguishes structures from other instructional strategies is that structures are repeatable and content-free. Let's take the structure RallyRobin as an example. In RallyRobin, students are in pairs and they take turns making brief oral responses to a question that has more than one possible answer. For example, the teacher may ask students to do a RallyRobin naming odd numbers. RallyRobin is the structure; naming odd numbers is the content. Having done RallyRobin with odd numbers, tomorrow the teacher could use RallyRobin again, this time having students name events from a story. Older students might be naming prime numbers or literary devices. RallyRobin is repeatable and content-free: We take out one content and put in another to create a new activity. RallyRobin can be used to have students name any content with multiple answers. For examples, the planets, the countries in Europe, things about which they are curious, or things for which students are grateful.

We work with a basic formula: *Structure + Content = Activity*. Because structures are content-free, any one structure can generate an infinite number of activities. They can be thought of as activity generators. Given any one structure, we can insert different content every day, generating new activities every day. In this formulation, a lesson is a series of sequenced activities. These activities can follow any type of lesson plan. For example, we might use one structure to create a set for the lesson, a different structure to give students input, another for guided practice, another for individual practice, and yet another structure for closure.

Structures make the life of a teacher easy; once a teacher knows a range of structures, the teacher simply delivers the content via structures. With practice, teachers implement structures effortlessly. It is analogous to learning to drive. When we first learn to drive a car, we have to think a lot: When do I start braking? When do I put on the turn signal? Is it safe to pass? How much space do I need to change lanes . . . ? After considerable practice, we drive effortlessly, free to have a conversation or to think about other things. Similarly, when we first learn a new language, we think a lot about the vocabulary, sentence structures, subject–verb agreement. Later we obtain fluency in the language and don't think about the language at all; we think about what we want to say. When a teacher becomes fluent in a structure, the teacher no longer needs to think about the structure, the teacher thinks about what she wants to teach.

A great many teachers have told me that using structures has transformed their teaching. With traditional teaching, student come alive when the bell rings; when structures are used, students come alive in class. Perhaps my favorite comment from a teacher came from an older teacher who said, "I was looking forward to retirement, but now, using structures, I look forward to each day of teaching."

Functions of Structures

Although my basic research on cooperation and the impact of situations on cooperativeness began in 1968, it was not until 1980 that Kagan Publishing and Professional Development began developing and training teachers in cooperative learning structures. In the nearly 40 years since then, we have developed over 280 cooperative learning structures. Why so many structures? Different structures determine different types of interaction and allow for the acquisition of different social skills, character virtues, thinking skills, and mastery of different types of content.

To take a simple example, let's contrast RallyRobin with Timed Pair Share. If we want students to respond to a question that has many possible answers, we would choose RallyRobin. In RallyRobin students take turns stating answers. If we want students to explain an answer in depth, we would choose Timed Pair Share. In Timed Pair Share students have one turn each to share for a predetermined amount of time.

Some structures have very specific functions. Find-My-Rule is designed to promote inductive reasoning. In Find-My-Rule the teacher places objects or names of objects one at a time in an unlabeled graphic organizer; after each object is placed, students interact to attempt to infer the rule the teacher is using to sort the objects. Logic Line-Ups (Kagan, 2001), in contrast, is used to foster deductive reasoning. Students are given rules about the order of objects, and each student assumes the role of one object. Their job is to line up in order to respect the conditions of each rule. Other structures, in contrast, are multi-functional. For example, a RoundRobin (each student in a team shares in turn) may be used, among other things for mastery (practice skip counting); thinking skills (name consequences of World War II); teambuilding (name fun weekend activities); or processing a lesson (name important concepts in the lesson).

In training teachers in the functions of structures we distinguish ten main functions, divided into two categories: interpersonal and academic. See Figure 5.3: Structure Functions. Over the years we have developed many structures for each function. For example, Paraphrase Passport is a communication skill structure; it enhances listening and taking the role

Structure Functions			
Interpersonal		Academic	
Function	**Goal**	**Function**	**Goal**
Classbuilding	Know and bond with classmates	**Knowledge-building**	Learn facts, master information
Teambuilding	Know and bond with teammates	**Procedure learning**	Acquire skills, procedures
Social Skills	Acquire social skills	**Processing Info**	Move content to long-term memory; verbalize learning
Communication Skills	Acquire communication skills	**Thinking Skills**	Acquire range of thinking skills
Decision-making	Acquire decision-making skills	**Presentations**	Create presentations; acquire presentation skills

Figure 5.3 Structure functions

of the other. Talking Chips is another communication skill structure; it enhances listening and turn-taking.

In planning activities for their students, we encourage teachers to first determine the functions they want to accomplish. Are they trying to foster a thinking skill, have students learn new facts, or practice new skills? Having determined the functions, they draw from those structures that are efficient in reaching those goals. Just as we would not use Logic Line-Ups to learn new facts, we would not use the Flashcard Game to foster thinking skills. With time, teachers draw effortlessly from their toolbox of structures to help students acquire desired skills. They choose structures tailored to their goals.

After having mastered the initial ten functions of structures, teachers may choose advanced workshops in the Structural Approach and learn new structures tailored to additional functions. For example, the brain has numerous independent memory systems and we have developed structures to place content in each of those memory systems. In the same way, we have developed structures to engage and develop Fifteen Thinking Skills (Kagan, 2003, 2005); Twenty-One Character Virtues (Kagan, 2000); Five Dimensions of Emotional Intelligence (Kagan, 2001, 2020); Eight Multiple Intelligences (Kagan & Kagan, 1998, 2006); and Five Stages of Language Acquisition (Kagan, 1993, 2013; Kagan & High, 2002). My major focus in the last decade has been to develop structures to implement six principles of brain-friendly teaching (Kagan, 1999, 2001b, 2006a, 2009, 2014).

Key 3. Teams

Teams

There are four types of teams: heterogeneous, random, homogeneous, and student-selected. Further, teams can be of different sizes. In the Structural Approach, we highly recommend students spend most of their time in heterogeneous teams of four.

Why Heterogeneous Teams?

We recommend teams of four, each team consisting of a high achiever, a high middle, a low middle, and a low achiever. Heterogeneous teams by academic achievement level maximize the chance of cross-ability tutoring. If everyone is at the same achievement level, they have little to learn from each other. Further, we recommend heterogeneous teams by gender, and by race, to improve cross-sex and cross-race relations.

Homogeneous teams by achievement level lead to winner and loser teams with negative impact on self-image and self-esteem for the low achievement teams. Random teams run the risk of having all the difficult or unmotivated students on one team. Self-selected teams usually devolve into homogeneous teams by ability level and run the risk of more off-task behavior as friends seek out friends.

We do recommend occasional breakout from the heterogeneous base team into random, and self-selected teams, but only for limited times and for special projects. For example, we might allow students to self-group into interest teams for an investigation project. Occasional breakouts into homogeneous teams to work with students with common needs are also possible, but to maximize achievement, and improve cross-sex and cross-race relations, it is important that students spend most of their time in heterogeneous teams.

Why Teams of Four?

Maximum simultaneous interaction occurs in pairs, and teams of four break evenly into two sets of pairs. For pair work we often say, turn to your "face partner," the person seated across from you, or turn to your "shoulder partner," the person seated next to you. During pair work, teams of three or five leave someone out. Teams larger than four cut down active engagement during teamwork. For example, to complete a RoundRobin it takes six minutes in a team of six but only four minutes in a team of four.

Re-forming Teams

We recommend forming new teams each six to ten weeks depending on the academic schedule. By having students work in different teams, we maximize the opportunity to learn new social skills (learning to get along with one person involves different skills than getting along with another). Further, some students are difficult to work with and we don't want the other three to always be on a team with that person. In addition, re-forming teams creates novelty and variety, energizing the class.

Knowing who to put on teams, how long to keep teams together, how to re-form teams, when to use random teams, and when to use heterogeneous teams contributes to enhanced academic and social outcomes.

Key 4. Management

Efficient cooperative learning requires adopting different management techniques. For example, because students are often interacting in pairs, as teams, and even as a class as a whole, the teacher needs an efficient quiet signal. Rather than begging for student attention, the teacher may raise her hand, a signal for all students to do the same and focus on the teacher. Quickly the teacher obtains full, alert attention. Because we may want to call on one team or one individual on each team, we need efficient ways of selecting students, so we have developed mechanical and electronic "student selectors." Because we want teams to engage in a structure for a specified amount of time or for individuals in the teams each to have the same amount of time to share, we need timers.

As we give instructions to engage in a structure, we can create chaos or efficient engagement depending on our management tools. We need to "trigger" action. For example, we may want students to do a grouping structure, StandUp—HandUp—PairUp. In StandUp—HandUp—PairUp, students get up from their seats, put a hand up while looking for a partner, find a partner, give the partner a high five, and put their hands down. It is simply one of the many grouping structures. We begin instructions with a phrase to *trigger* the action: "When I say go, you will do a StandUp—HandUp—PairUp." We then continue giving the directions to students. If we do not trigger the action by saying "When I say go . . . ," students begin standing and moving as soon as we say we are going to do a StandUp—HandUp—PairUp. This creates chaos, so students do not hear the rest of the directions. We have developed dozens of cooperative learning management tools that make the implementation of Kagan Structures more efficient (Kagan, 2009).

Key 5. Teambuilding

Teammates are not likely to encourage and tutor each other if they do not know or like each other. Brain studies demonstrate maximum cognitive performance occurs in the context of inclusion and safety (Kagan,

2014). Thus, we want to put teambuilding in place. We identify five aims of teambuilding and provide structures for each (Kagan, 2009). The five aims of teambuilding are (1) getting acquainted; (2) forming a team identity; (3) structuring for mutual support; (4) valuing individual differences; and (5) developing synergy. We have developed structures and activities to implement each of these goals (Kagan et. al., 1997).

Teambuilding occurs any time teammates enjoy working with each other and bond with each other. Thus, teambuilding in the Structural Approach is an ongoing process rather than something that occurs only occasionally as a special activity. For example, the structure Team Statements involves each student first writing their own statement on a topic, say a definition of democracy. They then each read their statement to the team, receiving validation. They then attempt to come up with a Team Statement each student can endorse more fully than their own initial individual statement. In the process there is mutual support, valuing differences, and developing synergy. Thus, a great deal of teambuilding in the Structural Approach occurs while students work on academic tasks.

> Classbuilding and teambuilding removes the awkwardness of sitting next to someone you might have never been given the opportunity to know.
> —Leeanne Loewe, Student, Lehigh Senior High School

Key 6. Classbuilding

Classbuilding does for the class what teambuilding does for the team. The five aims of classbuilding are the same as the five aims of teambuilding but directed toward classmates rather than teammates. There are specific classbuilding structures (Kagan et al., 1995). For example, in Corners students each go to the corner of the room corresponding to their choice. For example, they might choose their favorite season: fall, winter, spring, or summer. Once in their corners, students do a RallyRobin with a partner naming reasons they most enjoy that season. Then they share out and students from other corners paraphrase with a partner. Thus, there is getting acquainted, mutual support (within corners), and valuing individual differences (across corners).

Like with teambuilding, a great deal of classbuilding occurs while students are engaged in academic tasks. For example, with corners the content might be which of four poems students like most, or which of four alternative hypotheses they favor to explain a finding. When teambuilding and classbuilding structures are used to explore academic content, students get to know each other better, experience mutual support, and come to appreciate and value individual differences.

Key 7. Social Skills

The structural approach to cooperative learning departs from other approaches to social skills. Rather than teaching lessons on social skills, social skills are embedded in the structures. For example, while students are doing a Timed Pair Share, they are practicing active listening. The teacher gives a gentle reminder for students to face their partner and give undivided attention. Because students are practicing the social skills repeatedly (each time a structure is used), the social skills are acquired. This acquisition model is very different from a learning model. When we give a lesson on a social skill, students learn about the social skill, but it does not become stably part of their repertoire. Lessons place the social skills in the semantic memory. Semantic memory stores facts and information but does not necessarily change behavior. A student may know it is good to be cooperative (semantic memory), but that does not make the student more cooperative. If we read a book on how to drive a car, we have information in semantic memory, but that does not mean we can drive a car. Structures, in contrast, place social skills in procedural memory. When we have practiced driving a car many times, we can drive the car without thinking about it; that skill is in procedural memory. By the repeated use of social skills embedded in the structures, social skills simply become procedural memories—the way students interact with each other without even thinking about it. In other words, *learning about* social skills is quite different from *acquiring* social skills.

If we give a lesson on active listening or taking turns, when we check back on students in a month, students are not spontaneously practicing active listening or turn-taking. If instead in that month we repeatedly have students use structures that engage active listening and turn-taking, at the end of the month students are more often spontaneously engaging in active listening and turn-taking. Structures socialize students.

The Structural Approach to social skills is validated by the data and teacher comments presented later in this chapter demonstrating how structures lead to decreases in disruptive behaviors and increases in positive social behaviors.

Are the Seven Keys Necessary?

Kagan Structures can be used as stand-alone instructional strategies without implementing the Seven Keys. A teacher can do a RallyRobin and create greater engagement, learning, and enjoyment of class and content even if the teacher has not done any teambuilding or classbuilding, has not carefully assigned students into heterogeneous teams of four, has not taught or modeled social skills, does not know efficient cooperative learning management techniques, has not learned about the function of structures, and has never heard about PIES.

Ignoring the Seven Keys to Success, however, leads to haphazard implementation and can lead to misuse and even failure of the structures. For example, a teacher who does not know there is an advantage in creating heterogeneous teams of four and seating the highest and lowest achiever in each group kitty corner in the team will not release the full power of cooperative learning. A teacher unacquainted with the functions of structures might use a Timed Pair Share for students to answer a high-consensus short-answer question. The students will be sitting with time running and nothing to say. Timed Pair Share only works for long-answer responses. To take another example, a teacher who tells students we are going to do a StandUp—HandUp—PairUp without prefacing their statement with "When I say go" is likely to have students getting up from their desks before the teacher has completed his instructions.

Seven Keys to Success in the Structural Approach		
Key to Success	**Example**	**Importance**
Basic Principles (PIES)	Timed Pair Share	Students support each other, all participate, participation is about equal or at least equitable, and participation is maximized
Structures	RoundRobin for brief answers; Timed RoundRobin for long answers	Using long-answer responses without adding a timed response leads to very unequal participation
Teams	Teams of four are better than teams of three or five or more	Teams of four break into two pairs, and pair work maximizes simultaneous participation. Teams of three or five leave one student out during pair work
Management	Before having students interact, we "Trigger" their responses. That is, we say "*When I say go*"	Triggering action allows better understanding of directions and more focused attention
Teambuilding	Celebrity Interview	Students feel accepted and appreciated in their teams. Teambuilding helps equalize status in teams
Classbuilding	Traveling RallyInterview (Students ask several questions of a classmate before traveling to interview another classmate)	By getting to know and interact with everyone in the class students feel safer, feel part of the class, and learn more
Social Skills	Paraphrase Passport	Students learn to listen more empathetically; students feel heard and accepted

Figure 5.4 Seven Keys to Success in the Structural Approach

The Seven Keys are contextual elements that unlock the full power of the Structural Approach to cooperative learning. When structures are surrounded by these contextual elements, implementation is much more efficient and more powerful.

A list of the Seven Keys to Success is presented in Figure 5.4, along with an example of how to put that key in place and why the key is important. Each of the Seven Keys is presented in depth in our basic book, *Kagan Cooperative Learning* (Kagan & Kagan, 2009).

Teachers A, B, C

At any one moment, there are three distinct ways we can structure a classroom. In our trainings, we nickname these three ways of structuring interaction as Teacher A, Teacher B, and Teacher C. Distinguishing these three ways of structuring the classroom is one of the most helpful tools teachers have to transition into doing true cooperative learning. Teacher A uses traditional instructional strategies; Teacher B uses group work; Teacher C uses Kagan Structures. In short, Teacher A does not have students work with others; Teacher B has students work with others but does not implement all the PIES principles; and Teacher C has students work together using structures that implement all four of the PIES principles.

Many teachers use Teacher B methods but think they are doing true cooperative learning. When they learn to distinguish Teachers A, B, and C, they catch themselves doing group work and move up to doing true cooperative learning.

Let's examine how Teachers A, B, and C elicit oral and written responses.

Teacher A: Traditional Instructional Strategies

For both oral and written responses, the traditional teacher has students work alone. That is, they either answer a teacher's question without talking with classmates or they work alone on a worksheet.

Oral Responses: TSQA

I have worked with teachers and students in over 40 countries. This has given me an opportunity to observe teaching in learning in many parts of the globe. Based on those observations I can say with confidence that the most common way teachers attempt to elicit oral responses from students is to use the traditional structure I call Teacher-Student Question-Answer (TSQA). TSQA has the following five steps:

1. The teacher asks the class a question.
2. The students who wish to answer raise their hands.

3. The teacher calls on one.
4. The chosen student answers.
5. The teacher responds to the answer.

If we do a PIES analysis, we discover TSQA lacks all of the essential elements of cooperative learning.

POSITIVE INTERDEPENDENCE

The students are answering on their own so the gains of one are not directly tied to the gains of another and the students do not need each other for task completion. In fact, often during TSQA students are competing with each other to be called upon and many are even glad when a classmate fails to answer correctly because it affords them an opportunity to be called upon and receive teacher approval and peer admiration.

INDIVIDUAL ACCOUNTABILITY

Students can choose not to raise their hands, and so performance is not required of all students.

EQUAL PARTICIPATION

More motivated and higher achieving students are called on more; some may not be called upon at all. We call most on those who least need the practice and least on those most in need of practice.

SIMULTANEOUS INTERACTION

TSQA involves no simultaneous interaction: The teacher calls on students one at a time. In a class of 30, 1/30th of the class or about 3% of the students are talking at any one time. Further, the teacher talks about twice as long as the students because the teacher talks twice for each time a student responds (asking the question and then responding to the answer). Using TSQA with a class of 30 students takes well over an hour to give each student one minute to verbalize their thinking. In contrast, using a structure like Timed Pair Share in which 50% of the class is verbalizing at any one moment takes a little over two minutes to give each student one minute to verbalize her/his thinking.

Beyond failing to pass the test of PIES, there are other major problems with structuring using TSQA. Three of the most important problems:

1. *Non-representative Sample.* By calling on volunteers, the teacher is calling on those students who are most likely to know the answer.

Thus, the teacher inadvertently creates an illusion that the class is learning the content better than they actually are.
2. *Increased Achievement Gap.* Without intending the teacher calls most on the high achievers (who quickly raise their hands, anxious to be called upon) and least on the low achievers (who are hesitant to raise their hands). Because the high achievers are more engaged, they learn at a higher rate, increasing the achievement gap.
3. *Structured Boredom.* Because the teacher calls on students one at a time, 29 of the 30 students in the class are not engaged at any one time, creating boredom. The overwhelming prevalence of boredom among students in traditional classrooms has been well documented repeatedly for many years (Goodlad, 1984). In a study of 11,848 students from 21 public schools in ten states, 86% stated they were bored in class and 63% gave as a reason: "teaching methods not interesting." (NAIS Research, 2015)

Written Responses: Solo Worksheet Work

To elicit written responses, the traditional teacher relies on a structure called Solo Worksheet Work. Usually Solo Worksheet Work follows direct instruction on a skill and is designed to have students solve problems to practice the target skill. To implement Solo Worksheet Work, the teacher gives each student a worksheet and instructs students to complete the worksheet alone. Worksheets are then turned in to the teacher who corrects and grades them and returns them to the students.

If we do a PIES analysis, we discover Solo Worksheet Work lacks essential elements of cooperative learning.

POSITIVE INTERDEPENDENCE

The students work alone, so there is no interdependence. The gains of one do not help another. In fact, when worksheets are graded and passed back, students often compare grades, hoping to do better than others. Solo Worksheet Work involves a latent competition.

INDIVIDUAL ACCOUNTABILITY

There is individual accountability as each student is individually accountable for his/her worksheet performance.

EQUAL PARTICIPATION

There is equal participation as all students complete their own worksheet.

SIMULTANEOUS INTERACTION

Students are not interacting, but they are all performing at the same time.

Beyond failing to pass the test of PIES, there are other major problems with structuring using Solo Worksheet Work. Three of the most important problems:

1. *Delayed Feedback*. Students do not receive corrective feedback until after the teacher has had time to correct and pass back the papers. By then, many students have forgotten doing the problems and simply scan their paper to look for their grade. This traditional approach to correcting mistakes leads to no new learning.
2. *Emphasis on Grades, Not Learning*. If you ask students, why they do their worksheets most will say "to pass the course" or "to get a good grade." Learning becomes the means, not the end. We learn in order to get a good grade. As we will see, in cooperative learning the emphasis is placed on learning, not grades.
3. *Competitive Social Comparison*. When students receive their graded papers, they compare. Who did better than whom? This reinforces a competitive social orientation with emphasis on winning, not learning.

Teacher B: Group Work

For both oral and written responses Teacher B relies on unstructured group work. Students work together, but they structure their own interaction. Although Teacher B may want equal participation and individual accountability, the teacher has not structured for those outcomes, and so it may or may not occur. I am fond of saying Group Work is wishful thinking.

Oral Responses: Turn-N-Talk, Group Discussion

To elicit oral responses Teacher B has students talk with each other but does not structure the interaction. The most common Teacher B structure to elicit oral responses in pairs is Turn-N-Talk. The teacher poses a question or topic and then merely says, "Turn to your partner and talk it over." To elicit oral responses in larger groups the teacher uses Group Discussion, simply directing students to talk over the topic in their group.

POSITIVE INTERDEPENDENCE

Students benefit from hearing the ideas of others in their group, but they are not interdependent. That is, one student may choose not to verbalize her/his ideas, so task completion does not depend on participation of everyone.

INDIVIDUAL ACCOUNTABILITY

A student may choose not to speak and so is not held accountable.

EQUAL PARTICIPATION

Imagine a very verbal student paired with a shy student. Participation is likely to be quite unequal. When a high achiever is paired with a low achiever, it is the high achiever who does most or all the talking. Without intending, Teacher B calls most on those who least need the practice and least on those who most need the practice.

SIMULTANEOUS INTERACTION

Turn-N-Talk is very strong in simultaneous interaction. During Turn-N-Talk 50% of the class is talking at any one moment; during Group Discussion 25% of the class is talking at any one moment.

Written Responses: Group Problem-Solving

Teacher B gives a worksheet or problem to students in teams and instructs them to "solve it as a group." Teacher B may encourage students to work together and to listen to everyone's ideas but does not use structures that ensure individual accountability or equal participation.

POSITIVE INTERDEPENDENCE

Students gain from the work of others, but task completion is not dependent on participation by all. In fact, often in unstructured group work, a few students do most or even all the work while others take a free ride.

INDIVIDUAL ACCOUNTABILITY

Students are not held individually accountable. Some can sit back and let others do most or even all the work.

EQUAL PARTICIPATION

Participation is usually quite unequal, especially when students differ in motivation and/or ability. Group work often leads to "hogs" and "logs."

SIMULTANEOUS INTERACTION

Group Work is strong in simultaneous interaction: If it is a pair project, 50% of the class is working at any time; if it is a group project, at least 25% of the class is working at any one moment.

It is important to note that, without intending, both Teacher A and Teacher B enhance the achievement gap. Why? Without intending they are structuring, so the high achievers are responding most. Teacher A calls most on the students who least need the practice and calls least on those students who most need the practice! Teacher B allows the high achievers in each pair or group to do most or even all the talking or most or even all of the work on the group project.

Teacher C: Cooperative Learning

Oral Responses: RallyRobin, Timed Pair Share

To elicit oral responses Teacher C has students talk with each other but uses carefully designed structures to ensure all four PIES principles are in place. To ensure equal participation and individual accountability, Teacher C usually structures using time or turns. As we have seen in RallyRobin, each student has the same number of turns; in Timed Pair Share, each student has the same amount of time to share. In groups of four for brief responses, Teacher C might do a RoundRobin. For longer responses, Teacher C might use a Timed RoundRobin in which each student is allotted the same amount of time.

POSITIVE INTERDEPENDENCE

Students gain from the ideas of their partner or teammates, and the structure cannot be completed unless each contributes.

INDIVIDUAL ACCOUNTABILITY

Students are each accountable: Their teammates see or hear their contributions.

EQUAL PARTICIPATION

Time (for long responses) or turns (for brief responses) ensure equal participation.

SIMULTANEOUS INTERACTION

Pair work maximizes active engagement: 50% of the class are talking at once; with oral responses in teams of four, 25% of the class are talking at any one time. Compare these high rates of simultaneity with TSQA, in which only 3% are talking at once.

Written Responses: Sage-N-Scribe, Continuous Simultaneous RoundTable

There are many true cooperative learning structures that have students respond in writing. Some are coupled with oral responses; others are a form of sustained silent writing.

SAGE-N-SCRIBE

For worksheet practice, Teacher C may use Sage-N-Scribe. In Sage-N-Scribe, partners take turns solving problems. The Sage verbalizes her/his thinking, while the Scribe records. Scribes coach if necessary and praise their Sage when the problem is complete. Students switch roles for each new problem. Sage-N-Scribe can be used for content other than worksheets such as practicing correct athletic moves, adding the next step to a circuit board, or, for little ones, practicing tying one's shoes.

CONTINUOUS SIMULTANEOUS ROUNDTABLE

In Continuous Simultaneous RoundTable, students each begin writing on their own piece of paper. At a signal by the teacher or timer, or when each has finished and put a thumb up, all students pass their paper to their teammate on their left. All students then add their response to the paper they received, and the process continues without students talking. The papers may go around the group a number of times. The content can be team stories, drawings, or solving a problem on one of the four related worksheets. Sometimes, Continuous Simultaneous RoundTable is used to create four lists. For example, each paper has the name of a character from a book or story, or the name of a person from history. Each time the paper is passed, students add one adjective to describe the character. Similarly, each paper might have the name of a planet in the solar system, and students add facts they know about each planet.

POSITIVE INTERDEPENDENCE

In Sage-N-Scribe, the skill of the Sage is passed along to the Scribe and coaching by the Scribe improves the performance and learning of the Sage. Task completion depends on both students performing their roles. Similarly, in Continuous Simultaneous RoundTable all contribute and students view and learn from the contributions of their teammates.

INDIVIDUAL ACCOUNTABILITY

Each must perform in front of their partner (Sage-N-Scribe) or teammates (Continuous Simultaneous RoundTable).

EQUAL PARTICIPATION

Turns equalize participation in both structures.

SIMULTANEOUS INTERACTION

One hundred percent of the students are performing at once in Sage-N-Scribe (one describing what to write; the other writing). Similarly, 100% of the students are performing at any one time in Continuous Simultaneous Round-Table because at any moment each is writing on the paper before them.

By examining Teachers A, B, and C, we see that classrooms can be structured differently. By performing a PIES analysis on the structures teachers use, we find only Teacher C, who uses true cooperative learning structures, implements the PIES principles. The underlying premise of the Structural Approach is that cooperative learning is most effective for engaging all students and boosting student learning when PIES are in place. The use of structures facilitates the consistent implementation of the powerful PIES principles.

Teacher Training in the Structural Approach

Because the Structural Approach to cooperative learning is structure-based rather than lesson-based, teacher training in the Structural Approach is quite different from other approaches to cooperative learning (Kagan, 1998, 2001c). Teachers experience and practice the steps of structures and then are coached not on their cooperative learning lessons but rather on individual structures. This unique coaching model, called Kagan Coaching (Kagan, 2006c), developed by Laurie Kagan, eliminates the traditional pre- and post-coaching conference sessions; it is laser focused on a single structure in the moment of teaching.

Kagan Trainers

Kagan trainers undergo an extraordinarily rigorous preparation to become certified. Almost all trainers begin by using Kagan Structures as a full-time teacher for years. There are two programs for becoming a certified Kagan Trainer: the School Trainer Program and the Kagan Associate Trainer Program. Laurie Kagan developed both programs, along with their associated lesson plans and PowerPoint slides.

Kagan School Trainer Program

The first step in becoming a certified Kagan School Trainer is to attend the Kagan five-day cooperative learning training. Following the basic training, prospective trainers must use the training full-time in their classroom for a minimum of one year, practicing the structures. They are also encouraged to practice the structures in classrooms of different grade levels and with different content. Following their year of practice, prospective trainers apply for the School Trainer Program. Part of the application requires applicants to submit a video of themselves using structures. Not all applicants who submit a video are accepted. If accepted, they enter the School Trainer Program, which, when completed, certifies them to train Kagan Structures, but in their own school only.

Kagan Associate Trainer Program

Those who wish to become a certified Kagan Associate Trainer take steps in addition to those taken by the school trainers. They submit a two-part video showing themselves using Kagan Structures with students and training teachers in the steps of a Kagan Structure. If accepted, the prospective trainer attends a personalized mock training, with a certified Kagan Trainer. The next step is an intensive train the trainer workshop that has been affectionately called "Kagan Boot Camp." At Boot Camp, prospective trainers learn how to teach Kagan Cooperative Learning to educators. If the trainer passes the rigorous Boot Camp, they provide their first training under supervision of a senior Kagan Certified Trainer. If that goes well, they then become certified to conduct Kagan trainings.

For both the School Trainers and the Associate Trainers there are updates at which trainers learn and practice the latest improvements in the Kagan Cooperative Learning workshop. Different trainers are certified to offer different workshops. Kagan Professional Development offers 32 distinct workshops; the workshops are offered in one-day to five-day formats.

One reason Kagan training of trainers is so rigorous and scripted is that we conduct a great number of workshops and a school or district may choose to have a multi-day workshop on any topic with days between sessions. A school may have a different trainer on day 1 than on day 2, so it is extremely important that day 2 trainers know exactly what was trained on day 1. Another reason Kagan training is so tightly scripted is that there is a very tight workshop alignment. That is, in each of the 32 Kagan workshops, participants learn structures not taught in other workshops, so a participant can take workshop after workshop, being assured they will learn not just new content but also new structures. A few of the many workshops offered by Kagan are Kagan Cooperative Learning,

Brain-Friendly Teaching, Emotion-Friendly Teaching, and Win-Win Discipline. Kagan offers workshops applying the structural approach to specific areas of the curriculum (e.g., high school math, STEM, elementary social studies), to students with specific needs (e.g., high-risk students, disruptive students), and to specific educational approaches (e.g., multiple intelligences, Brain-Friendly Teaching).

Kagan Professional Development now has 17 full-time staff trainers and 51 part-time Associate Trainers in the United States. In addition, there are 87 International Certified Trainers who work in over 14 countries. The Kagan Cooperative Learning workshops and resources have been translated into a dozen different languages.

Workshops

The primary tools for teacher training in the Structural Approach are workshops for teachers, instructional coaches, and administrators. Kagan offers one-day, two-day, five-day workshops in a variety of formats and venues. In addition to single school and district-wide workshops, Kagan offers US tours as well as summer and winter academies. Kagan offers approximately 50 US tours a year. The workshops cover a wide range of content-specific and grade-level specific topics, always with a focus on how to use Kagan Structures to make curriculum more engaging. Over the past eight years in the United States, Kagan has provided an average of 1,765 training days a year, reaching an average of 58,628 teachers who teach over five million students per year. In addition, Kagan Professional Development has provided workshops in 47 countries.

Coaching

Coaching in the Structural Approach is conducted using a distinct model of coaching called Kagan Coaching developed by Laurie Kagan. Teachers are coached in real-time during brief structure-based sessions. Just as the football coach does not wait until the game is over to give his players feedback, Kagan Coaches give teachers feedback as they teach, allowing immediate practice of improved teaching. Because coaching sessions focus on only one structure, Kagan Coaches can see an average of 15 teachers a day. This efficiency has allowed Kagan Professional Development to coach more than 4,000 teachers a year for the last nine years in the United States. Kagan Coaching is used also in the countries in which Kagan has certified Kagan trainers. The model allows site-empowerment because principals and instructional leaders accompany the coach and debrief after each coaching session, learning the essential elements of Kagan Structures and Kagan Coaching.

An article describing how Kagan Coaching differs from traditional coaching includes Figure 5.5 (Kagan, 2006c):

Traditional vs. Kagan Coaching™

	Traditional	Kagan Coaching™
Unit of observation	Broad: Whole lesson	Focused: One structure
Time expended	Hours: Pre-observation; observation; post-observation	15-minute observation of one structure
Documentation	Complicated	Simple
Relevance of feedback	Potentially irrelevant	Relevant
Immediacy of feedback	Delayed	Immediate
Immediacy of correction	Delayed	Immediate
Implementation	Questionable	Assured
Site empowerment	None	Multi-level

Figure 5.5 Traditional versus Kagan Coaching™

Teacher Resources

Because Kagan Structures are used at all grades in all academic content, there is a very wide range of teacher resources available.

Books

To support teachers in implementation of Kagan Structures, Kagan Publishing offers general theory and method books, grade-level and content-specific books, as well as structure-specific books. To support administrators, Kagan offers Co-op Meetings, a very comprehensive binder on how to set up and manage faculty meetings using Kagan Structures. Kagan Publishing offers 131 books, 83 of which have been translated into different languages.

Cooperative Learning Support Resources

Kagan Publishing also offers a range of manipulatives and electronic resources to support cooperative learning. For example, ManageMats facilitate managing student teams by automatically assigning student numbers to teammates and student letters to shoulder and face partners. Software resources include student selectors (mechanical and electronic devices to efficiently choose who goes first in the team or pair), timers, and software for forming and reforming teams. Software, developed by Miguel Kagan, is available also to lead students through the steps of various structures in a game-like fashion. With Kagan Structure software, the teacher merely clicks to advance the class to each new step of a structure. Additional cooperative learning support resources include Learning Cubes, Learning Chips, dice, spinners, posters, flip charts, and learning kits.

What Does the Research Say?

Research indicates implementation of Kagan Structures results in a range of positive outcomes, including increased academic achievement, reduced high-low achievement gaps, reduced race-based achievement gaps, improved outcomes for students with disabilities, increased student satisfaction, increased time on task, decreased disruptive behaviors, increased prosocial behaviors, improved race relations, and decreased probability of school violence. Research supporting those outcomes is sampled in the following sections.

Increased Academic Achievement

Many schools report dramatic improvements in academic achievement following implementation of Kagan Structures. There are far too many of these studies to overview here.

There are far too many of these studies to overview here. Here, we focus on just a few illustrative studies.

An independent research team at the State University of New York (SUNY) published a series of research studies looking at, among other things, the academic achievement of students when traditional versus Kagan Structures were implemented (Haydon, Maheady, & Hunter, 2010; Maheady, Michielli-Pendl, Mallette, & Harper, 2002; Maheady, Michielli-Pendl, Harper, & Mallette, 2006; Maheady, Mallete, Harper, & Sacca, 1991; McMillen et al., 2016).

Results indicated very strong improvements in achievement across all studies. The studies include students of different grade levels and in different academic content areas. A summary of effect sizes in the studies revealed a remarkable 0.92 effect size that translates into a 32-percentile gain. This is an effect size substantially larger than the effect size of 0.59 in a meta-analysis of a range of cooperative learning studies (Hattie, 2009). It is also somewhat larger than the effect size of 0.86 of cooperative learning studies meeting the criteria of being at the highest quality (Johnson & Johnson, 1989). See Figure 5.6: Academic achievement gains with Kagan Structures.

High School Chemistry

Implementing just one structure, Numbered Heads Together, in substitution for TSQA produced dramatic gains for struggling learners in high school chemistry. The SUNY team used an ABAB design within a single chemistry

Academic Achievement Gains with Kagan Structures		
Study	Effect Size	Percentile Gain
1. Numbered Heads vs. TSQA (Maheady et al., 2006)	0.95	33.0
2. Numbered Heads + Incentive vs. TSQA (Maheady et al., 2006)	0.98	33.5
3. Numbered Heads vs. TSQA (Maheady et al., 1991)	0.78	28.2
4. Numbered Heads + Incentive vs. TSQA (Maheady et al., 2006)	0.96	33.2
5. Show Me vs. TSQA (Maheady et al., 2002)	0.90	31.5
6. Numbered Heads vs. TSQA (Maheady et al. 2002)	0.95	33.0
7. Numbered Heads vs. TSQA (Haydon et al, 2010)	0.89	31.2
Average	0.92	31.9

Figure 5.6 Academic achievement gains with Kagan Structures

class to determine the impact of switching between TSQA to Numbered Heads Together (McMillen et al., 2016). Students in the class were performing very poorly: Their baseline using traditional methods to review their chemistry content was a below passing average of 53% on weekly quizzes. When the teacher switched to Numbered Heads Together to review the content, achievement jumped to an average of 75%. When the teacher returned to traditional TSQA, achievement decreased to 59%. Finally, when once again the teacher used the Kagan Structure, achievement accelerated to 72%.

High School Algebra

At Lehigh Senior High School teachers were frustrated at the performance of their students in algebra. The algebra teachers formed a professional learning community and decided to increase engagement. They took the five-day Kagan Cooperative Learning workshop and implemented the structures in Algebra classes.

> Kagan provided the tools we needed—classbuilding and teambuilding activities to change the culture of the classroom to one that was trusting, a culture where students were comfortable interacting. Kagan Structures gave them the tools to make learning accountable and interactive. Algebra classrooms transformed from ones that reluctant math students dreaded to ones that they looked forward to attending. Students became learners and teachers among their peers. They were able to learn and grow from their interactions with each other. By the end of the year, we improved our algebra scores by 17%. This brought us from the bottom of

our district performance to the top of the list. We have consistently remained at the top since, closing the achievement gap among our at-risk students.

(Corey, 2017)

School-wide Achievement

Dramatic increases in achievement following the implementation of Kagan Structures have been documented school-wide. In 2004, prior to the adoption of Kagan Structures at Mills Hill School in the United Kingdom only 30% of the Mills Hill learners scored above national averages in combined English and mathematics. Following the adoption of Kagan Structures school-wide, over 70% of the Mills Hill students scored above national averages (Lee, 2009).

> During the period 2004 to 2008, Mills Hill School implemented the National Literacy and Numeracy lessons alongside the majority of UK primary schools. This included the curriculum entitlement and an exploration of teaching and learning approaches. It could be hypothesized that the national initiative could have been the lever for the changes in learner attainment. However, if this was true, we would expect other schools implementing the initiative to experience similar gains. This was clearly not the case:
>
> The national strategies have had an impact for learners but Kagan Structures for Engagement has been the significant lever of change for Mills Hill. In 2004, our school was in the top 30% of school nationally. Our rate of improvement has outpaced other schools—we are now in the top 6% of schools. I attribute this significant and rapid rate of progress to the high impact Kagan has had for our learners.
> —Darran Lee, Headteacher Mills Hill

Achievement Gains Across Content and Grade Levels

Research studies document significant achievement gains resulting from the implementation of Kagan Structures at almost every grade level, in many content areas, and with a range of populations. For example, gains have been documented for students with disabilities (Haydon et al., 2010), adults (Major & Robinette, 2004), and college students (Murie, 2004). The structures result in significant gains across grade levels and academic content. For example, research studies show significant gains in 4th grade writing (Kennedy, 2000); 5th grade math (Cline, 2007); 6th grade social studies (Dotson (2001); 6th grade science (Maheady et al. (2002); 9th grade science (McMillen et al., 2016); high school chemistry (Mele, 2001); high school journalism (Howard, 2006); and high school algebra (Van Wetering, 2009). Further, Kagan Structures have produced substantial multi-year gains school-wide (Lee, 2009; Winters, 2013; McColgan, 2013).

Reduced Achievement Gaps

High-Low Achievement Gap Reduced

The SUNY studies reveal Kagan Structures reduce the achievement gap between high- and low-achieving students. For example, in one study when Traditional Q&A was used, far more students had failing grades than when Numbered Heads Together was implemented:

> It is significant that no student had a failing average under the Numbered Heads Together condition, and six pupils had maintained averages above 90%. In contrast, when TSQA was used, six students had failing averages and only one child maintained an average exceeding 90%.
>
> (Maheady et al., 1991)

Race Achievement Gap Reduced

Perhaps the study that most reveals how Kagan Structures reduce the achievement gap was conducted in a school district in Florida (Kagan, 2007). The district was performing lower than state averages on the state-mandated tests of basic achievement: the Florida Comprehensive Assessment Test (FCAT). This lower-than-state-average achievement was predictable because the district was located in a lower-income area compared to state averages, and income level of parents is a strong predictor of achievement test performance.

When the district opened a new school in an area of the district that had lower income than district averages, they knew the state-mandated achievement scores would be lower than district averages unless something was done to boost achievement. They brought in Laurie Kagan to teach all of the teachers a range of Kagan Structures and to coach the teachers using Kagan Coaching. State-mandated testing at the end of the year revealed that compared to district averages, the Kagan School posted dramatic increases in both achievement and dramatic reductions in achievement gap for both math and reading. District percent proficient in math was 60% and reading 56%. In contrast, the Kagan School posted substantially higher in both math at 81% and reading at 79%. With regard to the black–white achievement gap the district had black students scoring 47% lower than white students in math and 43% lower in reading. In contrast, the Kagan School showed dramatically reduced race achievement gaps: math, 25%; reading, 27%. In sum, after only one year, the school located in a poorer area of the district, compared to district averages, scored dramatic increases in achievement and very substantial decreases in race-achievement gaps.

Progressive Reduction of Achievement Gap

As teachers increasingly integrate Kagan Structures into their everyday lessons, engagement and achievement increase, decreasing the achievement gap. This was illustrated dramatically in the classroom of Dana Hensley, a fifth-grade teacher at Bossier Elementary School (Hensley, 2016). At first Dana was using Kagan Structures as occasional activities:

> It was not on a lesson-by-lesson basis; it was more of a drop everything and let's do a Kagan Structure approach. It was not until I continued to notice more and more students being unsuccessful in science that I really stepped up my understanding of Kagan and began implementing structures into every lesson I taught in my science class. It was then that I began working smarter and not harder!

Quarter by quarter Dana began integrating more structures into her daily science lessons. As she did, the achievement gap in her class decreased.

Dana's class went from 38% of the class failing at outset, to 17% in the next quarter, to 7% in the following quarter, to finally not a single student failing. Perhaps equally important was the shift in attitudes among students:

> The more I added new structures, the more excited my students became about being in science class, and I heard more and more students saying, "Man it is already time to go; this class goes by so fast. Mrs. Hensley, what are we going to be doing tomorrow? Can we do this Kagan again?" It was nice for me to hear them so interested in learning.

Improved Outcomes for Students With Disabilities

Prior research has demonstrated that students with disabilities are better accepted and maintain stronger friendships with non-disabled students when mainstreamed into classrooms using cooperative learning compared to classrooms using traditional methods (Armstrong, Johnson, & Balow, 1981; Ballard et. al., 1977; Madden & Slavin, 1983). Research reveals that using a Kagan method dramatically increased achievement among students with disabilities (Haydon et al., 2010). The study compared language arts achievement of seventh-grade students with disabilities using traditional and Kagan instructional strategies. Results: In the traditional class students averaged 42%; in the Kagan class students averaged 62%.

Increased Student Satisfaction

Across the SUNY studies, measures of student satisfaction indicated a strong preference for the Kagan Structures. In the high school chemistry study just described, over 80% of the students agreed that Kagan Structures:

- Better helped them learn
- Was fair for all
- Helped them get along better with others
- Should be used in other classes, and
- Other students thought them smarter!

Researchers adapted the Kagan Structure Spend-A-Buck to assess student satisfaction. Students were given play money and were asked to spend it on which instructional strategy they preferred, TSQA versus the Kagan Structure Numbered Heads Together. Results indicated very strong preference for the Kagan Structure: Students spent an average of 79 cents on TSQA and an average of $18.71 on the Kagan Structure (Maheady et al., 2006). That's a ratio of 23.7 to 1 in favor of the Kagan Structure!

To test the attitude of students toward using Kagan Structures an elementary teacher, Danielle Gradone, administered a questionnaire to her students every two weeks for an eight-week study (Gradone, 2015). Mrs. Gradone used a wide range of Kagan Structures and included structures in every lesson. Following the eight weeks, students responded very favorably toward Kagan Structures on a questionnaire that included questions like "Structures help me communicate with other" and "Structures help me to participate more in class." Eighty-nine percent of responses were favorable (strongly agree and agree) compared to 11% unfavorable (disagree and strongly disagree).

Increased Time on Task

Several of the SUNY studies of Kagan Structures measured time on task of students using Kagan Structures versus Traditional Q&A. In all cases, time on task was significantly greater when Kagan Structures were used. More time on task was consistent across grade levels and subject content areas including third-grade social studies (Mahedy et al., 1991), sixth-grade science (Mahedy et al., 2006), and seventh-grade language arts among students with disabilities (Haydon et al., 2010). The greatest improvement occurred among students with disabilities: Using Traditional

Q&A, students were on task 63% of the time; using the Kagan Structure Numbered Heads Together the students were on task 97% of the time!

Decreased Disruptive Behaviors

As classroom teachers and whole schools implement Kagan Structures, they experience a remarkable decrease in disruptive behavior and discipline referrals. Years ago, when I first began teaching teachers how to use Kagan Structures, I frequently got a question from administrators and responded as follows:

> **Administrator:** *What is the new discipline program you are implementing?*
> **My response:** *No. I don't train teachers in discipline. I am simply teaching teachers cooperative learning structures.*
> **Administrator:** *You must be training teachers in some new discipline program. Referrals for discipline have declined dramatically.*

At that time, I made note of these conversations, but I filed it away mentally as I was focused on developing and training cooperative learning structures. Over the years, individual teachers have documented decreases in disruptive behavior in their own classes following the implementation of Kagan Structures. Further, principals and others have documented decreases in school-wide discipline problems when Kagan Structures are put in place.

Disruptive behaviors decrease dramatically when Kagan Structures are introduced. In some schools the number of discipline referrals is cut in half or more within a year of implementing Kagan Structures school-wide.

Drop in Elementary School Discipline Referrals

The dramatic impact of Kagan Structures in reducing discipline referrals is illustrated by what happened at Mills Hill Primary School in the United Kingdom (Lee, 2009). When Kagan Structures were introduced, the average number of discipline referrals per class each term was cut about in half. For several years prior to the institution of Kagan Structures, beginning in 2002, the school had recorded the number of discipline referrals to the headmaster (equivalent to the principal in US schools). The number of referrals prior to the introduction of Kagan Structures hovered between 25 and 30 per class each term. Headmaster Darran Lee indicated this was "a significant problem." When Kagan Structures were introduced, the number of referrals dropped to about half pre-Kagan levels and maintained that much lower average for years. Darran Lee stated that within months Kagan Structures were having "a significant impact in reducing the number of behavior incidents across school."

Drop in High School Discipline Referrals

Lehigh Senior High documented similar dramatic decreases in disruptive behavior following the implementation of Kagan Structures (Corey, 2017). At Lehigh, average student discipline referrals per class decreased 58% in one year following the implementation of Kagan Structures.

Progressive Decline of Discipline Problems

As Kagan Structures become part of the culture of the school, declines in disruptive behavior are progressive year after year. At Sage Elementary School, following the institution of Kagan Structures in the 2009–2010 school year, discipline referrals dropped each year (Kramer, 2014). Over a four-year period following implementing Kagan Structures, discipline referrals per 100 students dropped in half: Across the four years, discipline referrals decreased as follows: Year 1: 60.27; Year 2: 51.34; Year 3: 37.50; and Year 4: 27.45.

Why Do Structures Decrease Disruptive Behavior?

Decline in disruptive behaviors following the implementation of Kagan Cooperative Learning Structures can be attributed to many factors, including:

1. Engaged students are less disruptive.
2. Students acquiring social skills and improved social reactions are less disruptive.
3. The structures are a management system that keeps students focused.
4. Students enjoy class and content more and so are less inclined to disrupt class.

Increased Prosocial Behaviors

Inverse Relation: Disruptive versus Prosocial Behaviors

There is an inverse relationship between disruptive behaviors and positive behaviors. As students learn positive social skills and establish positive social relations, disruptive behaviors decline. This inverse relationship was plotted at Madison Camelview Elementary School from 2011 to 2014.

Madison Camelview Elementary School is a Title I school with 84% free and reduced lunch, a 28% ELL population, and a 10% special education population. It is also a diverse campus with 3% Asian, 10% black, 56% Hispanic, 11% Native American, and 20% white. Under the direction of principal Michael Winters, Madison Camelview implemented Kagan Structures school-wide (Winters, 2015):

> The implementation of Kagan had a dramatically positive impact on student behavior. With full Kagan implementation, negative behaviors decreased while positive referrals skyrocketed. Students received discipline referrals for typical behaviors disrupting the educational environment and/or process. Students earned positive referrals for positive behaviors. Here are some behaviors for which students typically earned a positive referral:
>
> - Finding money on campus and turning it in
> - Helping a friend who dropped his/her books
> - Picking up trash without being asked
> - Helping to clean the cafeteria without being asked
> - Holding a door for a teacher whose hands were full
> - Being an excellent coach to a partner or team

Within three years, positive referrals more than tripled (from 75 to 280), and discipline referrals were reduced to a fourth of what they were (from 200 to 48).

Disruptions Down, Social Skills Up

Stacey Magnesio conducted a study of the impact of Kagan Structures on disruptive and positive behaviors in her fourth-grade class (Magnesio & Davis, 2010). She had been having serious problems with disruptive behavior and decided to institute three Kagan Structures: RoundRobin, RallyCoach, and Quiz-Quiz-Trade. She plotted the number of disruptive behaviors per student each week using the ABCD Tally Chart (Kagan, Kyle, & Scott, 2004). The ABCD Tally Chart records aggression, breaking the rules, confrontations, and disengagement for each student. Frequency of disruptive behaviors declined week after week when Stacey introduced Kagan Structures. Frequency of disruptive behaviors decreased each week: Week 1: 83; Week 2: 63; Week 3: 51; Week 4: 32; Week 5: 19; Week 6: 7.

To determine if this decline in disruptive behavior was associated with an increase in positive behaviors, Stacey used five-minute time sample observations of selected students, recording incidents of listening attentively, praising others, respecting differences, staying on task, and taking turns. The frequency of positive behaviors in fact increased dramatically as incidents of disruptive behaviors declined. Week 1 positive behaviors averaged about three per student. By Week 3 they averaged around 7 per student. By Week 6 students averaged 12 positive behaviors.

Mrs. Magnesio noted the decline in the need to deal with disruptive behavior freed up time to focus on academics:

> This made a powerful impact on my classroom. Not only were the students getting better at working together as the weeks went by, I was able to spend more time teaching and less time lecturing my students about being team players and working together.

Progressive Improvement of Positive Behaviors

Positive behaviors become the norm as Kagan Structures are implemented school-wide. This was revealed at Cheatham Elementary School (Winters, 2013). The school plotted a number of positive referrals for unrequested positive behaviors from 2007 to 2011 using the same method described in the Camelview study.

Following the implementation of Kagan Structures school-wide, positive referrals increased each year and had skyrocketed from only 46 in the 2007–2008 school year to 475 three years later in 2010–2011—more than ten times increase!

The positive behavior of students was noticeable to outside visitors:

> We would also hear a great deal of praise from outside visitors. Literally every outside visitor, including district office staff, would comment on how polite and well-mannered our students were. At first this surprised me because dealing with the behavior issues on a day-to-day basis I didn't always see that, but they did. The positive behavior became the expectation and the norm.
> (Winters, 2013)

Improved Race Relations

As a professor in the School of Education at the University of California, Riverside, I developed the Riverside Cooperative Learning Project, a multi-year project to train student teachers in cooperative learning methods and to assess the impact of cooperative learning. One question we addressed was the impact of cooperative learning on race relations (Kagan, Zahn, Widaman, Schwarzwald, & Tyrell, 1985; Kagan, 2006b).

To test the impact of cooperative learning structures on race relations, 35 student teachers were randomly assigned to teach using either cooperative learning structures or traditional instructional strategies for six weeks. The student teachers taught approximately 900 students. The students were 66% white, 20% Mexican American, and 13% black, proportionally divided in the traditional and cooperative learning classes.

To assess the impact of cooperative learning on race relations among the students, we administered a measure of intimacy among students, the Interpersonal Relations Assessment Technique (IRAT). The IRAT has been validated on thousands of students; it is a unidimensional scale with high coefficients of reproducibility and scalability (Schwarzwald, & Cohen, 1982). It allows each student to indicate his or her willingness to engage in different intimacy behaviors with each of their classmates by writing a 1 or 0 under each intimacy item for each classmate. The behaviors vary in intensity of intimacy from sitting next to a student to inviting him or her home or telling secrets with that student. Five intimacy items were used. The items had predetermined Gutman properties chosen from 100 intimacy items, so agreement with a high-level intimacy item indicated agreement with all the less intimate items below it. For example, surprisingly, the Gutman analysis revealed that telling secrets with a classmate is a more intimate item than inviting the classmate home. That is, students willing to tell secrets with a classmate were also willing to invite that classmate home, but students willing to invite a classmate home might or might not be willing to tell secrets with that classmate. The items did not appear in intimacy order in the IRAT. In order of intimacy, the items were as follows:

- Sit next to him or her in class
- Loan him or her a pencil or book in class
- Invite him or her to your home
- Be his or her best friend
- Tell secrets to him or her

The IRAT was administered to all students in the traditional and cooperative learning classes. Results demonstrated that in only six weeks, race-relations were radically improved when cooperative learning structures were implemented. In classrooms taught with traditional instructional strategies, students increasingly self-segregated along race lines; in classrooms taught with cooperative learning methods, this self-segregation did not occur: friendship choices remained integrated. In the following sections, we present and discuss the results indicating that compared to traditional instructional strategies, cooperative learning reduces segregation.

Traditional Instruction Produced Racial Self-Segregation

Using traditional instructional strategies, with age, students progressively self-segregated. That is, students at grades 2–4 were color-blind with regard to friendship choices. They chose classmates of their own race only 5% more often than classmates of other races, a nonsignificant difference. In contrast, by grades 5–6, students chose friendships in part based on the race of the other; they chose their own-race classmates 26% more often than classmates of other races. Further, in the traditional classrooms students chose the highest levels of intimacy almost exclusively among students of their own race.

Cooperative Learning Instruction Produced Integration

In the classrooms using cooperative learning the picture was quite different. Race was not a significant predictor of friendship choices at both the younger and the older grades. That students choose their friendships without significant regard to race of the other indicates cooperative learning led to far greater integration of students along race lines.

The difference in self-segregation among students in the cooperative versus traditional classrooms was highly significant statistically, $p < 0.0001$. When traditional instruction was used, with increasing age students increasingly choose those of the same race as friends. In contrast, when cooperative learning was implemented, students didn't use race as a basis for friendship choices; they chose in a more integrated way.

The observed difference between how students oriented to those of other races in cooperative versus traditional classrooms is best attributed to the difference in the instructional strategies used in those classrooms. There were no special race relations or anti-racism programs taught in the cooperative learning condition. The near eradication of racial discrimination in friendship choices was the result of students working cooperatively in mixed-race teams. As a result of working together cooperatively in mixed-race teams, cooperative learning virtually eliminated race-based friendship choices.

> Take a moment and imagine how society would be different if all students throughout their time in school spent a substantial amount of class time learning in racially integrated teams which included occasional teambuilding activities.

This radical transformation of race relations in just six weeks by novice teachers is quite remarkable but understandable if we contrast social relations in traditional versus cooperative learning classrooms. In traditional classrooms students do not work together. Many do not even know the names of their classmates. They talk only with the teacher. They simply do not get to know each other. If you then ask students who they would like to sit next to or invite home, they have only the race of their fellow classmates upon which to decide. In contrast, in the cooperative learning classroom, which includes integrated student teams, teambuilding, and cooperative projects and learning tasks, students come to know each other as individuals, not merely as members of a racial group. Through teambuilding activities students get to know each other and appreciate individual differences. Cooperative projects and cooperative learning include mutual support activities, tutoring, coaching, praising, and celebrating. Students experience themselves as on the same side, working together to reach common goals. Through this process students get to know the humor, intellect, feelings, thoughts, and perspectives of their classmates. When then asked who they want to sit next to or invite home, they can decide based on knowing their classmates as individuals, not just as members of a racial group. In essence, cooperative learning makes possible the vision of Martin Luther King Jr., who dreamed of a time when students would relate to each other by the quality of their character, not the color of their skin. The ability of cooperative learning to eliminate self-segregation of students along race lines has extremely important implications for the future of race relations in society.

Decreased Probability of School Violence

Mass school shooting are on a rapid rise in the United States (Springer, 2018). There has been more than one school shooting a week in the first 20 weeks of 2018 in which someone was hurt or killed, not counting the shooter (Ahmed & Walker, 2018). Schools are spending billions of dollars attempting to mitigate the consequence. They are hiring armed guards, installing metal detectors, video surveillance, securing entrances and exits, and even installing bullet-proof rooms within classrooms. All of these efforts are reactive. To suggest a medical analogy, they are treatment-oriented rather than prevention-oriented. When a treatment orientation to polio was used, for years thousands of individuals a year became cripples or died. Following the adoption of a prevention orientation developed by Dr. Salk, polio has been almost completely eliminated.

Studies of the motivation of students who resort to extreme violence in schools combined with studies on the impact of cooperative learning suggest we can adopt a proactive prevention model to school violence and racially reduce the incidence of school shootings.

Two months after the Columbine tragedy in 1999, experts from the US Department of Education and the US Secret Service collaborated to study the "school shooter" phenomenon (Daniels, 2018). They were looking to discover something that was common to most shooters with the hope that shooters could be identified prior to their violent acts. At first, the attempt of the secret service to profile shooters was frustrating. They found most shooters were doing well in school, came from intact families, and were mostly white males. Further, the shooters had planned their attacks and broadcast their intentions. These initial findings provided "no accurate or useful 'profile' of students who engaged in targeted school violence."

Then emerged a critical finding: Most shooters had been rejected by their peers and had been bullied! This finding together with established outcomes of cooperative learning gives us the key to inoculating students against violence. We know that cooperative learning produces buddies rather than bullies. Cooperative experiences create a cooperative predisposition, which in turn predicts positive social relations and the absence of bullying and aggression (Choi, Johnson, & Johnson, 2011).

I am reminded of the parable of two men standing by the edge of a fast-moving stream. A man is being washed downstream, struggling not to drown. The men rush in and save the man. While they are attending to the half-drowned man, another man is washed downstream, screaming for help. Again, they jump in and pull him out. While they are attending to this second victim a third man is washed down stream. This time, as one of the two rescuers runs to jump in to save the new victim, but the other man begins walking upstream. The one who is about to jump in the stream yells at his partner, "Aren't you going to help?" His partner replies, "I am going to help. I am going to see who is pushing them in."

In my view, to reduce the problem of school violence we need to walk upstream. We need to change the culture in schools so that students are not set against each other. We need to structure student interactions so that students adopt a cooperative social orientation. To the extent we do this, students will not want to put each other down, create in- and outgroups, attempt to gain status by besting someone else. Most importantly, students will not ostracize and bully their classmates. Being accepted rather than bullied, students will not experience rage and will not turn violent.

Many school shootings are the product of a massive, unintended training program in social orientation. Let's examine how schools foster a social orientation that turns students against each other and leads them to put down, make fun of, bully, and outcast some individuals.

Massive, Unintended Training in Social Orientation

There are only three possible social orientations: against, alone, and with. Or to put it in other words, at any moment we can orient toward others in one of only three ways: We are competitive, individualistic, or cooperative.

Traditional instructional strategies, without intending and without many educators realizing it, on a consistent basis orient students competitively or individualistically. Students do not work with each other. This consistent orientation of students toward competition and individualism occurs year after year. Those social orientations become default orientations. Ultimately, our students adopt in life the social orientation they adopted year after year in school. Without intending traditional schooling is a massive training program in competitive and individualistic social orientations.

The consequence of this massive training program is seen when students leave school. If a person sees another needing help, and has a competitive social orientation, they have a secret smile to themselves, saying, "I am better than he is." If a person sees another needing help and has an individualistic social orientation, they say to themselves, "That is not my problem; I need to take care of myself." In contrast, if someone with a cooperative social orientation sees someone in need, they ask, "How can I help you?"

As simple as Kagan Structures are, they have the potential of correcting a very one-sided training program in social orientation. There are times competition is called for. There are times individualism is adaptive. But to make competition and individualism the default orientations of our students is not healthy for our students or for our society. We need to balance the diet. Kagan Structures are a simple way to balance competitive and individualistic orientations with a cooperative social orientation. When competitive and individualist orientations are no longer their default orientations, our students will be more likely to act cooperatively when that is adaptive. In the process of fostering a cooperative social orientation in our students, we make it a better world.

Why Do Structures Produce Gains?

How can we explain the dramatic gains structures produce in increasing achievement, increasing positive behaviors, and decreasing disruptive behaviors? Although PIES is not the whole story, it is much of the story. When we put Kagan Structures in place, we are putting in place four very powerful principles: Positive Interdependence, Individual Accountability, Equal Participation, and Simultaneous Interaction. These four principles directly determine outcomes, and the outcomes they produce interact to further elicit additional positive gains.

Figure 5.7, "Kagan Structures yield gains," illustrates how structures produce PIES and how in turn PIES produce academic, social, and psychological gains. After describing the direct paths between the PIES principles and the three types of gains, we examine how the gains in turn interact to accelerate each other.

Positive Interdependence

When students are on the same side and a gain for one produces a gain for another, they are motivated to encourage, tutor, coach, and praise

Kagan Structures Yield Gains

Basic Principles (PIES)

- Positive Interdependence
- Individual Accountability
- Equal Participation
- Simultaneous Interaction

Positive Outcomes

Positive Interdependence:
- Cooperative Social Orientation
- Tutoring, Coaching, Helping
- Encouraging, Praising, Celebrating
- Positive Social Skills & Behaviors, Character Development
- Decreased Disruptive Behaviors
- Improved Peer and Race Relations
- Enhanced Belonging, Safety
- Liking for Class, Content, School
- Increased Achievement

Individual Accountability:
- Motivation to Perform
- Enhanced Participation
- Status Equalization
- Communication Skills
- Thinking Skills
- Improved Self-Esteem
- Liking for Class, Content, School
- Growth Mindset
- Increased Achievement

Equal Participation:
- Active Engagement by All
- Status Equalization
- Improved Peer and Race Relations
- Improved Self-Esteem
- Liking for Class, Content, School
- Increased Achievement

Simultaneous Interaction:
- Maximized Engagement
- Increased Time on Task
- Decreased Boredom, Mind Wandering
- Liking for Class, Content, School
- Decreased Disruptive Behaviors
- Increased Achievement

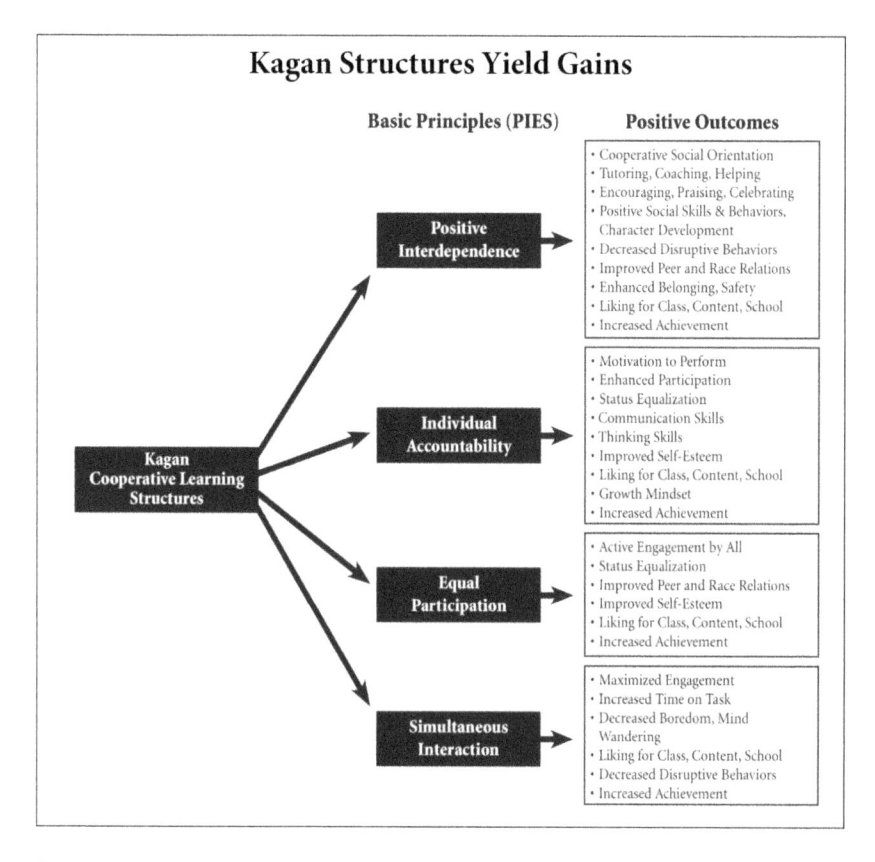

Figure 5.7 Kagan Structures yield gains

each other, which in turn leads to greater academic achievement. It also produces a "same-side" cooperative social orientation that improves social relations. Students develop positive social skills, social relations, and character virtues like caring, compassion, and responsibility to others. Further, students who like each other are less likely to fight, reducing discipline problems. Finally, positive interdependence among teammates and classmates produces a sense of belonging and safety as well as liking for school and class.

Individual Accountability

When students know they must perform and will be held accountable for their performance, their academic performance improves (Slavin, 1983). Individual accountability increases on-task behavior, and on-task students are less disruptive. When students must perform in cooperative learning groups they enhance their communication skills, and in answering questions posed by the teacher and teammates they develop thinking skills. When individual accountability is in place, the meta-communication to students is that your effort is what counts, supporting a growth mindset.

Equal Participation

By having the lower-achieving and shyer students participating just as much as the higher-achieving and more outgoing students, we increase the achievement of students who otherwise would be reluctant to participate. This decreases the achievement gap and increases overall achievement. As otherwise disengaged students see their efforts make a difference in increasing school achievement, they adopt a growth mindset. Further, improved achievement boosts self-esteem and social status. Students who are achieving more, feel better about themselves and are not marginalized in class. As students participate more equally in learning activities, they are less likely to be disruptive.

Simultaneous Interaction

Students who are more engaged achieve more and are less likely to be disruptive. The meta-communication to students when we call on a few students to respond is "some have something of value to share." The meta-communication when simultaneous interaction has all students responding is "everyone has something of value to share." This in turn increases self-esteem. Simultaneous interaction produces enhanced engagement of all students, increasing achievement, liking for class, school, and academic content. Enhanced engagement reduces discipline problems because engaged students are not disruptive.

Interactions Among Positive Outcomes

Teachers and administrators explaining the radically reduced discipline referrals that result from implementing Kagan Structures are consistent in their explanations: Greater engagement and improved social skills and relations leaves students less time for and less motivation for disruptions. They note also that teachers freed from dealing with discipline issues can focus more on academics. Thus, one positive outcome (fewer discipline problems) creates another positive outcome (enhanced achievement). The positive outcomes interact to reinforce each other.

There are a number of ways positive outcomes reinforce each other. To detail a few: As self-esteem, feeling of belonging and safety are increased, students are free to focus on academics, so achievement is enhanced. As interpersonal skills and liking for teammates and classmates are increased, students are more likely to encourage and tutor each other, increasing achievement. As achievement is increased, self-esteem is enhanced. There are implications for brain functioning: The sense of belonging and safety produced by positive interdependence puts the amygdala into a state of quiescence, freeing the prefrontal cortex to function more fully. This enhances the ability to think, problem-solve, and be creative. There are other interactions that could be spelled out, but what is clear is that we have a very synergistic set of processes in place once we implement the Kagan Structures, which put PIES in place.

How Can We Support This Instructional Revolution?

I have now presented keynotes and workshops in over 40 countries. In each country I have gone into classrooms to observe teaching and learning. I can say with confidence that worldwide the most common structure used by teachers to elicit student engagement is TSQA. As we have seen, TSQA violates the PIES principles and produces boredom and mind wandering more than engagement.

I have asked myself why teachers worldwide have so exclusively settled on a very inefficient instructional strategy. After studying the brain, I think I have an answer. Two brain processes combine to make TSQA so ubiquitous: mirror neurons and myelination.

Mirror Neurons

Mirror neurons explain how our brains fire as if we were doing the action or having the feeling that we observe in others. Our brains mimic the brains of people we observe. If we observe a disgusted face, the insula in our brain, which registers disgust, fires. If we watch someone pick up an object, the motor cortex in our brain fires as if we were picking up that object. Athletes improve by watching videos of outstanding performances by great athletes. Mirror neurons are the basis for empathy. They are how we know what others are feeling. What do mirror neurons have to do with why teachers call on one rather than engaging all students? The research on mirror neurons tells us that all of us went into training to become teachers when we first entered school. As we saw teachers using TSQA, our brains fired as if we were doing that.

Myelination

Year after year as we were watching our teachers call on one student at a time, neural tracks were being formed. Our brains were firing as if we were doing TSQA. Because we watched this structure year after year, those neural tracks became highly myelinated. Myelin is a fatty substance that wraps around neural tracks that repeatedly fire, making them much more efficient and harder to forget. Highly myelinated neural tracks can fire without conscious attention. We can do TSQA without much or any thought or planning.

That TSQA responses are so highly myelinated means the job of adopting Kagan Structures on a regular basis is very difficult. Using the structures on an occasional basis won't do it; our brains will fall back into their default network. There is only one way to overcome highly myelinated habits: practice. This is why in training the Structural Approach we emphasize taking one structure and practicing it over and over until it is so highly myelinated that it becomes a default network in the brain. Our goal is to make structures highly myelinated neural tracks.

Thus, as effective and as simple as they are—after all, how hard is it to do a RallyRobin?—it is not easy to obtain widespread implementation of structures. Why? Teachers teach the way they were taught, and repetition of behaviors creates highly myelinated neural circuits that are difficult to overcome. It is much easier to learn a new habit than to unlearn an old habit. Many teachers complete their initial training in the Structural Approach to cooperative learning and are fully convinced the structures are a better way to teach. They know it is foolish to call on one if in the same amount of time they could call on everyone. Nevertheless, in spite of this knowledge, some continue to call on one. Cognitive knowledge does not overcome procedural knowledge. The only way to overcome a habit is to replace it with a stronger habit. So too is it with structures. Teachers need to practice a structure, say RallyRobin or Timed Pair Share, so often that it becomes a highly myelinated neural pathway, making it more natural to use that structure than TQSA. Eventually, teachers begin to use specific structure sequences often enough that those sequences become the basis for lessons.

When we first learn a new language, we have to think hard about vocabulary, sentence structure, verb–subject agreement, and so on. It is exhausting. But at some point, that semantic knowledge becomes procedural knowledge: Instead of knowing about the language, we know the language; we become fluent in the language. At that point we no longer think about the language, we think about what we have to say. So, too, is it with structures: With practice we become fluent in a structure, and at that point we no longer think about the structure, we think about what we want to teach.

My dream is that enough teachers become fluent in enough structures that when their students first become teachers, those students will teach the way they were taught—they will teach with structures!

Final Note

Structures are very simple. Yet they have a very profound impact. By implementing structures, we increase achievement; decrease the achievement gaps; increase satisfaction with school; make teaching and learning more joyful; foster the acquisition of social skills; improve social relations; improve race relations; reduce disruptive behaviors; and reduce the probability of school violence. In addition, perhaps most importantly, we foster in students a cooperative social orientation.

In short, as simple as they are, implementing structures promises to address the most important educational and societal issues facing the nation. There are no more important issues for our country than improving academic achievement, reducing educational inequalities, and improving race relations. Employers are demanding schools equip students with communication skills and teamwork skills to prepare them to take their place in the fast-changing, interdependent workplace of the 21st century. Those skills cannot be acquired when teachers have students working only alone or in competition. For success in the workplace and in life, our students need to adopt a cooperative orientation, not during an occasional lesson, but as the way we orient toward each other on an ongoing basis.

References

2014 NAIS report on the high school survey of student engagement. *NAIS Research*, 2015, pp. 1–53.

Ahmed, S., & Walker, C. (2018, May 18). There has been, on average, 1 school shooting every week this year. *CNN*. Retrieved from www.cnn.com/2018/03/02/us/school-shootings-2018-list-trnd/index.html

Armstrong, B., Johnson, D., & Balow, B. (1981). Effects of cooperative vs. individualistic learning experiences on interpersonal attraction between learning-disabled and normal-progress elementary school students. *Contemporary Educational Psychology, 6*, 102–109.

Ballard, M., Corman, L., Gottlieb, J., & Kaufman, M. J. (1977). Improving the social status of mainstreamed retarded children. *Journal of Educational Psychology, 69*, 605–611.

Choi, J., Johnson, D. W., & Johnson, R. (2011). Relationships among cooperative learning experiences, social interdependence, children's aggression, victimization, and prosocial behaviors. *Journal of Applied Social Psychology, 41*(4), 976–1003.

Cline, L. (2007). Impacts of Kagan cooperative learning structures on fifth-graders' mathematical achievement. *Kagan Online Magazine*. San Clemente, CA: Kagan Publishing, Fall 2007. Retrieved from www.kaganonline.com/free_articles/research_and_rationale/319/Impacts-of-Kagan-Cooperative-Learning-Structures-on-Fifth-Graders-Mathematical-Achievement

Corey, J. (2017). At Lehigh Senior High School, "It's all about engagement!" *Kagan Online Magazine*. San Clemente, CA: Kagan Publishing. Fall 2017. Retrieved from www.kaganonline.com/free_articles/research_and_rationale/461/At-Lehigh-Senior-High-School—It-s-All-About-Engagement!-

Daniels, J. (2018). *If you want to know about how to stop school shootings, ask the Secret Service*, Scientific American, The Conversation US, February 27,

2018. Retrieved from www.scientificamerican.com/article/if-you-want-to-know-how-to-stop-school-shootings-ask-the-secret-service/

Dotson, J. (2001). Cooperative learning structures can increase student achievement. *Kagan Online Magazine*. San Clemente, CA: Kagan Publishing, Winter 2001. Retrieved from www.kaganonline.com/free_articles/research_and_rationale/311/Cooperative-Learning-Structures-Can-Increase-Student-Achievement

Goodlad, J. I. (1984). A place called school: Prospects for the future. New York, NY: McGraw-Hill Book Co.

Gradone, D. (2015). Increasing student participation, interest, and communication with cooperative learning structures. *Kagan Online Magazine Issue #53*. San Clemente, CA: Kagan Publishing. Retrieved from www.kaganonline.com/free_articles/research_and_rationale/421/Increasing-Student-Participation-Interest-and-Communication-with-Cooperative-Learning-Structures

Hattie, J. (2009). *Visible learning: A synthesis of over 800 meta-analyses relating to achievement.* New York, NY and London: Routledge.

Haydon, T., Maheady, J., & Hunter, W. (2010). Effects of numbered heads together on the daily quiz scores and on-task behavior of students with disabilities. *Journal of Behavioral Education, 19,* 222–238.

Hensley, D. (2016). You will see results! *Kagan Online Magazine, Issue #54*. San Clemente, CA: Kagan Publishing. Retrieved from www.kaganonline.com/free_articles/research_and_rationale/428/You-Will-See-Results

Howard, B. (2006). Cooperative learning structures improve performance and attitudes of high school journalism students. *Kagan Online Magazine*. San Clemente, CA: Kagan Publishing, Spring 2006. Retrieved from www.kaganonline.com/free_articles/research_and_rationale/312/Cooperative-Learning-Structures-Improve-Performance-and-Attitudes-of-High-School-Journalism-Students

Johnson, D. K., & Johnson, R. T. (1989). *Cooperation and competition theory and research.* Edina, MN: Interaction Book Company.

Kagan, M. (2001). *Logic line-ups.* San Clemente, CA: Kagan Publishing.

Kagan, M. (2007). Closing the achievement gap. San Clemente, CA: *Kagan Online Magazine*. San Clemente, CA: Kagan Publishing, Spring 2007. Retrieved from www.KaganOnline.com

Kagan, M., Kagan, S., & Kagan, L. (1995). *Classbuilding.* San Clemente, CA: Kagan Publishing.

Kagan, M., Kagan, S., & Kagan, L. (1997). *Teambuilding.* San Clemente, CA: Kagan Publishing.

Kagan, S. (1993). The structural approach to cooperative learning. In D. Holt (Ed.), *Cooperative learning: A response to linguistic and cultural diversity.* McHenry, IL: Center for Applied Linguistics and Delta Systems, Inc.

Kagan, S. (1998). Staff development and the structural approach to cooperative learning. In C. Brody & N. Davidson (Eds.), *Professional development for cooperative learning: Issues and approaches.* New York, NY: Teachers College Press.

Kagan, S. (1999). Kagan structures enhance brain engagement! *Kagan Online Magazine*. San Clemente, CA: Kagan Publishing. Retrieved from www.kaganonline.com/free_articles/dr_spencer_kagan/277/Kagan-Structures-Enhance-Brain-Engagement!

Kagan, S. (2000). The structural approach to character development. *Kagan Online Magazine*. San Clemente, CA: Kagan Publishing. Retrieved from www.kagan

online.com/free_articles/dr_spencer_kagan/291/The-Structural-Approach-to-Character-Development

Kagan, S. (2001a). Kagan structures for emotional intelligence. *Kagan Online Magazine*. San Clemente, CA: Kagan Publishing. Retrieved from www.kagan online.com/free_articles/dr_spencer_kagan/278/Kagan-Structures-for-Emotional-Intelligence

Kagan, S. (2001b). Kagan structures are brain-based. *Kagan Online Magazine*. San Clemente, CA: Kagan Publishing. Retrieved from www.kaganonline.com/free_articles/dr_spencer_kagan/276/Kagan-Structures-are-Brain-Based

Kagan, S. (2001c). Kagan structures and learning together: What is the difference? *Kagan Online Magazine*. San Clemente, CA: Kagan Publishing. Retrieved from www.KaganOnline.com

Kagan, S. (2003). Kagan structures for thinking skills. *Kagan Online Magazine*. San Clemente, CA: Kagan Publishing. Fall 2003. Retrieved from www.kaganonline.com/free_articles/dr_spencer_kagan/280/Kagan-Structures-for-Thinking-Skills

Kagan, S. (2005). Rethinking thinking—Does bloom's taxonomy align with brain science? *Kagan Online Magazine*. San Clemente, CA: Kagan Publishing. Retrieved from www.kaganonline.com/free_articles/dr_spencer_kagan/289/Rethinking-Thinking-Does-Bloom-s-Taxonomy-Align-with-Brain-Science?

Kagan, S. (2006a). Toward a brain-based pedagogy. In S. Feinstein (Ed.), *The praeger handbook of learning and the brain, volume two*. Westport, CT: Praeger Publishers.

Kagan, S. (2006b). Cooperative learning: The power to transform race relations. *Teaching Tolerance Magazine*, Fall 2006.

Kagan, S. (2006c). Kagan coaching. *Kagan Online Magazine*. San Clemente, CA: Kagan Publishing. Retrieved from www.kaganonline.com/free_articles/dr_spencer_kagan/273/Kagan-Coaching

Kagan, S. (2009). Cooperative learning structures for brain-compatible instruction. In J. Cooper, P. Robinson, & D. Ball (Eds.), *Small group instruction in higher education: Lessons from the past, visions of the future* (2nd ed., 2003). Stillwater, OK: New Forums Press.

Kagan, S. (2013). Kagan cooperative structures promote language acquisition. *Kagan Online Magazine*. San Clemente, CA: Kagan Publishing. Retrieved from www.kaganonline.com/free_articles/dr_spencer_kagan/414/Kagan-Cooperative-Structures-Promote-Language-Acquisition

Kagan, S. (2014). *Brain-friendly teaching: Tools, tips, & structures*. San Clemente, CA: Kagan Publishing.

Kagan, S. (2020). *Emotion-friendly teaching: Accelerating Social-Emotional Learning (SEL)*. San Clemente, CA: Kagan Publishing.

Kagan, S., & High, J. (2002). Kagan structures for English language learners. *ESL Magazine*, 5(4), 10–12.

Kagan, S., & Kagan, M. (1998). *Multiple intelligences: The complete MI book*. San Clemente, CA: Kagan Publishing.

Kagan, S., & Kagan, M. (2006). Multiple intelligences structures—Opening doors to learning. *Kagan Online Magazine*. San Clemente, CA: Kagan Publishing. Retrieved from www.kaganonline.com/free_articles/dr_spencer_kagan/285/Multiple-Intelligences-Structures-Opening-Doors-to-Learning

Kagan, S., & Kagan, M. (2009). *Kagan cooperative learning*. San Clemente, CA: Kagan Publishing.

Kagan, S., Kyle, P., & Scott, S. (2004). *Win-win discipline*. San Clemente, CA: Kagan Publishing.

Kagan, S., & Madsen, M. C. (1971). Cooperation and competition of Mexican, Mexican-American, and Anglo-American children of two ages under four instructional sets. *Developmental Psychology, 5*(1), 32–39.

Kagan, S., & Madsen, M. C. (1975). Experimental analyses of cooperation and competition of Anglo-American and Mexican children. *Developmental Psychology, 6*, 49–59. Reprinted in Lindgren, H. (Ed.). *Children's behavior: An introduction to research studies*. Palo Alto: Mayfield Publishing.

Kagan, S., Zahn, G. L., Widaman, K. F., Schwarzwald, J., & Tyrell, G. (1985). Classroom structural bias: Impact of cooperative and competitive classroom structures on cooperative and competitive individuals and groups. In R. E. Slavin, S. Sharan, S. Kagan, R. hertz-Lararowitz, C. Webb, & R. Schmuck (Eds.), *Learning to cooperate, cooperating to learn* (pp. 277–312). New York, NY: Plenum.

Kennedy, K. (2000). Test scores show Kagan structures work at long hill elementary school. *Kagan Online Magazine*. San Clemente, CA: Kagan Publishing, Summer 2000. Retrieved from www.kaganonline.com/free_articles/research_and_rationale/329/Test-Scores-Show-Kagan-Structures-Work-At-Long-Hill-Elementary-School

Kramer, M. (2014). Discipline referrals decrease dramatically at Sage elementary. *Kagan Online Magazine*. San Clemente, CA: Kagan Publishing. Spring/Summer 2014. Retrieved from www.kaganonline.com/free_articles/research_and_rationale/387/Discipline-Referrals-Decrease-Dramatically-at-Sage-Elementary

Lee, D. (2009). Mills hill school—A journey towards success. *Kagan Online Magazine*. San Clemente, CA: Kagan Publishing. Fall 2009. Retrieved from www.kaganonline.com/free_articles/research_and_rationale/326/Mills-Hill-SchoolA-Journey-Towards-Success,2

Madden, N. A., & Slavin, R. E. (1983). Cooperative learning and social acceptance of mainstreamed academically handicapped students. *Journal of Special Education, 17*, 171–1982.

Magnesio, S., & Davis, B. (2010). A teacher fosters social competence with cooperative learning. *Childhood Education*, Summer 2010. Reproduced in *Kagan's Online Magazine*, San Clemente, CA: Kagan Publishing. Fall/Winter 2010. Retrieved from www.kaganonline.com/free_articles/research_and_rationale/185/A-Teacher-Fosters-Social-Competence-With-Cooperative-Learning

Maheady, L., Mallete, B., Harper, G. F., & Sacca, K. (1991). Heads together: A peer-mediated option for improving the academic achievement of heterogeneous learning groups. *Remedial and Special Education, 25*(1), 25–33.

Maheady, L., Michielli-Pendl, J., Harper, G., & Mallette, B. (2006). The effects of numbered heads together with and without an incentive package on the science test performance of a diverse group of sixth graders. *Journal of Behavioral Education, 15*(1), 25–39.

Maheady, L., Michielli-Pendl, J., Mallette, B., & Harper, G. F. (2002). A collaborative research project to improve the academic performance of a diverse sixth grade science class. *Teacher Education and Special Education, 1*(25), 55–70.

Major, E., & Robinette, J. (2004). Kagan structures add power to corporate classes. *Kagan Online Magazine*. San Clemente, CA: Kagan Publishing, Fall 2004. Retrieved from www.kaganonline.com/free_articles/research_and_rationale/323/Kagan-Structures-Add-Power-To-Corporate-Classes

McColgan, B. (2013). From failing to the top 5%. *Kagan Online Magazine*. San Clemente, CA: Kagan Publishing, Summer 2013. Retrieved from www.kaganonline.com/free_articles/research_and_rationale/383/From-Failing-to-the-Top-5-

McGaugh, J. L. (2003). *Maps of the mind. Memory and emotion: The making of lasting memories*. New York City, NY: Columbia University Press.

McMillen, C., Mallette, B., Smith, C., Rey, J., Jabot, M., & Maheady, L. (2016). The effects of numbered heads together on the science quiz performance of 9th grade students. *Journal of Evidence-Based Practices for Schools*, 1(15), 65–89.

Mele, J. (2001). Kagan cooperative learning creates explosive results in high school chemistry. *Kagan Online Magazine*. San Clemente, CA: Kagan Publishing, Summer 2001. Retrieved from www.kaganonline.com/free_articles/research_and_rationale/321/Kagan-Cooperative-Learning-Creates-Explosive-Results-in-High-School-Chemistry

Murie, C. (2004). Effects of communication on student learning. *Kagan Online Magazine*. San Clemente, CA: Kagan Publishing, Summer 2004. Retrieved from www.kaganonline.com/free_articles/research_and_rationale/313/Effects-of-Communication-on-Student-Learning

Nelson, L., & Kagan, S. (1972). Competition. *Psychology Today*, 6, 53–91. Reprinted in *Readings in developmental psychology today* (2nd ed.). New York, NY: Random House, 1977. Also reprinted in text with associated films, cassette, and workbook. Huntington, NY: Instructional Communications Technology, Inc., 1974.

Schwarzwald, J., & Cohen, S. (1982). Relationship between academic tracking and the degree of interethnic acceptance. *Journal of Educational Psychology*, 74(4), 588–597.

Slavin, R. (1983). *Cooperative learning*. New York, NY: Longman.

Springer. (2018, April). Rapid rise in mass school shootings in the United States, study shows: Researchers call for action to address worrying increase in the number of mass school shootings in past two decades. *ScienceDaily*. Retrieved from www.sciencedaily.com/releases/2018/04/180419131025.htm

Wetering, V. J. (2009). Kagan structures and high school algebra. *Kagan Online Magazine*. San Clemente, CA: Kagan Publishing. Spring 2009. Retrieved from www.kaganonline.com/free_articles/research_and_rationale/324/Kagan-Structures-and-High-School-Algebra

Winters, M. (2013). Principal becoming exemplary with Kagan. *Kagan Online Magazine*. San Clemente, CA: Kagan Publishing. Fall/Winter 2013. Retrieved from www.kaganonline.com/free_articles/research_and_rationale/371/Becoming-Exemplary-with-Kagan

Winters, M. (2014). Earning a grades with Kagan. *Kagan Online Magazine*. San Clemente, CA: Kagan Publishing. Fall 2014/Winter 2015. Retrieved from www.kaganonline.com/free_articles/research_and_rationale/398/Earning-A-Grades-with-Kagan.

Chapter 6

Student Team Learning and Success for All

A Personal History and Overview

Robert E. Slavin and Nancy A. Madden

Student Team Learning (STL) is a set of approaches to cooperative learning that emphasize academic achievement as the main outcome and are designed to be used all year as a routine part of daily instruction. STL mainly includes Student Teams-Achievement Divisions (STAD) and Teams-Games-Tournament (TGT), plus programs for particular subjects, such as Cooperative Integrated Reading and Composition (CIRC), Student Team Writing (STW), and Team Accelerated Instruction (TAI) in mathematics. Success for All (SFA) is a whole-school reform model for disadvantaged elementary and middle schools. It adds to cooperative learning elements such as tutoring for struggling readers, parent involvement approaches, social-emotional learning methods, and more.

This chapter has two sections. First, it contains a personal history of the intellectual and pragmatic journey that led us to create, evaluate, and disseminate these programs. This chapter is the only place this story has been published. Second, it contains a section describing our theoretical perspective, main programs, and the research on them. This story has been told frequently, but it is important, we think, to include it with the personal history to help readers understand what we are talking about and what we think we offer to the practice of education.

Student Team Learning: A Personal History

Our approach to cooperative learning began in 1970, when I (Bob) was a sophomore and Nancy was a freshman at Reed College, in Portland, Oregon. We were psychology majors, both very interested in the possibilities of making schools exciting places, where learning was social and engaged the energies and enthusiasm of all students, especially students at risk.

As often as we could, we walked around the rain-swept streets of Portland, trying out ideas about education. Initially, we were thinking that group simulation games might be the key to making schools engaging and exciting, but we had opportunities to try them out and realized that it was what the groups did together, more than the simulation games, that held the greatest potential. Still, in the summer of 1970, we got a small grant to create a science program called WorldLab, in which young adolescents would learn and apply lab science in order to solve the problems of made-up countries on a made-up planet. Later, we both did undergraduate theses on applications of WorldLab. And we were still walking in the rain, trying out new thoughts, new approaches.

In an educational psychology class, I came upon a book by James Coleman (1961), entitled *The Adolescent Society*. In it, Coleman was wondering, as Nancy and I did, why the academic part of school was so boring and unengaging, while the sports parts were so exciting. He hypothesized that the difference was that in academics, one person's success causes another's failure. In contrast, in sports, each team member's success increased the chances that others would succeed, because their team would succeed. Therefore, students encourage and assist each other's hard work and engagement in sports, while discouraging hard work and engagement in academics. Strivers in academics get bad names, such as "nerds" or "geeks," while strivers in sports are "stars."

Coleman, like us, followed this idea into an interest in simulation games, and "It's Academic!" tournaments. But the core concept was just what we'd been chewing on. I taught for a year after Reed, waiting for Nancy to graduate, and then I went off to Johns Hopkins University for only one reason. Coleman was there.

As it happened, Coleman left the year I came, 1973, so I worked with David DeVries, creator of Teams-Games-Tournaments (TGT) (DeVries & Slavin, 1978). TGT not only used teams like those we later used in other models but also used academic games in which students competed to win points for their teams. I worked on TGT, but two years later DeVries left academia. I quickly finished my Ph.D. and took his now-empty position.

Nancy was teaching emotionally disturbed children in Baltimore, and then got a degree in clinical psychology, but we still worked together on cooperative learning. Seeing the difficulty of getting teachers to use the games of TGT or the simulations of WorldLab, we created a simpler program, *STAD*, in 1975 (Slavin, 1977, 1978, 1980). STAD involves students working in four- to five-member teams to help each other master content introduced by the teacher. Students then take individual quizzes, and teams are recognized based on the average team score.

Our Approach to Cooperative Learning

STAD and other cooperative learning programs we have developed at Johns Hopkins University have distinct characteristics, not only in the program procedures but also in the role of research and development in our work.

For us, like many others, teams are heterogeneous groups of four or five. The teams sit together, and they have team names and a responsibility to ensure the success of all team members.

We place a great deal of emphasis on two key factors: group goals and individual accountability (Slavin, 1978, 1980, 1981, 1983, 1995, 2014). Group goals mean that the team is working together to achieve success, and they can earn recognition or small rewards for doing so. Individual accountability means that in achieving their group goals, teams have to ensure that every member of the team is mastering the material the group is studying (Slavin, 1983, 1995). The purpose of the combination of group goals and individual accountability is to try to make sure that team members are teaching each other, explaining difficult ideas, helping each other study, and encouraging each other's success. These structures are intended to prevent the "free rider" problem of group work, in which one student works and three students watch them do it. It is also intended to prevent the "bully," the team member who takes over and tells others what to do. When there is a group goal and individual accountability, the team cannot succeed if only one or a few members are learning. All must learn.

We recognize that there are different structures for different objectives. Writing or project-based learning, for example, need structures different from studying math, science, or reading. But whatever the academic goal, there is a way to ensure that groupmates work eagerly together but cannot do each other's work.

Our focus on achievement as the principal goal of cooperative learning also affects our research. We are uninterested in short-term lab studies or artificial experiments. Instead, our studies generally operate in real classrooms in real schools over extended time periods, often a whole school year or more. We value studies that use traditional measures of traditional academic content. We respect more theoretically driven studies as steps on the way to larger and longer experiments, but before anyone claims that evidence supports any program, cooperative learning or anything else, we want to see evidence from experiments that took place in schools over extended periods.

In the mid-1970s, we became aware of other groups also working on cooperative learning: David and Roger Johnson, Elliot Aronson, Shlomo and Yael Sharan, and others. Each had their own ideas about how cooperative learning should be done, and each had different objectives. From the outset, we set as our goal creating practical approaches that could be used to help students learn traditional academic subjects, reasoning that these subjects have always driven the practice of education and always would, so if we expected to give large numbers of students the joy of working in teams, we'd need to help teachers use them to accomplish their basic goals.

By the late 1970s we were holding big workshops at Johns Hopkins and doing large-scale, year-long studies to evaluate many forms of cooperative learning. Around 1980, however, we recognized a problem. Much as teachers loved cooperative learning and loved the workshops, they had a lot of difficulty teaming up cooperative methods with the academic content they had to teach. We created blackline masters and other practical supports to help teachers apply STAD to reading, math, grammar, and other topics in many grade levels. The quality of implementation gained dramatically.

In the early 1980s, when Nancy gave up her clinical work and came to work at Johns Hopkins, we took another major step. We created a complete approach to upper-elementary math, called Team-Assisted Individualization (TAI). Much more than blackline masters, it combined individualization with cooperative learning. Students worked within teams on material at their instructional level, with the teacher providing leveled lessons. Teammates helped each other succeed on their individualized content. Evaluations found TAI to be one of the most effective initiatives we ever engaged in (Slavin, Leavey, & Madden, 1984), but teachers found it hard to implement, because students were working on so many different levels.

We also made a complete approach to upper-elementary reading and writing, called Cooperative Integrated Reading and Composition, or CIRC (Stevens, Madden, Slavin, & Farnish, 1987), which was also very effective and not so difficult to implement. CIRC involves students working not only in teams on reading and writing activities but also at times in reading groups, with all activities contributing to team scores and recognition.

As we worked with more and more schools, we began to see that the school, not individual teachers, was the essential unit of change. We created and studied a whole-school program called the Cooperative Elementary School, which mixed various cooperative learning approaches with a focus on mainstreaming, parent involvement, and whole-school leadership. Again, the outcomes were very promising (Stevens & Slavin, 1995a, 1995b).

Success for All

In 1987, a major change happened. We were approached by Buzzy Hettleman, a former Maryland State Secretary of Human Resources, about creating a successful approach for inner-city schools in Baltimore. This was the fruition of the ideas we'd been discussing since Portland. We already had many of the necessary components in place, but between fall of 1986 and fall of 1987, we had to create a beginning reading program, a tutoring model, an assessment model, and much more. Success for All uses cooperative learning in pre-K to eighth grade. It also provides struggling readers with tutoring and helps schools build school-wide leadership, assessment, parent involvement, and other features focused on disadvantaged schools.

We did all of this with many collaborators in the Baltimore City Public Schools, and our very first school was a rousing success. We expanded to four more Baltimore schools, and they were very successful as well (Madden, Slavin, Karweit, Dolan, & Wasik, 1993). Our early schools averaged effect sizes of +0.50 and +0.75 for the lowest quarter of students. A follow-up of these schools showed effects lasting through eighth grade, and there were major reductions in grade failures and special education referrals (Borman & Hewes, 2002).

From that point, our efforts shifted decidedly from teacher-by-teacher cooperative learning to school-by-school reform, still incorporating cooperative learning at all grade levels, but also incorporating tutoring, parent involvement, pre-kindergarten, and other elements.

From 1988 throughout the 1990s, Success for All grew at a rapid rate. Evidence from large-scale, usually randomized evaluations continued to support the effects of SFA (Borman et al., 2007; Rowan, Correnti, Miller, & Camburn, 2009; Quint, Zhu, Balu, Rappaport, & DeLaurentis, 2014). Success for All now operates in about 1000 schools in the United States, 150 in the United Kingdom, and smaller numbers in the Netherlands and Canada. We created and evaluated Student Team Writing (Madden, Slavin, Logan, & Cheung, 2011), and evaluated our preschool and kindergarten approaches (Chambers, Cheung, & Slavin, 2016).

Student Team Learning: Theory, Programs, and Research (Portions of This Section Are Adapted From Slavin (1995))

Theoretical Perspectives on Cooperative Learning

Although there is a fair consensus among researchers about the positive effects of cooperative learning on student achievement, discussed in this chapter, there remains a controversy about why and how cooperative learning methods affect achievement, and most importantly, under what conditions cooperative learning has these effects. Different groups of researchers investigating cooperative learning effects on achievement begin with different assumptions and conclude by explaining the achievement effects of cooperative learning in quite different theoretical terms. In earlier work, Slavin (1995) identified motivationalist, social cohesion, and cognitive as the three major theoretical perspectives on the achievement effects of cooperative learning.

The *motivationalist perspective* presumes that motivation is the single most impactful part of the learning process, asserting that the other processes such as planning and helping are driven by individuals' motivated self-interest. Motivationalist-oriented scholars focus more on the reward or goal structure under which students operate (Slavin, 1995, 2009). Methods derived from this perspective emphasize the use of group goals and individual accountability, meaning that group success depends on the individual learning of all group members (see later).

By contrast, the social cohesion perspective (also called "social interdependence theory") suggests that the effects of cooperative learning are largely dependent on the cohesiveness of the group. This perspective holds that students help each other learn because they care about the group and its members and come to derive self-identity benefits from group membership (Johnson & Johnson, 1998). In essence, students will engage in the task and help one another learn because they identify with the group and want one another to succeed. This perspective is similar to the motivationalist perspective in that it emphasizes primarily motivational rather than cognitive explanations for the instructional effectiveness of cooperative learning. However, motivational theorists hold that students help their groupmates learn primarily because it is in their own interests to do so. Social cohesion theorists, in contrast, emphasize the idea that students help their groupmates learn because they care about the group. A hallmark of the social cohesion perspective is an emphasis on teambuilding activities in preparation for cooperative learning, and processing or group self-evaluation during and after group activities. Social cohesion theorists have historically tended to downplay or reject the group incentives and individual accountability held by motivationalist researchers to be essential. They emphasize, instead, that the effects of cooperative learning on students and on student achievement depend substantially on the quality of the group's interaction. For example, Cohen (1986, pp. 69–70) stated

> if the task is challenging and interesting, and if students are sufficiently prepared for skills in group process, students will experience the process of groupwork itself as highly rewarding . . . never grade or evaluate students on their individual contributions to the group product.

Cohen's (1994) work, as well as that of Shlomo and Yael Sharan's (1992) group investigation and Elliot Aronson's Jigsaw (Aronson, Blaney, Stephan, Sikes, & Snapp, 1978), may be described as social cohesiveness theories. Cohen, Aronson, and the Sharans all prescribe forms of cooperative learning in which students take on individual roles within the group, which Slavin (1983) calls "task specialization" methods. In Aronson's Jigsaw method, students study material on one of four or five topics distributed among the group members. They meet in "expert groups" to share information on their topics with members of other teams who have the same topic and then take turns presenting their topics to the team. In the Sharans' group investigation method, groups take on topics within a unit studied by the class as a whole and then further subdivide the topic into tasks within the group. The students investigate the topic together and ultimately present their findings to the class as a whole. Cohen's Finding Out/Descubrimiento program has students play different roles in discovery-oriented science activities.

The major alternative to the motivationalist and social cohesiveness perspectives on cooperative learning, both of which focus primarily on group norms and interpersonal influence, is the *cognitive perspective*. The cognitive perspective holds that interactions among students will in themselves increase student achievement for reasons that have to do with mental processing of information rather than with motivation. Cooperative methods developed by cognitive theorists involve neither the group goals that are the cornerstone of the motivationalist methods nor the emphasis on building group cohesiveness characteristic of the social cohesion methods.

One example of the cognitive perspective is Davidson's (1990) small-group discovery method of learning mathematics. Based on Dewey's philosophy,

> interest in the mathematical topics and activities is to provide the primary source of motivation.... The ideal goal is to provide a learning environment in which all topics are perceived as interesting, valuable, or useful to the students.

Students learn mathematics by doing mathematics together in small groups. They make conjectures, state and prove theorems, and develop techniques for solving various classes of problems (Davidson, 1990, pp. 337–338).

Integrating Alternative Perspectives

The alternative perspectives on cooperative learning may be seen as complementary, not contradictory. For example, motivational theorists would not argue that the cognitive theories are unnecessary. Instead, they assert that motivation drives cognitive process, which in turn produces learning (Slavin, 1995). They would argue that it is unlikely over the long haul that students would engage in the kind of explanations to each other found by Webb (2008) and others to be essential to profiting from cooperative activity unless the learning of their teammates is important to them. Similarly, social cohesion theorists might hold that the utility of extrinsic incentives must lie in their contribution to group cohesiveness, caring, and pro-social norms among group members, which could in turn affect cognitive processes.

A simple path model of cooperative learning processes, adapted from Slavin (1995), is diagrammed in Figure 6.1. It depicts the main functional relationships among the major theoretical approaches to cooperative learning.

Figure 6.1 begins with a focus on group goals or incentives based on the individual learning of all group members. That is, the model assumes that motivation to learn and to encourage and help others to learn activates cooperative behaviors that will result in learning. This would include both motivation to succeed at learning tasks and motivation to interact in the group. In this model, motivation to succeed leads to learning directly and also drives the behaviors and attitudes that lead to group cohesion, which in turn facilitates the types of group interactions that yield enhanced learning and academic achievement. The relationships are conceived to be reciprocal, so that motivation to succeed leads to the development of group cohesion, which may reinforce and enhance motivation. By the same token, the cognitive processes may become intrinsically rewarding and lead to increased motivation and group cohesion.

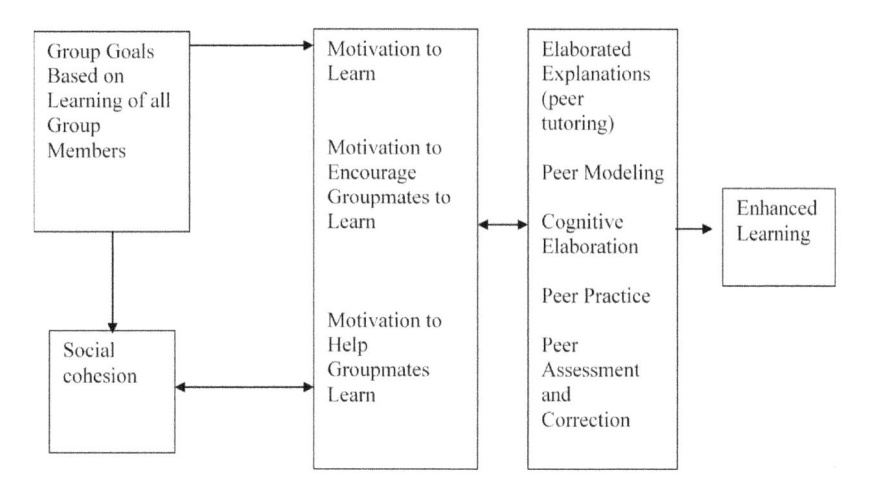

Figure 6.1 Integration of theoretical perspectives on cooperative learning effects on learning

Group Goals (or Rewards) and Individual Accountability

Considerable evidence from practical applications of cooperative learning in elementary and secondary schools supports the position that group rewards are essential to the effectiveness of cooperative learning, with one critical qualification. Use of group rewards enhances the achievement outcomes of cooperative learning, if and only if attaining the group rewards is based on the individual learning of all group members (Slavin, 1995). Most often, this means that team scores are computed based on average scores on quizzes, which all teammates take individually without teammate help. For example, in STAD (Slavin, 1994), students work in mixed-ability teams to master material initially presented by the teacher. Following this, students take individual quizzes on the material, and the teams may earn certificates based on the degree to which team members have improved over their own past records. The only way the team can achieve their rewards is by ensuring that all team members have learned, so the team members' activities focus on explaining concepts to one another, helping one another practice, and encouraging one another to achieve. In contrast, if attaining group rewards is based on a single group product (e.g., the team completes one worksheet or solves one problem), there is little incentive for group members to explain concepts to one another, and one or two group members may do all the work (see Slavin, 1995, 2009).

A 1995 review of 99 studies of cooperative learning in elementary and secondary schools that involved durations of at least four weeks compared achievement gains in cooperative learning and control groups (Slavin, 1995). Of 64 studies of cooperative learning methods that provided group rewards based on the sum of group members' individual learning, 50 studies (78%) found significantly positive effects on achievement, and none found negative effects (Slavin, 1995). The median effect size for these 64 studies was $d = +0.32$ (32% of a standard deviation separated cooperative learning and control treatments).

In contrast, studies of methods that used group goals based on a single group product or provided no group rewards found few positive effects, with a median effect size of only $d = +0.07$. Comparisons of forms of cooperative learning with and without group rewards within the same studies found similar patterns; group rewards based on the sum of individual learning performances were necessary to the instructional effectiveness of the cooperative learning models (e.g., Fantuzzo, Polite, & Grayson, 1990; Fantuzzo, Riggio, Connelly, & Dimeff, 1989).

Why are group rewards and individual accountability so important? To understand this, consider the alternatives. In some forms of cooperative learning, students work together to complete a single worksheet or to solve one problem. In such methods, there is little reason for more able students to take the time to explain what is going on to their less able groupmates or to ask their opinions. When the group task is to *do* something, rather than to *learn* something, the participation of less able students may be seen as interference rather than help. It may be easier in this circumstance for students to give each other answers than to explain concepts or skills to one another. More aggressive students may dominate the group, and others may avoid participating, letting others do the work (and the learning).

When the group's task is to ensure that every group member *learns* something, it is in the interests of every group member to spend time explaining concepts to his or her groupmates and to ask groupmates for explanations and help in understanding the topic of study. Studies of student behavior within cooperative groups have found that the students who gain most from cooperative work are those who give and receive elaborated explanations (Webb, 1985, 2008). In contrast, giving and receiving answers without explanations were *negatively* related to achievement gain. Group rewards and individual accountability motivate students to give elaborated explanations and to take one another's learning seriously, instead of simply giving answers.

While research has focused on group rewards (usually recognition for achieving a given group score), there are other ways groups can achieve group goals that need not involve scores or recognition. For example, a community might decide to build a garden together, and all share in the produce. The garden and its vegetables are not a "reward," but the dynamic is the same: Group members collaborate to achieve something of value to them. So the concept of "group rewards" can be expressed more broadly as "group goals," although in schools, it is usual that group goals are to achieve a standard set by the teacher, for which groups receive recognition or small privileges.

Student Team Learning: Programs and Research

As noted earlier in this chapter, two concepts are central to all STL methods: *group rewards* and *individual accountability*. Using STL techniques, teams earn certificates or other team rewards if they achieve above a designated criterion. *Individual accountability* means that the team's success depends on the individual learning of all team members. This focuses the activity of the team members on explaining concepts to one another and making sure that everyone on the team is ready for a quiz or other assessment that they will take without the help of teammates.

Four principal Student Learning methods have been extensively developed and researched. Two are general cooperative learning methods adaptable to most subjects and grade levels: Student Teams-Achievement Divisions (STAD) and Teams-Games-Tournament (TGT). The remaining two are comprehensive curriculums designed for use in particular subjects at particular grade levels: Team-Assisted Individualization (TAI) for mathematics in grades 3–6 and Cooperative Integrated Reading and Composition (CIRC) for reading and writing instruction in grades 3–5. Middle school adaptations of CIRC are called Student Team Reading and the Reading Edge.

STAD

In STAD (Slavin, 1994), students are assigned to four-member learning teams mixed in performance level, sex, and ethnicity. The teacher presents a lesson, and the students work within their teams to make sure that all team members have mastered the lesson. Finally, all students take individual quizzes on the material, at which time they may *not* help one another.

Students' quiz scores are compared to their own past averages, and points are awarded based on the degree to which students meet or exceed their own earlier performances. These points are then summed to form team scores, and teams that meet certain criteria earn certificates or other rewards. The whole cycle of activities, from teacher presentation to team practice to quiz, usually takes three to five class periods.

STAD has been used in a wide variety of subjects, including mathematics, language arts, and social studies. It has been used from grade 2 through college. STAD is most appropriate for teaching well-defined objectives, such as mathematical computations and applications, language usage and mechanics, geography and map skills, and science facts and concepts. In STAD, students work in four-member heterogeneous teams to help each other master academic content.

Numerous studies of STAD have found positive effects of the program on traditional learning outcomes in math, language arts, science, and other subjects (Barbato, 2000; Mevarech, 1985; Reid, 1992; Slavin, 1995; Slavin & Karweit, 1984). Across 11 comparisons that met standard inclusion criteria (e.g., use of control groups, minimum duration of 12 weeks, measures not made by researchers), nine of which used random assignment to conditions, the sample-size-weighted effect size was +0.14. These studies involved a total of more than 4000 students in grades 3–12.

TGT

TGT (Slavin, 1994) uses the same teacher presentations and teamwork as in STAD but replaces the quizzes with weekly tournaments. In these, students compete with members of other teams to contribute points to their team score. Students compete at three-person tournament tables against others with a similar past record in mathematics. Table assignments rotate to keep the competition fair. The winner at each tournament table brings the same number of points to his or her team, regardless of which table it is; this means that low achievers (competing with other low achievers) and high achievers (competing with other high achievers) have equal opportunity for success. As in STAD, high-performing teams earn certificates or other forms of team rewards. TGT is appropriate for the same types of objectives as STAD. Several studies of TGT have found positive effects on achievement in math, science, and language arts (Slavin, 1995).

TAI

TAI (Slavin, Leavey, & Madden, 1986) shares with STAD and TGT the use of four-member mixed-ability learning teams and certificates for high-performing teams. However, where STAD and TGT use a single pace of instruction for the class, TAI combines cooperative learning with individualized instruction. Also, where STAD and TGT apply to most subjects at grade levels, TAI is specifically designed to teach mathematics to students in grades 3–6 (or older students not ready for a full algebra course). Across five comparisons (two randomized) involving almost 3000 students, the sample-size-weighted effect size for TAI was +0.19.

CIRC

CIRC is a comprehensive program for teaching reading and writing in the upper elementary grades (Stevens et al., 1987). In CIRC, teachers use reading texts and reading groups, much as in traditional reading programs. However, all students are assigned to teams composed of two pairs from two different reading groups. While the teacher is working with one reading group, the paired students in the other groups are working on a series of cognitively engaging activities, including reading to one another, making predictions about how narrative stories will come out, summarizing stories to one another, writing responses to reading comprehension questions, and practicing spelling, decoding, and vocabulary. Students work as a whole team to master the main idea and other comprehension skills. During language arts periods, students engage in writing drafts, revising and editing one another's work, and preparing for publications of team books.

In most CIRC activities, students follow a sequence of teacher instruction, team practice, team pre-assessments, and quizzes. That is, students do not take the quiz until their teammates have determined that they are ready. Certificates are given to teams based on the average performance of all team members on all reading and writing activities.

Research on CIRC and similar approaches has found positive effects in upper-elementary and middle school reading (Stevens & Durkin, 1992; Stevens et al., 1987; Stevens & Slavin, 1995a, 1995b). CIRC has been adapted as the upper-elementary and middle school components of the Success for All comprehensive reform model and is currently disseminated under the name *Reading Wings* by the Success for All Foundation (see Slavin, Madden, Chambers, & Haxby, 2009).

Success for All

Success for All (SFA) makes extensive use of cooperative learning, but also adds additional elements to transform entire schools. It was designed and first implemented in 1987 in an attempt to serve very disadvantaged schools, in which it is not practically possible to serve all struggling readers one at a time. The program emerged from our team's research at Johns Hopkins University, and since 1996 has been developed and disseminated by a non-profit organization, the Success for All Foundation (SFAF). SFA was designed from the outset to provide research-proven instruction, curriculum, and school organization to schools serving many disadvantaged students.

Success for All: Theory of Action (Portions of This Section Are Adapted From Cheung, Xie, Zhang, Neitzel, and Slavin (in press).)

The theory of action for SFA assumes that students must start with success, whatever this takes, in the expectation that early success builds a solid base for later learning, positive expectations for future success, and motivation to achieve. However, success in the early grades is seen as necessary but not sufficient. Evidence on the difficulties of ensuring long-term maintenance of reading gains from highly successful first-grade tutoring programs demonstrates that ensuring early grade success in reading cannot be assumed to ensure lifelong reading success. The designers of SFA intended to build maintenance of first-grade effects by continuing high-quality instruction and classroom organization, with an emphasis on cooperative learning, after an intensive early primary experience sets students up for success. Beyond cooperative learning, reading, and tutoring, the design seeks to build on students' strengths by involving their parents, teaching social-emotional skills, and ensuring high attendance.

The logic of Success for All is much like that of response to intervention (Fuchs & Fuchs, 2006), now often called Multi-Tier Systems of Support (MTSS). That is, teachers receive extensive professional development and in-class coaching to help them use cooperative learning and other proven approaches to instruction. Students who do not succeed despite enhanced teaching may receive one-to-small group (e.g., one-to-four) or, if necessary, one-to-one tutoring. Ongoing assessment, recordkeeping, and flexible grouping are designed to ensure that students receive instruction and supportive services at their current instructional level, as they advance toward higher levels. Program components focus on parent involvement, classroom management, attendance, and social-emotional learning, to solve problems that may interfere with students' reading and broader school success. Each school has a full-time facilitator to help manage professional development and other program elements, some number of paraprofessional tutors, and coaches from the non-profit SFAF, who visit schools approximately once a month to review the quality of implementation, review data, and introduce additional components.

Program Components

Success for All is a whole-school model that addresses instruction, particularly in reading, as well as school-wide issues related to leadership, attendance, school climate, behavior management, parent involvement, and health (see Slavin et al., 2009, for more detail). The program provides specific teacher and student materials and professional development to facilitate use of proven practices in each program component.

Research on Success for All

Success for All has been in existence for 33 years and currently (2020) provides services to about 1000 schools in the United States. About half of these use the full program, and half use major components (most often, the K-2 reading program). The program has placed a strong emphasis on research and evaluation and has always carried out or encouraged experimental or quasi-experimental evaluations to learn how the program is working and what results it is achieving for which types of students and settings. Studies of Success for All have usually been done by third-party evaluators (i.e., researchers unrelated to the program developers). They have taken place in high-poverty schools and districts throughout the United States and in other countries.

A recent synthesis of research on Success for All by Cheung, Xie, Zhang, Neitzel, and Slavin (in press) includes every study of reading outcomes carried out in US schools that evaluated the program using methods that meet a set of rigorous inclusion standards. The meta-analysis found a sample-size-weighted mean effect size across 17 high-quality studies of +0.24 on independent measures. Effects were largest for low achievers (usually students in the lowest 25% of their classes at pretest). For these students, the mean effect size was +0.54. Long-term effects of SFA, reported by Borman and Hewes (2002), indicate that by eighth grade, students who had been in SFA elementary schools were still scoring significantly better than were control students and were significantly less likely to have ever been retained or assigned to special education.

Conclusion

Research on cooperative learning over a 50-year period has found that under a set of well-defined circumstances, students working in structured small groups can learn significantly better than can students working in traditional classrooms. Positive learning outcomes depend on the use of programs in which students work toward group rewards and are individually accountable for learning the content the group is engaged with. Outcomes are generally enhanced if students are taught specific ways of working in groups dealing with both metacognitive and social strategies for making best use of the group learning setting. Providing sufficient training and follow-up to ensure high-quality implementation is also essential.

Although important research continues to appear, the basic principles have been established for many years, and there are many pragmatic training programs available. The STL programs provide one well-researched set of practical programs. Yet cooperative learning remains an innovative approach familiar to most teachers but not used as a regular part of instruction. Most school principals can lead a visitor to a teacher enthusiastically using cooperative learning programs that are demonstrably working for the students, yet the visitor will note on the way to see that teacher the many fellow-teachers in the same school who are teaching students in rows, or using informal forms of group work without group goals or individual accountability, which research has rarely supported. Studies of actual use of cooperative learning (e.g., Antil, Jenkins, Wayne, & Vadasy, 1998) find that most use of cooperative learning is informal, and does not usually incorporate the elements that research has repeatedly found to be essential.

There remains a need for development and evaluation of cooperative learning programs that solve key problems of teaching and learning in all subjects and grade levels, and for continued research to identify the conditions under which cooperative learning is most likely to be effective. The greatest need at this point, however, is to develop and evaluate forms of cooperative learning that can be readily and successfully adopted by schools on a large scale, and to study the impediments to successful adoption of cooperative strategies. There is also a continued need to combine cooperative learning with other elements to create whole-school approaches capable of making a substantial long-term impact on the achievement of disadvantaged students, as has been achieved by Success for All. After 50 years of research and application, cooperative learning still has much more to contribute to students' learning.

References

Antil, L. R., Jenkins, J. R., Wayne, S., & Vadasy, P. F. (1998). Cooperative learning: Prevalence, conceptualizations, and the relation between research and practice. *American Educational Research Journal, 35*(3), 419–454.

Aronson, E., Blaney, N., Stephan, C., Sikes, J., & Snapp, M. (1978). *The Jigsaw classroom*. Beverly Hills, CA: Sage.

Barbato, R. (2000). *Policy implications of cooperative learning on the achievement and attitudes of secondary school mathematics students*. Unpublished Doctoral Dissertation, Fordham University.

Borman, G. D., & Hewes, G. M. (2002). The long-term effects and cost-effectiveness of success for all. *Educational Evaluation and Policy Analysis, 24*(4), 243–266.

Borman, G. D., Slavin, R. E., Cheung, A., Chamberlain, A., Madden, N. A., & Chambers, B. (2007). Final reading outcomes of the national randomized field trial of success for all. *American Educational Research Journal, 44*(3), 701–703.

Chambers, B., Cheung, A., & Slavin, R. (2016). Literacy and language outcomes of balanced and developmental-constructivist approaches to early childhood education: A systematic review. *Educational Research Review, 18*, 88–111.

Cheung, A., Xie, C., Zhang, T., Neitzel, A., & Slavin, R. E. (in press). Success for All: A quantitative synthesis of evaluations. *Journal of Research on Educational Effectiveness*.

Cohen, E. G. (1986). *Designing groupwork: Strategies for the heterogeneous classroom*. New York, NY: Teachers College Press.

Cohen, E. G. (1994). *Designing groupwork: Strategies for the heterogeneous classroom* (2nd ed.). New York, NY: Teachers College Press.

Coleman, J. S. (1961). *The adolescent society*. New York, NY: The Free Press of Glencoe.

Davidson, N. (Ed.). (1990). *Cooperative learning in mathematics; A handbook for teachers*. Menlo Park, CA: AddisonWesley.

DeVries, D. L., & Slavin, R. E. (1978). Teams-games-tournament: Review of ten classroom experiments. *Journal of Research and Development in Education, 12*, 28–38.

Fantuzzo, J. W., Polite, K., & Grayson, N. (1990). An evaluation of reciprocal peer tutoring across elementary school settings. *Journal of School Psychology, 28*(4), 309–323.

Fantuzzo, J. W., Riggio, R. E., Connelly, S., & Dimeff, L. A. (1989). Effects of reciprocal peer tutoring on academic achievement and psychological adjustment: A component analysis. *Journal of Educational Psychology, 81*(2), 173–177.

Fuchs, D., & Fuchs, L. (2006). Introduction to response to intervention: What, why, and how valid is it? *Reading Research Quarterly, 41*(1), 92–128.

Johnson, D. W., & Johnson, R. T. (1998). *Learning together and alone: Cooperative, competitive, and individualistic learning* (5th ed.). Boston, MA: Allyn & Bacon.

Madden, N. A., Slavin, R. E., Karweit, N. L., Dolan, L., & Wasik, B. (1993). Success for all: Longitudinal effects of a schoolwide elementary restructuring program. *American Educational Research Journal, 30*, 123–148.

Madden, N. A., Slavin, R. E., Logan, M., & Cheung, A. (2011). Effects of cooperative writing with embedded multimedia: A randomized experiment. *Effective Education, 3*(1), 1–9.

Mevarech, Z. R. (1985). The effects of cooperative mastery learning strategies on mathematics achievement. *Journal of Educational Research, 78*(6), 372–377.

Quint, J., Zhu, P., Balu, R., Rappaport, S., & DeLaurentis, M. (2014). *Scaling up the success for all model of school reform: Final report from the Investing in Innovation evaluation*. New York, NY: MDRC.

Reid, J. (1992). *The effects of cooperative learning with intergroup competition on the math achievement of seventh grade students* (ERIC Document Reproduction Service No. ED355106).

Rowan, B., Correnti, R., Miller, R., & Camburn, E. (2009). *School improvement by design: Lessons from a study of comprehensive school reform programs.* Ann Arbor, MI: University of Michigan, Consortium for Policy Research in Education.

Sharan, S., & Sharan, Y. (1992). *Expanding cooperative learning through group investigation.* New York: Teacher's College Press.

Slavin, R. E. (1977). Classroom reward structure: An analytic and practical review. *Review of Educational Research, 47*, 633–650.

Slavin, R. E. (1978). Student teams and achievement divisions. *Journal of Research and Development in Education, 12*, 39–49.

Slavin, R. E. (1980). Cooperative learning. *Review of Educational Research, 50*, 315–342.

Slavin, R. E. (1981). Cooperative learning: A research synthesis. *Educational Leadership, 38*, 655–660.

Slavin, R. E. (1983). When does cooperative learning increase student achievement? *Psychological Bulletin, 94*, 429–445.

Slavin, R. E. (1994). *Using student team learning* (2nd ed.). Baltimore, MD: Success for All Foundation.

Slavin, R. E. (1995). *Cooperative learning: Theory, research, and practice* (2nd ed.). Boston, MA: Allyn & Bacon.

Slavin, R. E. (2009). Cooperative learning. In G. McCulloch & D. Crook (Eds.), *International encyclopedia of education.* Abington: Routledge.

Slavin, R. E. (2014). Make cooperative learning powerful: Five essential strategies to make cooperative learning effective. *Educational Leadership, 72*(2), 22–26.

Slavin, R. E., & Karweit, N. (1984). Mastery learning and student teams: A factorial experiment in urban general mathematics classes. *American Educational Research Journal, 21*(4), 725–736.

Slavin, R. E., Leavey, M. B., & Madden, N. A. (1984). Combining cooperative learning and individualized instruction: Effects on student mathematics achievement, attitudes, and behaviors. *Elementary School Journal, 84*, 409–422.

Slavin, R. E., Leavey, M. B., & Madden, N. A. (1986). *Team accelerated instruction mathematics.* Watertown, MA: Mastery Education Corporation.

Slavin, R. E., Madden, N. A., Chambers, B., & Haxby, B. (Eds.). (2009). *Two million children: Success for all.* Thousand Oaks, CA: Corwin.

Stevens, R. J., & Durkin, S. (1992). *Using student team reading and student team writing in middle schools: Two evaluations.* Baltimore, MD: Johns Hopkins University, Center for Research on Effective Schooling for Disadvantaged Students. Report No. 36.

Stevens, R. J., Madden, N. A., Slavin, R. E., & Farnish, A. M. (1987). Cooperative integrated reading and composition: Two field experiments. *Reading Research Quarterly, 22*, 433–454.

Stevens, R. J., & Slavin, R. E. (1995a). The cooperative elementary school: Effects on student achievement and social relations. *American Educational Research Journal, 32*(2), 321–351.

Stevens, R. J., & Slavin, R. E. (1995b). Effects of a cooperative learning approach in reading and writing on handicapped and nonhandicapped students' achievement, attitudes, and metacognition in reading and writing. *Elementary School Journal*, 95(3), 241–262.

Webb, N. M. (1985). Student interaction and learning in small groups: A research summary. In R. Slavin, S. Sharan, S. Kagan, R. Hertz-Lazarowitz, C. Webb, & R. Schmuck (Eds.), *Learning to cooperate, cooperating to learn*. New York, NY: Plenum.

Webb, N. M. (2008). Learning in small groups. In T. L. Good (Ed.), *21st century education: A reference handbook* (pp. 203–211). Los Angeles, CA: Sage.

Chapter 7

The Jigsaw Classroom
A Personal Odyssey Into A Systemic National Problem

Elliot Aronson

My initial excitement about investigating the benefits of cooperative learning did not come primarily from intense interest in public education per se or from negative feelings about the dangers of competition in the classroom and in society at large. Although, as a university professor, I have always been excited about the process of education, my major motivation stems from my deep and abiding fascination with the social psychology of ethnic and racial prejudice. Prejudice is ubiquitous around the world. In our own country, it has existed at least since the Puritans emigrated from England in 1620 to escape intolerance and immediately began practicing intolerance against Native Americans and, eventually, against everybody else in sight. For me, however, the issue is more than historical—it is deeply personal, as well. Indeed, I have been profoundly curious about prejudice and its possible reduction for almost my entire life—or, at the very least, since I was nine years old.

I was born the year before Hitler came to power as Chancellor of Germany and grew up overhearing the adults in my extended family talking, in hushed tones, about the terrible atrocities being committed against our relatives in Europe. I was too young to fully understand the horror of what was happening. But I was old enough to understand the kinds of less drastic things that were happening to me on a daily basis.

We were the only Jewish family in a virulently anti-Semitic neighborhood in a rundown, blue-collar city just north east of Boston. My parents insisted that I go to Hebrew School—which I did, walking to and from the school, in a dilapidated old building located in a small Jewish enclave about a 35-minute walk from my house. I took that walk both ways and tolerated the two hours of boredom, in the classroom, between those two long walks—four days a week in the late afternoon and early evening. On the way home, I was often the target of gangs of Jew-hating teenagers—sometimes they merely yelled anti-Semitic things at me, sometimes they pushed me around, and occasionally they roughed me up. I kept trying to find different routes home in an attempt to avoid trouble. I wasn't often successful. One of my most vivid childhood memories involved one of those unsuccessful maneuvers, one dark, cold, winter evening when I was nine years old. I was waylaid and roughed up by four or five teenaged tough guys calling me a dirty Jew and telling me to go back where I came from. (I was never sure where that was!).

After this drubbing, I spent about a half hour, sitting on the curb, nursing a bloody nose and a split lip, feeling very sorry for myself—and wondering how it was that these kids could hate me so much when they didn't even know me. I wondered whether they had been born hating Jews or had learned it from their parents. I wondered whether, if these kids had gotten to know me better (and discovered what a sweet and harmless little boy I was), they would like me a little more. And if they had gotten to like me more, would they then begin to hate other Jews less? I didn't realize it then, of course, but these were profound social-psychological questions.

Ten years later, when I was a sophomore at Brandeis University, majoring in economics, I was having a cup of coffee with a fellow student—an attractive young woman for whom I was beginning to have romantic feelings. Suddenly, she looked at her watch and realized that she had to run off to class. Because it was a large lecture class, I decided to go along with her—hoping to sit next to her, in the back of the lecture hall and perhaps hold hands. (Those were innocent times!) The class was introductory psychology and the professor was some guy named Abraham Maslow. As luck would have it, the topic of Maslow's lecture that day was racial and ethnic prejudice. Halfway through the lecture, much to my astonishment, Maslow began to raise some of the very same questions I had raised when I was nine years old, sitting on that curb, feeling sorry for myself. Sitting there, in the back of the lecture hall, I became enthralled with the gradual realization that there was an entire scientific discipline aimed at exploring these questions. I let go of the young woman's hand and began taking notes. I lost the girl but gained a vocation. The very next day I switched my major from economics to psychology. Eventually, I began to work closely with Maslow. Maslow, the founding father of humanistic psychology, was a warm and exciting mentor who inspired me to believe that psychology could and should be used to improve the human condition. I decided that was what I wanted to do with my life.

In my senior year, Maslow told me that he thought I might have some talent and, with the appropriate training, I could become an effective college teacher—or, perhaps, even a psychotherapist—so he encouraged me to go to graduate school, which I did. After getting an MA at Wesleyan, I went on to Stanford and entered their Ph.D. program. As luck would have it, I entered Stanford the same year that Leon Festinger arrived as a distinguished young professor. Festinger was in the process of developing an intriguing new theory that he called "cognitive dissonance." In my first year at Stanford, I enrolled in Festinger's graduate seminar and quickly became enamored of his brilliance and of the exciting heuristic fertility of dissonance theory.

Festinger could not have been more different from Maslow. For one thing, he was tough and demanding—with little or no tolerance for laziness or stupidity on the part of his students. Moreover, he didn't give a fig about using psychology to improve the human condition. After we worked together for several months and began to develop something of a friendship, he asked me, over drinks one night, what first got me interested in psychology? When I mentioned that it was Abe Maslow who had inspired me, he laughed.

> Look, kid, Maslow may be, as you say, a helluva nice guy but he's a dreamer. No matter how noble his ideas or how good his intentions might be, they are worthless if he can't put them to the test empirically. Psychology is a science. You want to do good? You can try—if you really want to. But the truth is, you can't do anything important in this discipline—good, bad, or indifferent—without being able to do good research.

Festinger was interested in only one thing: to learn how the human mind works.

During my three years at Stanford, under Festinger's guidance, my fellow students and I discovered a lot of interesting new things about how the mind works—many of which flew in the face of the conventional wisdom and dominant theory, radical behaviorism, of the time. For example, we learned that if a person goes through a difficult, embarrassing initiation in order to get into a discussion group, she thinks more highly of that group, afterward, than if she had gone through a mild initiation to gain admission (Aronson & Mills, 1959). The explanation in terms of dissonance theory is simple: Working hard to get into a discussion group is dissonant with anything about that group that, objectively speaking, is boring, tedious, or unpleasant. So the people in the severe initiation condition downplayed anything that was negative about the group and, in their own minds, emphasized all the things that were positive. The people, who merely went through a mild initiation to gain admission, felt less dissonance and therefore had less of a need to see the group in a positive light. In a similar vein, we learned that if a person tells a lie for a small bribe, he comes to believe that lie to a greater extent than if he told the same lie for a large bribe (Festinger & Carlsmith, 1959; Festinger & Aronson, 1960). After getting my doctorate and leaving Stanford, in collaboration with students of my own, I learned that if you threaten young kids with a small punishment to keep them from playing with an attractive, forbidden toy they come to dislike that toy to a greater extent than if you threaten them with a severe punishment for playing with it

(Aronson & Carlsmith, 1963). Likewise, we learned that, if you hurt a person, you dislike him more as a consequence (Kahn, 1966); we also learned that, if you are induced to do someone a favor, it greatly increases your liking for the recipient (Jecker & Landy, 1969).

These findings challenged the dominant theories at the time and expanded our understanding of human cognition and motivation. This excited me a great deal. But, by far, the most valuable things I learned in graduate school were the importance of doing good experiments—and how to do them. Leon Festinger was a master craftsman who taught experimental methodology partly by his own brilliant example and partly by sharp, often harsh criticism. He was delighted whenever one of us came up with a creative solution to a knotty methodological problem that had seemed unsolvable and, on the other side of the continuum, he would not tolerate sloppiness or corner cutting of any kind. The joy of designing and conduction an elegant laboratory experiment may have been the single most valuable thing I have ever learned as a student of psychology. In the process of falling in love with the art of experimentation, I seem to have lost sight of the reason why I had gotten interested in psychology in the first place. That is, I lost sight of my youthful desire to do something to improve the human condition.

And then, an interesting thing happened. In 1971, when I was a professor at the University of Texas, at Austin, happily doing basic research on cognitive dissonance theory and interpersonal attraction, the Austin public schools were finally desegregated and all hell broke loose. African-American, Anglo, and Mexican-American youngsters were in open conflict; fistfights were breaking out among these groups in corridors and schoolyards. It was a full 17 years after the landmark Supreme Court decision, in *Oliver Brown* v. *the Board of Education of Topeka Kansas* was rendered, overturning the previous ruling (*Plessy* v. *Ferguson*, 1896). In Plessy, the court had ruled that segregation by race was legal as long as the educational facilities were equal. In 1954, the court, partly on the basis of social psychological evidence, ruled that segregation itself had a deleterious effect on black children by making them feel less worthy than their white counterparts. In the words of Chief Justice Earl Warren,

> To separate minority children from children of similar age and qualifications solely because of their race generates a feeling of inferiority as to their status in the community that may affect their hearts and minds in a way unlikely to ever be undone.

In short, what the Supreme Court ruled was that the notion of "separate but equal" is a logical impossibility because the mere fact that they are being segregated lowers the self-esteem of minority children and, thus, constitutes unequal treatment under the law.

In 1954, on the day of the Supreme Court decision, I was in my senior year at Brandeis and I have a vivid memory of the exhilaration that so many of us felt at the time. Abe Maslow was practically dancing around his office: "This is the beginning of the end of prejudice!" he exclaimed. The reasoning seemed self-evident: If segregation lowers self-esteem, then integration should raise it; once the self-esteem of minority children was raised, their academic achievement would improve. Moreover, given the assumption that prejudice is based largely on ignorance and negative stereotypes, bringing minority kids and white kids together should decrease their reciprocal animosity.

Unfortunately, it didn't take long before it became clear that desegregation was not going to be easy and was not automatically going to produce the hoped-for results. In most places, it was typically followed by turmoil in the community and hostility in the classroom. Moreover (and perhaps, more important), contrary to our optimistic expectations, systematic research showed that following desegregation, prejudice in the schools was actually increasing, and, in most desegregated schools, the self-esteem and performance of minority kids were declining even further. Austin was certainly not an outlier. The situation in Austin was typical, albeit more dramatic, of what was happening in schools across the country.

In the midst of this uproar, the assistant superintendent of schools (who was a former graduate student and colleague of mine) called me to ask if I had any idea about what could be done. He wanted an end to the violence; I wanted to know why desegregation was not producing the benefits we had anticipated. Our interests dovetailed, and I accepted his invitation—but only with the proviso that he would help me implement any reasonable changes that I might recommend.

I embarked on this project with no preconceived notions. The first step was to find out exactly what was going on in those classrooms. So, I recruited a half dozen of my graduate students and we fanned out to observe several elementary school classes—mostly fifth and sixth grades. My instructions to the graduate students (and to myself!) were simple enough.

> Be unobtrusive; just sit quietly in the back of the room. After a while, the kids will forget you are there. As you observe, take nothing for granted. Some things are so common that it is easy to miss their importance. A good way to avoid that mistake is to imagine that you are a visitor from Mars and have never been in a classroom before; you are observing everything these Earthlings do for the first time in your life. Write every observation down. Then, make a list of your observations and rank-order your list in terms of the frequency of each behavior you observed.

At the end of the day, when we reconvened and shared our observations, one thing leapt out at us, something that anyone who has ever attended traditional public schools takes for granted. The typical classroom is a highly competitive place in which students vie against one another for the attention and praise of the teacher. A very frequent observation: The teacher stands in front of the room and asks a question. Immediately 10 or 12 hands shoot up. Some of the kids actually leap out of their seats in an attempt to be the one called on. When the teacher calls on one of the children, an audible groan or sigh emanates from some of the other hand-raisers because it is apparent that they are disappointed at having missed an opportunity to show the teacher how smart they are. Meanwhile, the kids who don't know the answer are looking down, squirming in their seats—apparently afraid of making eye contact with the teacher.

In Austin, as in most communities, in this competition the minority kids were virtually guaranteed to lose. The previous law, "Separate but equal," had been separate, all right, but things never had been equal. In Austin, there was residential segregation, and the schools in the black and Latino neighborhoods were substandard; as a result, the reading skills of the minority kids were approximately one full grade level behind those of the Anglo kids. So when the teacher would call for the answer to a question, it was primarily the white kids who raised their hands, hoping to be called on, and primarily the minority kids who squirmed in their seats, trying to look invisible. The competitive structure of the classroom, coupled with the uneven playing field, seemed to confirm (and might have even magnified) the children's existing stereotypes of each other: The Anglo kids saw the minority kids as stupid and lazy; the minority kids saw the Anglo kids as arrogant and pushy. If someone had intentionally designed a classroom structure aimed at making desegregation fail, they could not have done a better job. But it was not intentional. That is simply the way the classroom was structured.

What to do? It took only a few days to come up with a workable strategy. It seemed to come from out of nowhere. I am tempted to say it simply popped into my head, but that would be erroneous. As a social psychologist, I had a lot of knowledge of previous research on human interaction—knowledge that I was not even aware that I had. To put it succinctly, I was standing on the shoulders of giants such as Gordon Allport (1954), Morton Deutsch (1961), and Muzafer Sherif, Harvey, White, Hood, and Sherif (1961). Building on this earlier thinking and research, our specific intervention was a relatively simple one, consisting of restructuring the dynamics of the classroom from competitive to cooperative. We invented a technique that created small interdependent groups, designed to place students of different racial and ethnic backgrounds in a situation where they needed to cooperate with one another in order to understand the material. We called it the jigsaw classroom, because the process was like assembling a jigsaw puzzle, with each student contributing a vital piece to the total picture. For example, if the topic was "The Life of Eleanor Roosevelt," each child in the small group was assigned a paragraph describing a phase of Mrs. Roosevelt's life: (a) her childhood, (b) her marriage to her cousin, Franklin, (c) her serving as First Lady, (d) her subsequent work at the United Nations, and so on. Each child's task was to study that paragraph on her own, and then rejoin the group and report its contents to the others. The only access each child had to all the paragraphs and information, therefore, was by paying close attention to what each of the other children in the group had to say. Immediately after the jigsaw session, the teacher gave a written exam on the entire life of Eleanor Roosevelt. It is important to note that each child had a vital piece of the puzzle that the group needed. Although the children learned together and shared their information cooperatively, each student took the exam individually, and earned his or her own individual score.

As my assistants and I were setting up this design, I worried about what would happen if one kid, perhaps one who couldn't read very well, really did screw up. Then everyone in his jigsaw group would hate him even more. I remembered my experiences as an ardent teenage baseball player when the least talented player, the one chosen last, would be put in deep right field. The poor kid stands there, hoping and praying that no one will hit the ball to him, and then bingo, with the bases loaded and two outs, he's sent an easy fly ball—and drops it. Every kid's nightmare! I immediately thought of a way of ensuring against such a calamity in our classroom: After the students read their own paragraph a few times and learned it pretty well, they would join an "expert" group. This expert group would consist of one member from each of the jigsaw groups, all of whom had been assigned the identical paragraph. They would then rehearse their selection together, allowing the slower students to get up to speed, before rejoining their original team. The expert group made it almost impossible for a child to screw up completely by dint of failing to understand the assignment. Of course, it didn't make each child's performance flawless, nor did it eradicate a child's nervousness, but it did protect every child from being a drag on his or her classmates.

And so we began our pilot study, comparing a fifth-grade classroom divided into jigsaw groups with a control classroom structured as usual. In the beginning, it did not go smoothly. It seems that old competitive habits do not die easily. During the first few days, the children simply repeated the strategies that had value when they were trying to outperform their rivals. But, gradually—sometimes painfully—they began to realize that their competitive behavior had become dysfunctional. Take the example of a Mexican-American boy, whom I will call Carlos. English was his second language and, although he was fluent, he spoke with an accent that often evoked taunting or derisive laughter among the Anglo kids. So he usually kept quiet in class. But when we introduced jigsaw, he could no longer avoid talking; he was required to present the paragraph he had learned.

When Carlos began to recite his piece of the puzzle (Eleanor Roosevelt's middle years), he had learned the paragraph well, but he was nervous and frequently stumbled and mumbled. Initially, some of the other children sighed audibly, or looked away; one called him stupid. In a competitive classroom, this kind of behavior might actually be functional for the individual in that it often succeeds in throwing one's opponent off balance. But in a jigsaw classroom, the kids soon understood that their disparaging remarks and gestures would keep them from learning the piece of the puzzle that Carlos, and only Carlos, knew and that he was struggling to give them—and would thus prevent them from getting a high grade on the exam. They had to learn to be patient, to listen carefully, and to prompt Carlos by asking the kinds of questions that would help him articulate the information he had in his head but was having trouble stating. After a few jigsaw sessions, we were gratified to see several children becoming pretty good interviewers—a bit like pint-sized Terri Grosses! In the process, they gradually learned that Carlos was a lot smarter, a lot nicer, and a lot more interesting than they had previously thought.

Within a week or two of instituting jigsaw, there was a discernible, positive change in the classroom atmosphere. Visiting teachers in specialties such as art and music were among the first to notice it; they would spontaneously ask the classroom teacher what it was that he or she had been doing differently. After six weeks, we documented the changes empirically. We asked the children to rate how much they liked their classmates—all of them, not just those in their jigsaw group. We also asked them how much they liked school, and we validated their responses against their attendance records.

The formal data confirmed our casual observations: Compared to students in traditional classrooms, students of all ethnicities liked school more (absenteeism significantly declined) and liked each other more—across and within ethnic and racial groups. For white students, self-esteem and test performance remained constant. But the minority students in jigsaw classrooms showed a significant increase in self-esteem and their test performance averaged nine percentage points higher than those of minority students in traditional classrooms. This difference was highly significant both statistically and meaningfully. A black sixth grader might be earning a score of 72 on an exam in a traditional classroom, but his counterpart in a jigsaw classroom would earn an 81.

The jigsaw method proved to be teacher-proof. In replicating this study, we used a stringent test and we stacked the cards against jigsaw: We assigned to the control condition those teachers whom their principals had designated as being the best in each of the schools. Thus, the improved performance of children in the jigsaw classrooms could not be attributed to superior teaching but only to the method itself. Over the next few years, as we continued to implement the jigsaw technique, the findings remained the same. Moreover, the schools that adopted this approach became more truly integrated. In observing kids in the schoolyards during recess, we paid close attention to who was hanging out with whom. Whenever they had free time, students in traditional schools were clustering in groups according to race or ethnicity. Students in jigsaw schools were more likely to mingle interracially (Aronson & Patnoe, 1997).

I was elated. At long last, I had produced a scientifically sound answer to the question I had asked myself when I was nine years old, sitting on that curbstone. My students and I had shown that prejudice *can* be overcome and that children of different ethnic backgrounds can learn to like one another. What it takes is not simply *increased* contact but the right *kind* of contact. As Gordon Allport had written in *The Nature of Prejudice* (1954), "While it may help somewhat to place members of different ethnic groups side by side on a job, the gain is greater if these members regard themselves as part of a team." Following up on Allport's suggestion, my students and colleagues have shown why this is true: Working together toward a common goal, giving and receiving favors from others mitigate against finding things to dislike in those teammates and increase one's tendency to emphasize whatever good qualities one's teammates might have (Jecker & Landy, 1969).

In order to further explore and refine how this happens, we brought jigsaw out of the classroom and into the laboratory as a way of determining the impact of jigsaw on the kind of attributions people make. That statement needs a little explanation. Basically, there are two kinds of attributions we make as a way of understanding another person's behavior and the motivation behind it. The attributions we make are either dispositional (an aspect of his personality) or situational (a function of the situation he is in). For example, suppose you are driving along and another driver suddenly swings out of his lane and cuts you off. How would you account for this behavior? Making a dispositional attribution, you might say, "what a reckless, inconsiderate jerk!" Making a situational attribution, you might say, "Oh, the poor guy might have been having a bad day, or he might have had a temporary lapse of attention." Basically, most of us give our friends the benefit of the doubt by making situational attributions of their failures or of their thoughtless behavior—and we tend to make dispositional attributions toward strangers or enemies for the same behavior. In a series of laboratory experiments, my students and I showed that following a jigsaw-like experience with strangers, participants tended to give them the benefit of the doubt by attributing their failure to situational causes. However, when they had been engaging in competitive games, they attributed the failure of a stranger to dispositional causes (Aronson, Presser, Stephan, & Kennedy, 1978; Stephan, Burnham, & Aronson, 1979).

In addition, the dynamics of working as a team encourages the development of other valuable skills. Several years after the Austin experiments, my students at UC Santa Cruz and I speculated that one of the major abilities nurtured and expanded by working in jigsaw groups is empathy: the ability to take the perspective of another person and experience something akin to what he or she may be experiencing. We reasoned that, in the competitive classroom, the primary goal is simply to show the teacher how smart you are. You don't have to pay much attention to the other students. But the jigsaw situation is different. In order to participate effectively in the jigsaw classroom, each student needs to pay close attention to whichever member of the group is reciting. In the process, the participants begin to learn that great results can accrue if each of their classmates is approached in a way that is tailored to fit his or her special needs. For example, Alice may learn that Carlos is a bit shy and needs to be prodded gently, while Phyllis is so talkative that she might need to be reigned in occasionally. Peter can be joked with, while Serena responds only to serious suggestions. In order to do well in learning the material, it is a great advantage to be able to put oneself squarely in the shoes of your teammates.

One of my students, Diane Bridgeman speculated that, if this analysis is sound, then it should follow that working in jigsaw groups would lead to the sharpening of a youngster's general empathic ability. To test this notion, Bridgeman (1981 conducted) a clever experiment with ten-year-old children. Prior to her experiment, half of the children had spent two months participating in jigsaw classes; the others spent that time in traditional classrooms. Bridgeman showed the children a series of cartoons aimed at testing a child's ability to empathize—to put themselves in the shoes of the cartoon characters. For example, in one cartoon, the first panel shows a little boy looking sad as he waves goodbye to his father at the airport. In the next panel, a letter carrier delivers a package to the boy. In the third panel, the boy opens the package, finds a toy airplane inside, and bursts into tears. Bridgeman asked the children why they thought the little boy burst into tears at the sight of the airplane. Nearly all of the children could answer correctly—because the toy airplane reminded him of how much he missed his father. Then Bridgeman asked the crucial question: "What did the letter carrier think when he saw the boy open the package and start to cry?"

Most children of this age make a consistent error; they assume that everyone knows what they know. Thus, the youngsters in the control group thought that the *letter carrier* would know the boy was sad because the gift reminded him of his father leaving. But the children who had participated in the jigsaw classroom responded differently. Because of their experience with jigsaw they had developed the ability to take the perspective of the letter carrier; they realized that, not having witnessed the farewell scene at the airport he would be confused at seeing the boy cry over receiving a nice present. In the context of the cartoon letter-carrier, this may sound trivial. But the fact that the children, who learned to work cooperatively, developed the ability to put themselves in another person's shoes is a crucial precursor to compassion and prejudice reduction. From a scientific perspective, it helps me understand the dynamics underlying the success of jigsaw and, by extension, of all cooperative learning strategies.

In the 1970s, my students and I published our results in several peer-reviewed scientific journals, but I wanted our technique to be known not just to other psychologists but also to the general public, especially teachers and parents. So, once we were certain that our findings were robust—that is, after we had replicated our experiment in several classrooms in Austin, I wrote up our findings in a non-technical way and submitted the article to the popular magazine *Psychology Today* (Aronson, Blaney, Sikes, Stephan, & Snapp, 1975), where it was featured prominently, complete with full-color photos. I made a few hundred copies, sent them to school superintendents all over the country, and offered to train teachers free of charge. Then I sat back and waited for the requests to come pouring in.

How naïve! You can't give something away if nobody wants it and, at the outset, not many wanted it. When I followed up with phone calls, most of the superintendents and principals explained that they were doing just fine and didn't need an outsider to come into their schools and set up some new method. One of them was unusually candid. "Do you know what would happen if we instituted your technique?" he said. "My phone would be ringing off the hook with complaints from parents. 'Do you mean to tell me that some black kid is teaching my child? What are we paying the teachers for?'" It dawned on me that I had been invited to intervene in Austin primarily because the schools were in crisis. What I concluded at that moment was that, in most school systems that I had contacted, anything short of a crisis was characterized as "doing just fine."

I found this both disillusioning and heartbreaking. This was in sharp contrast with my feelings of elation as a scientist. The invention of the jigsaw classroom was one of the most exciting events of my professional life. Not only did our experiments demonstrate that, by changing the structure of the classroom from competitive to cooperative, desegregation could work the way so-called dreamers like Abraham Maslow hoped it would, but it also helped advance our knowledge and understanding of the psychology of human interaction. In one experiment after another, my students and I had shown over and over again that jigsaw was an effective, simple way to reduce prejudice and bullying, improve performance, and raise the self-esteem of minority students (e.g., Aronson, Bridgeman, & Geffner, 1978; Aronson, Lucker, Rosenfield, & Sikes, 1976; Aronson & Gonzalez, 1988; Aronson & Patnoe, 1997). We also succeeded in increasing children's liking for school and their ability to empathize with their classmates (Aronson & Bridgeman, 1979; Bridgeman, 1981). Moreover, on a highly personal level, it enabled me to broker a marriage between my two mentors—the humanistic idealist, Abraham Maslow, and the tough-minded, no-nonsense experimental scientist, Leon Festinger.

In sum, during the 1970s, the scientist in me was excited while the change agent in me felt like a total failure because of my inability to convince more than a few dozen school administrators to adopt jigsaw. Looking back on that decade through the lens of old age (and its alleged wisdom!), I have come to believe that I may have been far too impatient. It now seems clear to me that novel ideas often need time to marinate. And these ideas usually need a little luck as well. One unexpected piece of good luck came about in 1984 when, in commemoration of the 30th anniversary of the Supreme Court decision in *Brown* v. *Board of Education*, the United States Civil Rights Commission named Austin as a model city in which school desegregation had taken place in a relatively orderly manner and that the effects on the students were positive. They gave much of the credit to the jigsaw classroom. Another important event took place several years later, when, with the advent and burgeoning of the Internet, the Social Psychology Network (SPN) established a website for jigsaw,[1] from which teachers could download a wealth of material free of charge. To my immense gratification, the website quickly became one of the two or three most popular in the network. The jigsaw website contains a bibliography of the significant research on jigsaw, several curricula developed and submitted by classroom teachers as well as some of the basic material I had been presenting to interested teachers in workshops that I had been conducting around the country. For example, one component of these workshops is a guide for teachers called *Jigsaw in 10 easy steps*:

1. Divide students into four-, five-, or six-person jigsaw groups. Each group should be as diverse (in terms of ability, gender and race), as possible. The number of students in a group depends, in large part, on the nature of the material. We have found that groups consisting of fewer than four or greater than six are less effective.
2. Appoint one student from each group as the leader. Initially, the leader in each group should be the most mature or most respected student in that group. The leader's role is to keep the group on task and to help the recitations flow in an orderly fashion. After several

sessions, it might be useful to give each student an opportunity to be the leader.
3. Divide the day's lesson into four, five, or six segments—depending on the nature of the material. Each segment should be of equal or near equal length.
4. Assign each student to learn one segment.
5. Give students time to read over their segment and become familiar with it.
6. Form temporary "expert groups" by having one student from each jigsaw group join other students assigned the same segment. Allow students in these expert groups sufficient time to discuss the main points of their segment, to discuss strategies of how best to present the material, and to rehearse the presentations they will make to their jigsaw group. Again, it is important that the expert group be small enough to be effective. If there are eight or more students in an expert group, it would be best to divide the group in half.
7. Bring the students back into their jigsaw groups.
8. Ask each student to present her or his segment to the group.
9. Float from group to group, observing the process—intervening if necessary. As soon as it is feasible, it is best to intervene by whispering your intervention to the leader so that he can assert his authority. After a few sessions, you can begin to coach the group leader to intervene on her own.
10. At the end of each session, administer a brief quiz on the material. Students will quickly come to realize that these sessions are more than just fun and games but really count. This will accelerate their becoming adept at reciting, listening, and asking helpful questions.

Taken together, these two events, the recognition of jigsaw by the Civil Rights Commission and the Website provided by SPN, produced a dramatic increase in the popularity of the jigsaw method. It is now being used in thousands of classrooms in North America, and based on the encouraging mail I have been receiving from teachers around the world, and the requests to translate my books on the method (*The Jigsaw Classroom and Nobody Left to Hate*), jigsaw has gained considerable popularity in Europe and Asia as well. Also, I was pleased to see that a great many researchers, most of whom were not former graduate students of mine, have replicated and extended our own research findings (see, e.g., Nolan, Hanley, DiVietri, Harvey, 2018; Perkins & Saris, 2001; Singh, 1991; Van Ryzin & Roseth, 2018; Wallace, 1995; West & Lepper, 1991; Williams, 2004).

Interestingly (and perhaps, ironically), the fact that the jigsaw method had begun to flourish—in classrooms, from elementary schools to college campuses—as well as in research projects being conducted by a great many competent professionals, gave me permission, in effect, to turn the major focus of my own research elsewhere. And, so, my personal odyssey continues. As I mentioned at the beginning of this chapter, my initial interest in cooperative learning did not arise primarily from my role as an educator and possible change agent but as a mainstream social psychologist trying to learn something about how prejudice might be reduced and, more generally, about how the human mind works. Consequently, once it became apparent that jigsaw could be effective, and once my students and I had begun to uncover some of the underlying psychological causes of its effectiveness, I thought it might be time to step aside and become a cheerleader for the new wave of educational researchers who had picked up the baton. As a research-oriented social psychologist, I was eager to move on to new areas of research.

But where did I move? Well, as it turns out, the students and teachers were not the only beneficiaries of the jigsaw method. The years I spent designing and conducting jigsaw experiments had a profound impact on the content and direction of my scientific research. I now wanted to perform experiments that were not aimed exclusively at advancing theory and enhancing our understanding—what is commonly referred to as "basic research." I also was disinclined to perform experiments that were dealing solely with the solution of a practical problem, commonly known as applied research. My aim as a scientist became, whenever possible, to combine those two goals: to do experiments that would simultaneously advance theory (i.e. reveal something new about how the mind works), while, at the same time, being useful to society.

In sum, because, the jigsaw experiments convinced me that it was possible to influence individuals to change their own dysfunctional behavior—like those associated with prejudice and racism—I started looking around for other dysfunctional behavior. I didn't have to look far. At the time, we were in the midst of the AIDS epidemic without a vaccine or other medical solution in sight. But, because most infections were being spread by sexual contact and because condoms were a nearly perfect protection against AIDS and other sexually transmitted diseases, all we needed to do was convince sexually active people to use condoms regularly. Government agencies were spending millions of dollars on print and media advertising to try to convince people to practice safer sex. But it was becoming clear that these traditional communication strategies could only take us so far. For example, on most college campuses, the percentage of sexually active undergraduates regularly using condoms was small—hovering around 17%. After several false starts, my graduate students and I devised a strategy that tripled the percentage of sexually active students who used condoms every time they made love. This strategy is described thoroughly elsewhere (Aronson, Fried, & Stone, 1991; Stone, Aronson, Crain, Winslow, & Fried, 1994). Briefly, we hit upon an idea that eventually led us to invent a new paradigm for cognitive dissonance theory that sharpened our understanding of human cognition and motivation. We called it the hypocrisy paradigm. It is based on the assumption that virtually all people are highly motivated to see themselves as having integrity. As such, they will go to great lengths to avoid behaving hypocritically if at all possible. In our experiments, we induced sexually active college students to star in a video in which they composed and recited a communication aimed at convincing younger, less experienced teenagers to use condoms when having sex. We then confronted the participants with their own hypocrisy—that is, with the undeniable fact that they were not practicing what they were preaching to others. As mentioned earlier, the results were remarkable. Subsequently, we succeeded in applying that paradigm to a variety of societal problems like the conservation of energy (Stern & Aronson, 1994) and the conservation of water during a drought (Dickerson, Aronson, Thibodeau, & Miller, 1992). The results of these experiments were equally powerful.

It should be clear that, as a scientist, having moved on to other areas of research does not in any way imply that I had lost interest in jigsaw. Far from it. The personal gratification I experienced as a direct result of that invention continues to delight and inspire me—partly, as mentioned earlier, by seeing other researchers continue to explore the ramifications of jigsaw, and partly in the form of letters I receive from teachers and students who have benefitted from using that strategy. I would like to end this chapter by sharing one of these letters—one that I received some four decades ago and continues to touch me deeply.

Dear Professor Aronson:

I am a senior at the University of Texas. Today I got a letter admitting me to the Harvard Law School. This may not seem odd to you, but let me tell you something. I am the 6th of 7 children my parents had—and I am the only one who ever went to college, let alone graduate, or go to law school.

By now, you are probably wondering why this stranger is writing to you and bragging to you about his achievements. Actually, I'm not a stranger although we never met. You see, last year I was taking a course in social psychology and we were using a book you wrote, *The Social Animal*, and when I read about prejudice and jigsaw it all sounded very familiar—and then, I realized that I was in that very first class you ever did jigsaw in—when I was in the 5th grade. And as I read on, it dawned on me that I was the boy that you called Carlos. And then I remembered you when you first came to our classroom and how I was scared and how I hated school and how I was so stupid and didn't know anything. And you came in—it all came back to me when I read your book—you were very tall—about

6 1/2 feet—and you had a big black beard and you were funny and made us all laugh. And, most important, when we started to do work in jigsaw groups, I began to realize that I wasn't really that stupid. And the kids I thought were cruel and hostile became my friends and the teacher acted friendly and nice to me and I actually began to love school, and I began to love to learn things and now I'm about to go to Harvard Law School.

You must get a lot of letters like this but I decided to write anyway because let me tell you something. My mother tells me that when I was born I almost died. I was born at home and the cord was wrapped around my neck and the midwife gave me mouth to mouth and saved my life. If she was still alive, I would write to her too, to tell her that I grew up smart and good and I'm going to law school. But she died a few years ago. I'm writing to you because, no less than her, you saved my life too.

Sincerely,
"Carlos"

Note

1. www.jigsaw.org.

References

Aronson, E. (2000). *Nobody left to hate: Teaching compassion after Columbine.* New York, NY: Worth/Freeman.

Aronson, E., Blaney, N., Sikes, J., Stephan, C., & Snapp, M. (1975). The jigsaw route to learning and liking. *Psychology Today, February, 8*, 43–50.

Aronson, E., & Bridgeman, D. (1979). Jigsaw groups and the desegregated classroom: In pursuit of common goals. *Personality and Social Psychology Bulletin, 5*, 438–446.

Aronson, E., Bridgeman, D., & Geffner, R. (1978). Interdependent interactions and prosocial behavior. *Journal of Research and Development in Education, 12*, 16–27.

Aronson, E., & Carlsmith, J. M. (1963). Effect of severity of threat in the devaluation of forbidden behavior. *Journal of Abnormal and Social Psychology, 66*, 584–588.

Aronson, E., Fried, C., & Stone, J. (1991). Overcoming denial and increasing the intention to use condoms through the induction of hypocrisy. *American Journal of Public Health, 81*, 1636–1638.

Aronson, E., & Gonzalez, A. (1988). Desegregation, jigsaw and the Mexican-American experience. In P. Katz & D. Taylor (Eds.), *Eliminating racism.* New York, NY: Plenum.

Aronson, E., & Mills, J. S. (1959). The effect of severity of initiation on liking for a group. *Journal of Abnormal and Social Psychology, 59*, 177–181.

Aronson, E., & Patnoe, S. (1997). *Cooperation in the classroom: The jigsaw method.* New York, NY: Longman.

Aronson, E., Presser, N., Stephan, C., & Kennedy, J. (1978). Attributions to success and failure in cooperative, competitive and interdependent interaction y), *European Journal of Social Psychology, 8,* 269–274.

Aronson, E., Stephan, C., Sikes, J., Blaney, N., & Snapp, M. (1978). *The jigsaw classroom.* Beverly Hills, CA: Sage.

Bridgeman, D. L. (1981). Enhanced role taking through cooperative interdependence: A field study. *Child Development, 52,* 1231–1238.

Deutsch, M., & Collins, M. E. (1951). *Interracial housing: A psychological evaluation of a social experiment.* Minneapolis, MN: University of Minnesota Press.

Dickerson, C., Thibodeau, R., Aronson, E., & Miller, D. (1992). Using cognitive dissonance to encourage water conservation. *Journal of Applied Social Psychology, 22,* 841–854.

Festinger, L., & Aronson, E. (1960). The arousal and reduction of dissonance in social contexts. In D. Cartwright & A. Zander (Eds.), *Group dynamics* (pp. 214–231). Evanston, IL: Row & Peterson.

Festinger, L., & Carlsmith, J. M. (1959). Cognitive consequences of forced compliance. *Journal of Abnormal and Social Psychology, 58,* 203–211.

Jecker, J., & Landy, D. (1969). Liking a person as a function of doing him a favor. *Human Relations, 22,* 371–378.

Kahn, M. (1966). The physiology of catharsis. *Journal of Personality and Social Psychology, 3,* 278–298.

Nolan, J., Hanley, B., DiVietri, T., & Harvey, N. (2018). She who teachers learns: Performance benefits, of a jigsaw activity in a college classroom. *Scholarship of Teaching and Learning in Psychology, 4,* 93–104.

Perkins, D. V., & Saris, R. N. (2001). A "jigsaw classroom" technique for undergraduate statistics courses. *Teaching of Psychology, 28,* 111–113.

Sherif, M., Harvey, O. J., White, J., Hood, W., & Sherif, C. W. (1961). *Intergroup conflict and cooperation: The robber's cave experiment.* Norman, OK: Institute of Intergroup Relations, University of Oklahoma.

Singh, B. R. (1991). Teaching methods for reducing prejudice and enhancing academic achievement for all children. *Educational Studies, 17,* 157–171.

Stephan, C. M., Burnham, A., & Aronson, E. (1979). Attributions for success and failure after cooperation, competition, or team competition. *European Journal of Social Psychology, 9*(1), 109–114.

Stern, P. C., & Aronson, E. (1994). *Energy use: The human dimension.* New York, NY: W. H. Freeman.

Stone, J., Aronson, E., Crain, A. L., Winslow, M. P., & Fried, C. (1994). Inducing hypocrisy as a means of encouraging young adults to use condoms. *Personality and Social Psychology Bulletin, 20,* 116–128.

Van Ryzin, M., & Roseth, C. (2018). Cooperation in middle school. A means to improve peer relations in middle school and reduce victimization, bullying, and related outcomes. *Journal of. Educational Psychology, 110,* 1192–1201.

Walker, I., & Crogan, M. (1998). Academic performance, prejudice, and the jigsaw classroom: New pieces to the puzzle. *Journal of Community and Applied Social Psychology, 8,* 381–393.

Wallace, J. (1995). Cooperative learning in college classrooms: Getting started. *College Student Journal, 29,* 458–459.

West, S. C., & Lepper, M. R. (1991). Effects of structured cooperative contact on changing negative attitudes towards stigmatized social groups. *Journal of Personality and Social Psychology, 60,* 531–544.

Williams, D. (2004). Improving race relations in higher education: The jigsaw classroom as a missing piece to the puzzle. *Urban Education, 39,* 316–344.

Some Additional References to Jigsaw

Aronson, E. (1990). Applying social psychology to desegregation and energy conservation. *Personality & Social Psychology Bulletin, 16,* 118–132.

Aronson, E. (1991). How to change behavior. In R. Curtis & G. Stricker (Eds.), *How people change: Inside and outside therapy.* New York, NY: Plenum.

Aronson, E. (2000, May/June). Nobody left to hate: Developing the empathic schoolroom. *The Humanist, 60,* 17–21.

Aronson, E., Blaney, N. T., Stephan, C., Rosenfield, R., & Sikes, J. (1977). Interdependence in the classroom: A field study. *Journal of Educational Psychology, 69,* 121–128.

Aronson, E., Bridgeman, D., & Geffner, R. (1978). Interdependent interactions and prosocial behavior. *Journal of Research and Development in Education, 12,* 16–27.

Aronson, E., Bridgeman, D., & Geffner, R. (1979). The effects of cooperative classroom structure on student behavior and attitudes. In D. Bar Tal & L. Saxe (Eds.), *Social psychology of education.* Washington, DC: Hemisphere.

Aronson, E., & Goode, E. (1980). Training teachers to implement jigsaw learning: A manual for teachers. In S. Sharan, P. Hare, C. Webb, & R. Hertz-Lazarowitz (Eds.), *Cooperation in education* (pp. 47–81). Provo, UT: Brigham Young University Press.

Aronson, E., & Osherow, N. (1980). Cooperation, prosocial behavior, and academic performance: Experiments in the desegregated classroom. *Applied Social Psychology Annual, 1,* 163–196.

Aronson, E., & Thibodeau, R. (1992). The jigsaw classroom: A cooperative strategy for reducing prejudice. In J. Lynch, C. Modgil, & S. Modgil (Eds.), *Cultural diversity in the schools.* London: Falmer Press.

Aronson, E., & Yates, S. (1983). Cooperation in the classroom: The impact of the jigsaw method on inter-ethnic relations, classroom performance and self-esteem. In H. Blumberg & P. Hare (Eds.), *Small groups.* London: John Wiley & Sons.

Battle, J. (1981). Enhancing self-esteem: A new challenge to teachers. *Academic Therapy, 16,* 541–552.

Carroll, D. W. (1986). Use of the jigsaw technique in laboratory and discussion classes. *Teaching of Psychology, 13,* 208–210.

Desforges, D. M., Lord, C. G., Ramsey, S. L., Mason, J. A., Van Leeuwen, M. D., Dori, Y. J., & Herscovitz, O. (1999). Question-posing capability as an alternative evaluation method: Analysis of an environmental case study. *Journal of Research in Science Teaching, 36,* 411–430.

Lucker, W., Rosenfield, D., Sikes, J., & Aronson, E. (1977). Performance in the interdependent classroom: A field study. *American Educational Research Journal, 13,* 115–123.

Maring, G. H., Furman, G. C., & Blum-Anderson, J. (1985). Five cooperative learning strategies for mainstreamed youngsters in content area classrooms. *Reading Teacher, 39,* 310–313.

McManus, M. M., & Aiken, R. M. (1995). Monitoring computer-based collaborative problem solving. *Journal of Artificial Intelligence in Education, 6,* 307–336.

Purdom, D. M., & Kromrey, J. D. (1995). Adapting to cooperative learning strategies to fit college students. *College Student Journal, 29,* 57–64.

Wolfe, C. T., & Spencer, S. J. (1996). Stereotypes and prejudice: Their overt and subtle influence in the classroom. *American Behavioral Scientist, 40,* 176–185.

Chapter 8

Design for Change
A Teacher Education Project for Cooperative Learning and Group Investigation in Israel

Yael Sharan and Shlomo Sharan

> I cannot say whether things will get better if we change; what I can say is they must change if they are to get better.
> —Georg C. Lichtenberg, 18th-century experimental physicist

Introduction

Lichtenberg, quoted here, was one of many scientists, artists, and thinkers who, before and after their time, changed the status quo in their fields. They changed the way we think, act, create, and invent, and contributed to continuous progress. In contrast, until the second half of the 20th century, teaching methods had by and large remained constant. Despite sporadic efforts, the traditional format of one teacher standing in front of a class and lecturing to a roomful of passive students remained unchanged. For decades attempts to change the long-standing educational paradigm did not succeed in overcoming resistance to fundamental innovations.

A sweeping movement to break the mold and actively engage students of all ages in learning emerged in the 1960s and 1970s (see, e.g., the Schools Council Environmental Studies Projects, 1972). Many educational researchers and educational psychologists, some of whom are represented in this volume, perceived that a change was crucially needed. They came from different theoretical and cultural backgrounds and developed a variety of interactive methods and models, many of which were eventually grouped under the "umbrella" term "cooperative learning" (CL). Their efforts heralded a fundamental change in educational practice that has since spread worldwide.

The authors were exposed to the first stages of this dramatic change in education during a two-year stay in California, from 1971 to 1973. We had a chance to visit many different experimental schools, where teachers sought various ways to engage children in learning. These attempts resonated with the first author, whose first teaching post, in the late 1950s, was in a border village in Israel. Her students were children of immigrants from Iran, Kurdistan and Egypt, who did not relate to the prescribed curriculum or to the frontal style of teaching. Clearly, it was not possible to continue the traditional one-way communication from teacher to students by being a "banker," to borrow Paolo Freire's term (1970, p. 72), who deposits knowledge without taking time to explore the students' minds and lives; teaching had to bridge the gap between the students' worlds and the curriculum. That was the turning point in her teaching. The experimental atmosphere in California at the time offered many alternative examples of ways to bridge that gap.

Shlomo Sharan's earlier immersion in college in Dewey's philosophy had laid the foundation for his acceptance of the changes we witnessed. When he taught at the School of Education at Tel Aviv University, he realized the need for a book for Israeli teachers about the new methods we had witnessed in California. The book *Small Group Teaching* (1975/1976) written by both authors described various ways of engaging students in interactive groups (the term "cooperative learning" had not yet been coined).

In 1975 we learned that word of the development of multiple research-based interactive methods and models had encouraged a few courageous Israeli school supervisors to introduce them in their districts. They realized that these new methods and models of teaching created a need for a new approach to teacher education, one that would take into account the challenges these procedures presented to teachers and principals. At the time, the majority of Israel's teachers were wedded to the traditional transmission model of teaching that calls for imparting prescribed facts and ideas. Even schools in *kibbutzim*, which had originally pioneered new ways of teaching (mainly by the project method), had gradually conformed to the traditional transmission model. Clearly, teacher education for interactive methods, by now called cooperative learning, required drastic changes in teachers' instructional behavior, attitudes, and perceptions of teaching. Adopting CL called for teachers to move to the transaction model, which invites students to actively participate in the learning process, and, even beyond, to the transformation model, which enables learners to contribute to the formation of knowledge (Brody, 1998).

Typically, in the prevailing model of teachers' professional development at the time, one or two teachers from a school would attend a short-term course, generally with random colleagues from other schools. Participating teachers had little in common with one another beyond subject matter or grade level. Teachers would return to their schools and report on what they had learned, but they could not count on their colleagues' full acceptance of new ideas or mutual support for their implementation. It was the rare teacher who implemented new ideas on her own despite finding herself isolated among her colleagues. Teachers' professional development in Israel remained largely untouched by the growing discipline of planned change in schools and the developing strategies for collaborative whole-school cultures (see, e.g., Fullan, 1982/2015).

Shlomo Sharan was approached by one district supervisor to lead a professional development project that would introduce CL methods to three elementary schools in a low socioeconomic neighborhood. He initiated a project for teacher education for CL and Group Investigation (GI) that involved a team of researchers and teacher educators (including the first author). The project was based on several existing theories as well as on contemporary attempts to effect change in teaching and in teacher education. GI, for one, was based on Dewey's view of learning as the conduct of inquiry in a social context, as shaped by Thelen (Dewey, 1943; Thelen, 1972, 1981). Sharan incorporated Kurt Lewin's theory of, and method for, the effective management of groups (Lewin, 1948; Sharan, S., Sharan, Y., & Tan, I., 2013; Sharan, Y. & Sharan, S., 1992). The teacher education team relied on many of the activities for effective group management presented by Richard Schmuck and Patricia Schmuck (1971/2001).

A key element of the rationale for the teacher education project was the combination of Dewey's and Lewin's theories with the principles of constructivist psychology: Knowledge is conceived as what learners construct out of elements of information, feelings, and experience, not as something that simply exists in chunks in the external world to be swallowed whole (Sigel & Cocking, 1977). Members of the project teams firmly believed that merely presenting information to students, or asking them to read a passage in a book, would not transform information into knowledge.

A powerful inspiration for the team of teacher educators was the pioneering action research study carried out in the late 1940s by Alice Miel (1952) with her associates at Teachers College. They observed how over 75 teachers, in various elementary schools throughout the United States, implemented cooperative procedures. Observers meticulously recorded teachers' and pupils' actions and reactions, as well as the follow-up discussions with the teachers and pupils. The result was a wealth of information about how pupils and teachers cooperatively planned, executed, and evaluated a wide variety of projects. Some were as short as naming a goldfish; others involved the full investigation of a unit of study. Through the recorded discussions we could "see" and "hear" how teachers and pupils had acquired the skills and attitudes that created interactive classrooms.

Group Investigation

As part of the "umbrella" of CL procedures, GI incorporates the essential principle of positive interdependence, conceptualized by Deutsch (1949, 1973) and thoroughly developed and researched by Johnson D. and Johnson R. (see, e.g., Johnson, Johnson, & Holubec, 1998). Although CL methods and models vary in their goals and emphasize different skills, they all structure group members' interaction so that each member's efforts are required and indispensable for reaching the group's goal. A firm base in fundamental cooperative social and learning behaviors is an essential prerequisite for carrying out a GI project. CL social and learning skills were developed at the initial stages of the teacher training project and refreshed throughout, whenever necessary, to ensure an effective investigation.

As a CL model GI integrates interaction and communication among learners with the process of academic inquiry. In the course of a GI project learners take an active part in the investigation of a multifaceted problem that is, generally, part of the curriculum. The classroom becomes a social system built on cooperation in learning *within* groups and on coordination of learning *among* groups. Organizing learning in this way creates conditions that allow students, in collaboration with their classmates, to identify questions for inquiry, plan together the procedures needed to understand and research these questions, collect relevant information, and cooperatively (though not necessarily *collectively*) prepare a presentation of the results of their investigation, usually in some creative and interesting way (Sharan, S. et al., 2013; Sharan, Y. & Sharan, S., 1994/1999). These interactions are part and parcel of the six stages of GI, as shown in Table 8.1.

Table 8.1 Stages of group investigation

Stages of GI	Teacher's Role	Students' Role
I. Class determines sub-topics and organizes research groups	Leads exploratory discussions to choose sub-topics; facilitates organization of research	Generate questions of interest; sort them into categories; join a research group
II. Groups plan their investigation: what they will study; how they will carry out their investigation	Helps groups formulate their plan; helps maintain cooperative norms; helps find resources	Plan what to study; choose resources; assign roles and divide study tasks
III. Groups carry out their plans	Helps with study skills; continues to help maintain cooperative norms	Seek answers to their questions; locate information; integrate, summarize findings
IV. Groups plan their presentations	Organizes plans for presentations; coordinates plans with steering committee	Determine main ideas; plan how to present them and involve all groupmates
V. Groups present their findings	Coordinates presentations; facilitates feedback	Present their findings; class gives feedback
VI. Teacher and students evaluate individuals, groups, and class	Evaluates learning of new information, higher level thinking, and cooperative behavior; facilitates reflection	Reflect on learning as investigators and on group processes

GI is not an exclusive model, and at different stages of the investigation teachers may incorporate other CL procedures, as demonstrated in the examples of GI projects in Sharan, Y. (1995, 1998) and Sharan, Y. and Sharan, S. (1992). There is even room for direct instruction, as, for example, when all groups have the same difficulty in organizing their information, or when it is helpful to teach the whole class some basic facts about the general topic to facilitate their understanding of the kind of information they need to collect and how to make sense of it.

While there is no one way to teach teachers how to implement CL and GI, there is widespread consensus that experiential learning is an essential feature of any teacher education program for CL and GI (Brody & Davidson, 1998). The necessary change in teachers' perception of their role in CL cannot take root by learning *about* any CL method or model. Successful change programs combine experiential learning with the development of specific instructional skills, and coordination between the training workshops and classroom application (Cohen, E. G., Brody, C., & Sapon-Shevin, M., 2004; Sharan, Y., 2002).

The focus of this chapter is twofold: the design of the teacher education project for CL and GI, and the main research results of the project.

Experiential Workshops for Prospective Teachers of CL and GI

A marked innovation of the teacher education project was its duration; for 18 months the team of teacher educators planned and conducted 40 hours of experiential workshops with 50 elementary school teachers from three schools. Team members also observed teachers in their classrooms, met with them individually, and, when needed, demonstrated CL and GI procedures in classrooms (Hertz-Lazarowitz & Calderon, 1994/1999; Sharan, S., 1994/1999; Sharan, S. & Hertz-Lazarowitz, 1982; Sharan, Y., 2012a; Sharan, Y. & Sharan, S., 1987).

When the Israel Educational Television heard of the new trend in teacher education, they initiated the production of a series of 20 closed-circuit telecasts of real-time CL and GI activities in real classrooms, which were used in the training workshops. Shlomo Sharan served as the academic advisor to the production team (Reiner, Sharan, & Hertz Lazarowitz, 1981). Each workshop was accompanied by a study guide of related small-group activities, written by Rachel Hertz-Lazarowitz. The success of the project was enriched by the dedication of participating teachers, principals, and the district supervisor.

The workshops were based on two major principles: whole-school participation and experiential learning.

Whole-School Participation

True to the emerging trends in educational change programs, the principal and all teachers in each of the three schools were encouraged to attend the workshops. Most teachers were home-room teachers, a few were librarians, others taught special subjects (e.g., English, music, gym). (From here on we will refer to all participants as "teachers.") The majority of participants were graduates of teacher training colleges. Gradually, the teachers in each school created their unique learning community, regardless of rank, subject matter, or extent of implementation.

Experiential Learning

The most consistent feature of our teacher education program for CL and GI was the experiential learning model. In order to integrate the various principles and features of CL in general, and of GI in particular, we believed teachers had to actually experience them. This was clearly true at the time, when most teachers had been taught to prepare lessons in the traditional transmission style of teaching, as they themselves had experienced as students. It was our belief that by experiencing firsthand how CL transforms the nature of learning, teachers would recognize the benefits of a class as a learning community and of knowledge as a shared social construction.

The design of the workshops followed the basic sequence of the experiential learning cycle: experience, reflection, conceptualization, and planning (Kolb & Fry, 1975). Group formation varied: for some activities, teachers grouped according to grade level; for others, according to shared interest in a particular aspect of CL, in a specific topic they were to teach, or in a specific problem they had experienced in their classes. Occasionally, teachers stayed in the same group throughout the workshop, and other times group composition changed once or twice during the workshop.

What follows is the description of how, by carrying out the stages of the experiential learning cycle, teachers experienced firsthand the many personal and professional implications of CL and GI, as they worked together in pairs or groups of three or four for various purposes.

Experience

A few participants had heard of, and some had tried, Jigsaw (Aronson, E., Bridgeman, D. & Geffner, R., 1978), one or two cooperative structures (Kagan & Kagan, 1985/2009), and STAD (Slavin, 1980), but only as isolated procedures that did not include preparation for the cooperative behaviors involved, for teachers or for students, and with no continuation.

As they began to see connections between workshop activities and any previous exposure to CL methods, a few teachers recalled how they had applied one or two of them but had been at a loss as to what to do once the novelty wore off. For most participants, the variety of group tasks and activities that the workshops offered, and the discussions that followed, provided their first taste of collaborative decision-making as well as of collaborative planning of process and products.

In each workshop teachers had ample opportunities to take an active role in their own learning. A workshop typically began with the screening of a telecast that demonstrated a specific cooperative skill, such as group members taking turns in a discussion or leading a group discussion. Teachers then carried out similar activities, and also experienced several additional helpful skills, as suggested in the study guide. At first, for example, the topic was discussion skills, and the telecast showed small groups of students taking part in "buzz group" discussions, after which they reflected, in their own words, on what they felt and learned from the experience. The teachers then conducted reflective discussions in small "buzz groups" about what they had seen and took part in short-term activities that demonstrated additional discussion skills, for example, listening and taking turns. Throughout the project difficulties in carrying out the activity served as examples of what their students might experience, thus preparing teachers for any initial confusion or objections in their classrooms.

When the facilitators felt that the teachers had a firm understanding of the basic communication and social skills necessary for group work, they introduced GI. This phase of the workshops was enhanced by a series of films that followed students in a sixth-grade class as they carried out a GI project on ancient Greece. The films, produced by Israel Educational Television, were edited in two ways: according to the stages of GI, to depict how all groups carried out each stage of the investigation, as well as how each of the three groups carried out their complete investigations (one on democracy, one on sports, and a third on architecture and art in ancient Greece).

Reflection

The reflection component of the workshop encouraged teachers to share their thoughts, satisfactions, and doubts about the various cooperative strategies they experienced, and to discuss in detail their understanding of the CL and GI process and the extent to which they felt prepared to carry them out in their classrooms. Throughout they also related what they had learned from their pupils' reactions to CL and GI, which further enriched their understanding of the cooperative processes involved. The reflection process also heightened teachers' awareness of their own strengths and weaknesses as group members, as well as of facilitators of CL.

The experience of being a member of a cooperative group was invaluable; it offered teachers many opportunities to clarify misunderstandings about what happens when planning and learning with others. Teachers voiced questions such as: "What if one person dominates the group?" "Won't one person do all the talking?" "How can I hear what everyone's saying?" "What if students make mistakes and I won't know about it?" They also observed and reflected on the coping strategies that facilitators modeled.

Conceptualization

The conceptualization component of the experiential learning model lent order to participants' observations and reflections about their experience. Workshop facilitators did not directly teach the principles of CL and GI. At each session teachers shared their conclusions from the various cooperative procedures that they had experienced, in the workshop and in their classrooms.

Planning

Teachers' observations, reflections, and conceptualization at each workshop contributed to their readiness to plan gradual implementation in their own classrooms. Teachers regrouped, if necessary, according to grade levels or subject matter, at first to plan short-term activities, such as they had seen in the telecasts and had carried out in groups. Here, again, was an opportunity for them to practice equal participation and experience the cooperative construction of ideas. Although each teacher planned which CL procedure or stage of GI was appropriate for his or her class and subject, and when to apply it, the open exchange of ideas created a feeling of mutual support and encouragement among peers that they had not experienced in traditional professional development courses.

The next workshop session began with teachers' reports of their experience of classroom implementation, their reflection on the outcomes, the degree to which the principles were carried out, and ideas for further planning.

The Experiential Learning Cycle Resumes

Following teachers' reports, the experiential learning cycle began anew: teachers carried out a CL or GI related activity, or watched a telecast of a class carrying out a cooperative activity or a stage of GI, depending on the level of implementation they had reached. They then reflected on their impressions, discussed the principles involved, and planned further implementation. Throughout the project there was no pressure to rush from one stage of implementation to another; on the contrary, teachers were encouraged to feel confident in facilitating each stage in their classrooms before advancing to activities and learning procedures that required a higher level of competence (theirs and the students'). They were also encouraged to conduct as many team building and discussion-skill building activities as they felt necessary, and to repeat them when needed, even with one or two groups.

Over time the teachers of each school developed a common language about their understanding of CL and GI, as well as of ways of planning and implementing. Gradually teachers felt more competent in carrying out the multiple tasks that effective CL and GI require: modeling cooperative behaviors, designing cooperative procedures, monitoring group work and facilitating group processing. In addition, the experiential workshops expanded their role as teachers: they acquired the ability to evaluate their planning and implementation of CL and GI, as well as their students' progress in acquiring the relevant cooperative skills.

Although most teachers were enthusiastic about implementing CL and GI, a few found it difficult to give up the transmission model they were comfortable with. In these cases the workshop facilitators, who were also classroom observers, helped them identify their own and their students' behaviors that hindered learning in cooperative groups, and, together, planned how to develop appropriate skills.

Questions Teachers Ask

The more competent teachers became in facilitating CL and GI, the sooner they shed their centrality and accepted the decentralization of their authority. A crucial factor in this element of the change process was the type of questions teachers put to their students, in whole-class discussions and in group activities. Teachers grew accustomed to asking questions with more than one answer (or more than one source for the answer), not to hear the answers they had prepared but to learn what the students knew or thought. The ensuing variety of answers served as a catalyst for lively discussions and diverse investigations.

Freely voicing their opinions and ideas did not necessarily come easily to students. To encourage them to do so, teachers, in effect, established a new "contract" with their students, one that redefined the type of questions they asked. In the early stages of their implementation, when most lessons were mainly in the transmission mode, teachers took one small step and began with a multifaceted question. Instead of, for example, asking "How many cities are built near rivers?" a teacher might ask: "Why do you think cities are built on the banks of rivers?" Think-pair-share, by now a very popular procedure, was helpful in structuring discussions (Lyman, 1981). In time students learned to trust that they may say what they know or think about a topic without being told it was wrong or inappropriate.

As teachers and students gradually lived up to the terms of this new "contract," classrooms were filled with a richer variety of answers and ideas. Teachers often experienced an "aha" moment when, after they may have expected two or three answers, groups came up with many more, some of which had not occurred to the teacher. This moment was a turning point for many teachers, convincing them of the inherent variety of ideas in any classroom and of the potential contribution each student can make to learning, based on his and her understanding of the world, and interest in learning about it. This small step did not involve a major change in classroom organization, yet it was significant for setting the stage for CL and GI.

The new "contract" called for teachers to consistently react to students' ideas in several ways: to comment favorably and reinforce what students said without repeating their words; ask students to react to what a classmate said before the teacher did; inquire how students understood a concept before expressing their own understanding of the concept; ask students to elaborate on their initial responses; allow them "wait time" before answering a question (Sharan, Y., 2015). Quite often teachers were surprised by students' answers; for the first time students had an opportunity to say what *they* thought and knew, not what the teacher had in mind. Needless to say, the more teachers used multifaceted questions, the more they learned how their students thought and what their values were, which helped them choose appropriate CL activities.

Directions for a Cooperative Task

Teachers were encouraged to have students work in pairs for as long as it took (for both teachers and students) to adjust to discussing a question together, or to planning and carrying out a simple learning task. A particularly challenging hurdle many teachers found hard to overcome was how to formulate directions for carrying out a cooperative task in pairs and/or groups of four. Often directions were not sufficiently detailed; teachers assumed that students would understand how to proceed if told to "work together," or "discuss" a topic. We established a general rule that a group task begin with each member saying or writing what he or she knew or thought about the question put to the group, then share their answers with a partner, and, finally, with another pair. We encouraged teachers to have students advance to groups of four only when pair work went smoothly.

When workshop facilitators felt that individual guidance would be helpful, they met with teachers one-on-one to analyze their difficulties and, together, seek ways of overcoming them. For facilitators this was a profound learning experience; we quickly realized that we could not take for granted that all teachers would easily apply what they learned in the workshops, as experiential as they may be. Several teachers often benefitted from extensive individual follow-up to ease the transition from frontal teaching to CL and GI (Sharan, S., 1994/1999; Sharan, Y. & Sharan, S., 1992).

What Are the Effects of CL in General and Group Investigation in Particular?

The research team conducted intensive studies of the GI project to examine a wide range of the project's effects such as students' academic achievement, their spoken language, their intrinsic motivation to learn, their social interaction with one another, teachers' style of talking while teaching, and teachers' attitudes toward CL and GI, to name a few. A marked finding of these studies was that CL procedures, including the GI model, exert distinctly positive effects on both teachers and students, discernible in improved classroom climate. Initial participation in short- term and increasingly long-term GI projects gave students unprecedented control over their learning, which resulted in enhanced motivation to learn and deepened the personal meaning derived from learning, as opposed to that experienced in the traditionally taught classroom (Sharan, S. & Shaulov, 1990). What follows are a few additional significant findings from the body of research conducted in the three elementary schools, and subsequently spread to a few junior high schools. Readers are referred to the original publications for more detailed descriptions of the research and the findings.

Students' Language in the GI Classroom

A CL classroom is rarely quiet; learning in cooperative groups and carrying out a GI project require a great number of conversations between group members. One study (Sharan, S. & Shachar, 1988) assessed the effects of GI on achievement, social interaction, and verbal behavior among 351 students from nine eighth-grade classes. Both the social-interactive and cognitive intellectual features of the discussions carried out by young adolescent speakers were evaluated in this study, but we will focus here on the findings of the effects of GI on their verbal behavior.

Assessment of students' spoken language at the end of several months of experiencing GI was compared to peers in traditionally taught classes. Statistical analysis revealed that students in the GI group used more words than did their peers from the frontal classes. The same was true for the number of turns they took to speak during their discussions. In the original publication there are extensive details about the students' ethnic background that served as one of the independent variables in the study.

Academic Achievement and Social Relations in the GI Classroom

The general problem posed by another study was: "Does learning that emphasizes peer cooperation promote academic achievement and social relations among pupils in general and in mixed ethnic classes in particular, as compared to traditional instruction?" (Sharan et al., 1984).

The study focused on the effects of two CL methods, GI and Student Teams Academic Divisions (STAD) (Slavin, 1980), versus Whole-Class (W-C) instruction, on three sets of dependent variables: achievement in English language and literature, social attitudes and cooperative, and competitive behavior. The report compared the findings for each of three different instructional approaches in terms of classroom climate, students' pro-social behavior, and the dissemination of CL among teachers. Results demonstrated that pupils taught by GI registered greater improvement than their peers in the W-C classes on the entire English Language test and, in particular, on the Listening Comprehension section of the test. Pupils in the STAD classes also achieved higher scores than those in the W-C classes on the entire test and on the Listening Comprehension section. Direct instruction proved less effective for teaching language skills than the group methods.

Students' Perceptions of GI

In one of the more unique studies several hundred children, in grades 3–7, were asked to write letters to the researchers about what they thought and felt about their experience (Hertz-Lazarowitz, Sharan, & Shachar, 1981). Their letters were mailed directly to the researchers so that neither teachers nor peers would know what they wrote. Content analysis of the 400 letters identified 692 statements that were categorized and counted by independent judges. The category that appeared most frequently in students' statements was that they liked studying in small groups because they could help one another, thus promoting learning and preventing failure. The same study showed that the children made significantly more altruistic and cooperative decisions on a task that asked them to allocate resources to themselves and classmates.

Group Investigation in Ethnically Heterogeneous Classrooms

Another research problem posed by Sharan et al. (1984) was: Do three instructional methods (Group Investigation, STAD (Slavin, 1980), and W-C) exert differential effects on children's cooperative behavior cross-ethnically and with same-ethnic peers? The focus of the study was on overt social behavior, rather than on attitudinal change and/or friendship patters as expressed in socio-metric measures (Hansell & Slavin, 1981).

Results recorded by observers indicated that students who were experienced in CL and GI generated more cooperative behavior while performing the task than did either of the two other methods. STAD students displayed more cooperative behavior than did those in classes taught with the W-C approach; students in the GI and STAD classes were less competitive than those who studied in the classes taught by the W-C method.

A GI project assigns a portion of the task to different students without assigning them to a social role that may have implications for the minority–majority relationship between them. Each student investigates a particular subtopic in order to contribute his or her share to the final group product. All members acquire status in the group through reciprocal exchange (Sharan, Raviv, Kussell, & Hertz-Lazarowitz 1984).

The Effects of the Change Project on Teachers

To assess project participants' behavior, attitudes, and perceptions of CL and GI, researchers employed questionnaires, observations, and individual interviews. We will summarize a few of their findings, as presented by Lichtenson (1981), Sharan and Hertz-Lazarowitz (1982), and Hertz-Lazarowitz, Sharan, and Steinberg (1980). On an attitude questionnaire workshop participants registered a significant positive change in attitude toward their role, namely a reduction in their view of control as a basic goal of teaching and of education in general. Implementers of CL and GI were found to be less conservative and more willing to take risks, more spontaneous and imaginative, more open to feelings, and more socially oriented than were teachers who did not regularly implement the new methods in their classrooms.

One clear finding was that substantial implementation of CL and GI occurred during the second year of the project. In intensive interviews conducted with all participating teachers, those who consistently implemented CL and GI expressed greater openness to educational innovations and a greater sense of being able to cope with problems in the classroom than teachers who implemented infrequently. Their positive attitudes enabled them to slowly overcome their initial wariness of losing their authority in the classroom and their concern with issues of discipline and order.

Among the conclusions that the research team reached from questionnaires and interviews was that the more conservative teachers, who experienced difficulties in implementation, would have benefitted from more consistent help from the project team. Their difficulties stemmed mainly from the feeling that they didn't have adequate tools for dealing with students who did not cooperate in a group, who didn't like the children in their group, or who felt that they knew more than others and resisted having to "teach" them. These obstacles to cooperative behavior are familiar to teachers and teacher educators even today, and dealing with them requires a great deal of patience and flexibility. Given the teaching methods that prevailed at the time of the change project, it is understandable that many teachers began with resistant attitudes and had difficulty in adjusting to what seemed a drastic reduction of their control and authority. Whereas the benefits of CL have been established, they are not magic panaceas; mastering the multiple ways of achieving them requires consistent, gradual, and systematic effort on the part of teachers and students, as well as of teacher educators.

In Conclusion

Today, there is a broader understanding of the CL approach and its applications, and of the benefits of applying all CL methods, models, or their components to all levels of educational settings, including postsecondary, vocational, and university settings (Baloche, 2011). As teachers in more countries take up the challenges of implementing CL and GI in their classrooms, their efforts involve considerations that we were not aware of at the time of the project. The most obvious of them is the effect of cultural differences on the application of cooperation in schools, a topic widely discussed and researched but is outside the scope of this chapter.

Educational researchers continue to revisit many of the issues that were of concern in the 1970s and the 1980s, and continue to deepen our understanding of how CL and GI effect students' and teachers' behavior and learning, as well as relationships within the classroom and within the school (see, e.g., Tan, I. et al., 2006). Furthermore, CL and GI elements continually surface in various interactive and inquiry-based learning methods (to be implemented systematically) and models (whose stages can be applied flexibly), even if the origins of a particular procedure are not cited explicitly. Elements of CL and GI are increasingly applied in various forms and levels to digital and online collaborative learning environments (see, e.g., Jacobs & Seow, 2015; Shonfeld & Ronen, 2009; Shonfeld & Gibson, 2019; Stahl, 2017; Zaphiris & Ioannou, 2014).

Research studies in higher education continually examine CL's contribution to math, sciences, computer-mediated learning and distance learning, as presented in an overview of studies conducted in the first decade of the 21st century (Sharan, Y., 2012b). The overview reported on the application of cooperative procedures in a long list of other fields as well: business, engineering (e.g., CL in a soil mechanics undergraduate course), and music, economics, training of medical, physical therapy and nursing students; accounting, athletic training, interior design classes, psychology, nutrition courses, and more.

Issues concerning cultural diversity have understandably gained momentum as a focus of CL-related research. Included in this category in the overview were studies that examined the connection between CL and cross-ethnic friendship, multiethnic classrooms, racial identity, and how CL can be adapted to specific cultural norms (Thanh, 2011). Mobilizing CL for efforts to deal with cultural diversity has led to some very creative ideas, such as a study in India of the effects of middle school students' collaboration in a puppetry project in a multicultural design and technology program (Mehrotra, Khunyakari, Natarajan, & Chulalwalan, 2009).

Our intense contact with teachers and students during the change project supported our view that teaching and learning through CL and GI systematically develop habits of active participation, social interaction, inquiry, and reflection. These learning and social skills are essential to productive group processes, whether at work or in school. They are becoming increasingly important wherever there is genuine concern about initiating and managing productive teamwork, problem-solving, and continuous learning in schools and workplaces.

We hope that this chapter contributes to the ongoing international discourse about the teaching of, and teacher education for, CL and GI, so that they, indeed, do continue to "get better."

Note

The bibliography does not represent the vast number of publications on the subject of teacher education for CL and GI; we have restricted it to publications specifically relevant to the period in which our change project took place.

The authors are indebted to Aviva Davidson, who gave of her time and sharp eyes to improve the text, and to Lynda Baloche, Nomi Sharan Gazit, and Dan Zetland, for their helpful comments.

Bibliography

Aronson, E., Bridgeman, D., & Geffner, R. (1978). Interdependent interactions and prosocial behavior. *Journal of Research and Development in Education*, 12, 16–27.

Baloche, L. (2011). A brief view of co-operative learning from across the pond, around the world and over time. *Journal of Co-operative Studies*, 44(3), 25–30. ISSN 0961 5784

Brody, C. (1998). The significance of teacher beliefs for professional development and cooperative learning. In C. Brody & N. Davidson (Eds.), *Professional *development for cooperative learning: Issues and approaches* (pp. 25–48). Albany, NY: Suny.

Brody, C., & Davidson, N. (1998). Introduction: Professional development and cooperative learning. In C. Brody & N. Davidson (Eds.), *Professional development for cooperative learning: Issues and approaches* (pp. 3–24). Albany, NY: Suny.

Cohen, E. G., Brody, C., & Sapon-Shevin, M. (Eds.). (2004). *Teaching cooperative learning: The challenge for Teacher Education*. Albany, NY: Suny.

Deutsch, M. (1949). A theory of cooperation and competition. *Human Relations*, 2, 129–151.

Deutsch, M. (1973). *The resolution of conflict: Constructive and destructive processes*. Carl Hovland memorial lectures. New Haven, CT: Yale.

Dewey, J. (1943). *The school and society*. Chicago, IL: University of Chicago.

Freire, P. (1970). Pedagogy of the oppressed. New York, NY: The Continuum International Publishing Group, 72.

Fullan, M. (1982/2015). *The new meaning of educational change*. New York, NY: Teachers College.

Hansell, S., & Slavin, R. (1981). Cooperative learning and the structure of interracial friendships. *Sociology of Education*, 54, 98–106.

Hertz-Lazarowitz, R., & Calderon, M. (1994/1999). Facilitating teachers' power through collaboration: Implementing cooperative learning in elementary schools. In S. Sharan (Ed.), *Handbook of cooperative learning methods* (pp. 300–317). Westport, CT: Praeger.

Hertz-Lazarowitz, R., & Sharan, S. (1984). Enhancing prosocial behavior through cooperative learning in the classroom. In E. Staub (Ed.), *Development and maintenance of prosocial behavior* (pp. 423–444). Springer. https://doi.org/10.1007/978-1-4613-2645-8_26

Hertz-Lazarowitz, R., Sharan, S., & Shachar, H. (1981). What children think about small-group learning. In S. Sharan & R. Hertz-Lazarowitz (Eds.), *Changing schools: The small-group teaching project in Israel* (pp. 293–311). Ramot: Tel-Aviv University (Hebrew).

Hertz-Lazarowitz, R., Sharan, S., & Steinberg, R. (1980). Classroom learning style and cooperative behavior of elementary school children. *Journal of Educational Psychology*, 72(1), 99–106. https://doi.org/10.1037/0022-0663.72.1.99

Jacobs, G., & Seow, P. (2015). Cooperative learning principles enhance online interaction 1. *Journal of International Comparative*, 4(1), 28–38. https://doi.org/10.14425/00.76.07

Johnson, D. W., Johnson, R. T., & Holubec, E. (1998). *Circles of learning*. Edina, MN: Interaction Book Company.

Kagan, S., & Kagan, M. (1985/2009). *Kagan cooperative learning*. San Clemente, CA: Kagan Publishing.

Kolb, D., & Fry, R. (1975). Towards an applied theory of experiential learning. In C. L. Cooper (Ed.), *Theories of group processes* (pp. 33–57). London: Wiley.

Lewin, K. (1948). *Resolving social conflicts*. New York, NY: Harper's.

Lichtenson, Y. (1981). The small-group teaching project. In S. Sharan & R. Hertz-Lazarowitz (Eds.), *Changing schools: The small-group teaching project in Israel* (pp. 293–311). Ramot: Tel-Aviv University (Hebrew).

Lyman, F. (1981). The responsive classroom discussion. In A. S. Anderson (Ed.), *Mainstreaming digest* (pp. 109–113). College Park, MD: University of Maryland College of Education.

Mehrotra, S., Khunyakari, R., Natarajan, C., & Chulalwalan, S. (2009). Collaborative learning in technology education: D & T unit on puppetry in different Indian socio-cultural contexts. *International Journal of Technology and Design Education, 19*(1), 1–14.

Miel, A. (1952). *Cooperative procedures in learning.* New York, NY: Teachers College.

Reiner, T., Sharan, S., & Hertz-Lazarowitz, R. (1981). Planned change in schools. In S. Sharan & R. Hertz-Lazarowitz (Eds.), *Changing schools: The small-group teaching project in Israel* (pp. 55–80). Ramot: Tel-Aviv University (Hebrew).

Schmuck, R., & Schmuck, P. (1971/2001). *Group processes in the classroom.* Boston, MA: McGraw Hill.

School Council Environmental Project. (1972). *Case studies.* London: Hart-Davis Educational Publications.

Sharan, S. (1980). Cooperative learning in small groups: Recent methods and effects on achievement, attitudes, and ethnic relations. *Review of Educational Research, 150,* 241–271.

Sharan, S. (Ed.). (1990). *Cooperative learning: Theory and research.* New York, NY: Praeger.

Sharan, S. (1994/1999). Cooperative learning and the teacher. In S. Sharan (Ed.), *Handbook of cooperative learning methods* (pp. 336–348). Westport, CT: Praeger.

Sharan, S., Hare, P., Webb, C. D., & Hertz-Lazarowitz, R. (Eds.). (1980). *Cooperation in education.* Provo, UT: Brigham Young University.

Sharan, S., & Hertz-Lazarowitz, R. (1982). Effects of an instructional change program on teachers' behavior, attitudes, and perceptions. *Journal of Applied Behavioral Science, 18*(2), 185–201.

Sharan, S., Kussell, P., Hertz-Lazarowitz, R., Bejerano, Y., Raviv, S., & Sharan, Y. (1984). *Cooperative learning in the classroom: Research in desegregated schools.* Hillsdale, NJ: Lawrence Erlbaum Associates.

Sharan, S., Raviv, S., Kussell, P., & Hertz-Lazarowtiz, R. (1984). Cooperative and competitive behavior. In S. Sharan, P. Kussell, Y. Bejarano, S. Raviv, & Y. Sharan (Eds.), *Cooperative learning in the classroom: Research in desegregated schools* (pp. 73–106). Hillsdale, NJ: Lawrence Erlbaum.

Sharan, S., & Shachar, H. (1988). *Language and learning in the cooperative classroom.* New York, NY: Springer Verlag.

Sharan, S., & Sharan, Y. (1975). *Small group teaching.* Tel Aviv: Schocken (Hebrew).

Sharan, S., & Sharan, Y. (1976). *Small group teaching.* Englewood Cliffs, NJ: Educational Technology Publications.

Sharan, S., Sharan, Y., & Tan, I. (2013). The group investigation approach to cooperative learning. In C. Chinn, C. Hmelo-Silver, A. O'Donnell, & C. Chan (Eds.), *International handbook of collaborative learning* (pp. 351–369). New York: Taylor and Francis.

Sharan, S., & Shaulov, A. (1990). Cooperative learning, motivation to learn and academic achievement. In S. Sharan (Ed.), *Cooperative learning: Theory and research* (pp. 173–202). New York, NY: Praeger.

Sharan, S., & Tan, G. C. I. (2008). *Organizing schools for productive learning.* New York, NY: Springer.

Sharan, Y. (1995). Music of many voices: Group investigation in a cooperative high school classroom. In J. Pederson & A. Digby (Eds.), *Cooperative learning in the secondary school: Theory and practice* (pp. 313–339). New York, NY: Garland.

Sharan, Y. (1998). Enriching the group and the investigation in the intercultural classroom. *European Journal of Intercultural Studies, 9*(2), 133–140.

Sharan, Y. (2002). Essential features of a teacher education program for cooperative learning. *Asia Pacific Journal of Education, 22*(1), 68–74.

Sharan, Y. (2012a). What we can learn from the history of cooperative learning. In A. H. Jensen (Ed.), *Perspektiver pa cooperative learning* (pp. 43–56). Denmark: Dafolo.

Sharan, Y. (2012b). From the journals: To the field and back. *IASCE Newsletter, 31*(1), 15–16.

Sharan, Y. (2015). How can teachers' questions contribute to the cooperative classroom? *Better, 7*(1), 12–13.

Sharan, Y., & Sharan, S. (1987). Training teachers for cooperative learning. *Educational Leadership, 45*(3), 18–26. Reprinted in D. Beach (Ed.). *Programs and procedures in supervision.* Needham Heights, MA: Ginn.

Sharan, Y., & Sharan, S. (1992). *Expanding cooperative learning through group investigation.* New York, NY: Teachers College.

Sharan, Y., & Sharan, S. (1994/1999). Group investigation in the cooperative classroom. In S. Sharan (Ed.), *Handbook of cooperative learning methods* (pp. 97–114). Westport, CT: Praeger.

Shonfeld, M., & Gibson, D. (Eds.). (2019). *Collaborative learning in a global world.* Charlotte, NC: Information Age Publishing, Inc.

Shonfeld, M., & Ronen, I. (2009). *Online learning: Variations in groups of participants and tools.* Proceedings of EDEN, Gdansk, Poland.

Sigel, I., & Cocking, R. (1977). *Cognitive development from childhood to adolescence: A constructionist point of view.* New York, NY: Holt, Rinehart and Winston.

Slavin, R. E. (1980). Student team learning: A manual for teachers. In S. Sharan, P. Hare, C. Webb, & R. Hertz-Lazarowitz (Eds.), *Cooperation in education* (pp. 82–135). Provo, UT: Brigham Young.

Stahl, G. (2017). Group practices: A new way of viewing CSCL. *I.J. Computer Supported Collaborative Learning, 12*(1), 113–126.

Tan, I., Sharan, S., & Lee, C. (2006). *Group investigation and student learning: An experiment in Singapore schools.* Singapore: Marshall Cavendish Academic.

Thanh, P. T. H. (2011). An investigation of perceptions of Vietnamese teachers and students toward cooperative learning (CL). *International Education Studies, 4*(1), 3–12.

Thelen, H. A. (1972). *Education and the human quest: Four designs for education.* Chicago, IL: University of Chicago.

Thelen, H. A. (1981). *The classroom society.* London: Croom Helm.

Chapter 9

About Richard Schmuck's Contributions to the Study of Organization Development and Cooperation in Education

Richard Arends, Neil Davidson, and Richard Schmuck*

A social psychologist of education, Richard Allen Schmuck is Professor Emeritus of Educational Psychology at the University of Oregon, Eugene. He did research and development and taught there for 32 years. His specialties were classroom peer-group dynamics, and school-faculty organization development (OD), both largely focused on cooperative social processes. During a professional career of over 40 years at the University of Michigan, the University of California at Santa Barbara, Temple University, and the University of Oregon, Richard published 26 academic books and 199 scientific journal articles.

In 1971, Richard Schmuck published two co-authored books: one on organizational development in schools with Philip Runkel, the other on group processes in the classroom with Patricia Schmuck. The book on OD was based on research he and his colleagues at the University of Oregon had been conducting on strategies for helping school participants (primarily teachers and principals) develop more effective school processes. His work on group processes aimed at helping teachers create more socially, emotionally, and high-performing classrooms.

Addressing important problems faced by educators in the 1960s and 1970s, Schmuck's work was guided by ideas and theories from the fields of social psychology, group dynamics, and planned organizational change. In this chapter, we first describe Schmuck's contributions to the fields of OD and group processes and the relationships among these fields to cooperative learning (CL). The chapter concludes with a review of Schmuck's leadership over the years in the International Association for the Study of Cooperation in Education (IASCE) and his reflections on becoming an IASCE Pioneer.

Organization Development in Schools

In the early to mid-1970s, Richard Schmuck, Philip Runkel, and their colleagues at the University of Oregon published several research reports and books on OD in schools (1970, 1972, 1975, 1977). These described their work and research aimed at helping teachers and school principals develop skills in interpersonal communication, procedures to work more effectively in groups, and new ways of setting goals, solving problems, and making decisions. Even though OD as a change strategy had gained a foothold in business and industry in the 1950s, it was not until the work of Matthew Miles (1959, 1963) and Richard Schmuck and Philip Runkel (1970) that OD ideas and strategies were introduced in schools.

Introducing OD in schools can be viewed, in part, as a response to larger political and social issues of the 1950s and 1960s. Challenged by the Soviet Union's launch of Sputnik (the first earth satellite) in the late 1950s, Americans declared that education should become a higher priority and issued calls for reforming the ways schools were organized and what and how students were taught. The National Defense Educational Act (1958) and the Elementary Secondary Education Act (1965) provided a spate of new programs and policies that required an overhaul of the traditional curriculum with more emphasis on academic learning, student-centered, and inquiry approaches to teaching, and new ways for organizing schools and classrooms. Many of these reforms maintained that the "self-contained" classroom, where one teacher met all day with 30 students, should be replaced by teaching teams and more flexible schedules.

In 1961 University of Illinois professor, J. Lloyd Trump published a little book entitled *Guide to Better Schools: Focus on Change*. This book challenged the sanctity of the self-contained classroom in elementary schools and the fixed, six-period schedule in secondary schools. Other similar projects followed, such as a widely distributed film, "And No Bells Ring," and books like *The American High School Today* (1959) written by Harvard University President James Conant. The reforms offered by Trump, Conant, and others at the time contended that more cooperation was needed among teachers in schools. This put a strong emphasis on team teaching and more flexible schedules. These reforms required teachers to work together cooperatively rather than alone both inside and outside the classroom.

To make these new organizational structures work required a different set of skills and capabilities on the part of teachers, principals, and other school participants. The Oregon OD group led by Schmuck and Runkel developed intervention strategies aimed at helping school participants acquire these capabilities. Their strategies were based on the perspective that school organizations, like other organizations, are not singular identities but instead are constituted of a variety of groups and subsystems—that is, particular schools, teaching teams, subject matter departments, counseling departments, and central administration. Thus, the Schmuck-Runkel approach was to improve the capabilities and functioning of schools' intact subsystems. The following subsystem capabilities became the targets of their interventions.

Clarifying Communication

Much of what goes on in schools is affected by the communication processes used by the participants in the school. Communication effectiveness can be enhanced when members can raise and describe important issues precisely and listen to one another's messages and emotional feelings.

Establishing Goals

Goals in schools are often ambiguous and taken for granted. Effective subsystems communicate goals in precise writing and, on a continuous basis, take time to assess progress toward desired goals.

Working With Conflict

Conflict is a natural part of social life. Often, however, conflict in schools is avoided. Organizations as a whole and effective subsystem have norms that support the uncovering of conflict and means for resolving difficult conflict situations.

Improving Meetings

Meeting are places where important collaborative work is done. This is best accomplished in meetings where convening and recording functions are shared, where everyone participates, and where time is set aside to review how the meeting went.

Solving Problems

Often participants in schools ignore problems and/or lack systematic procedures for solving them. School subsystems become more effective when members see problems as natural, can state them precisely, and have specific procedures for solving complex problems.

Making Decisions

Choosing among competing goals or solutions to problems requires making decisions. In many schools, major decisions traditionally are made by those who have legitimate authority, such as the principal. Effective schools and subsystems have procedures for all participants to share in decisions and have clear expectations about who should make what decisions.

To test the effectiveness of their approach, in the late 1960s, Schmuck, Runkel, and their colleagues initiated research projects in two school districts, Kent, Washington, and Eugene, Oregon. The intervention and research in Kent (Schmuck & Runkel, 1970) was carried out in a junior high school and was designed to increase interpersonal communication, to develop new ways of group problem solving, and to help school participants become more responsive to student needs. An OD project in Eugene, Oregon labeled the "Multiunit Elementary School Project" (Schmuck, Murray, Smith, Schwartz, & Runkel, 1975) followed the initial project in Kent. Teachers in selected elementary schools were organized into teacher units (teams). In most instances, units were created by combining grades 1 and 2, grades 3 and 4, and grades 5 and 6. Teaching teams were encouraged to take responsibility for all the students in the unit, not just the 25 or 30 previously assigned to them in their self-contained classrooms. Principals were encouraged and coached to interact with members of the teaching units rather than solely with individual teachers. A leadership team consisting of a designated lead teacher from each unit helped coordinate and make school-wide decisions.

Teaching in teams required a set of behaviors on the part of teachers and principals different from those they traditionally possessed. Schmuck and his colleagues provided OD training and consultation for this purpose. Training and consultation aimed at improving teacher's skills in interpersonal communication, showing them how to work cooperatively, improving the effectiveness of team meetings, and illustrating how to use different approaches to solving problem, making decisions, and resolving conflict.

The multiunit project in Eugene and the junior high training in Kent had research as the primary focus, so obviously the OD consultants to the project would not stay involved forever. So, Schmuck and his colleagues asked, "once multiunit schools and teaming were fully implemented, how can they be maintained over time, become self-renewing, and be implemented in other schools in the districts or regions?" They proposed the creation of what they labeled "Cadres of Organization Specialists." Initially tried in Kent, and then in Eugene, district-based "Cadres of OD specialists" were established. The Multi-Unit Project provided an ideal setting for creating a district-based "Cadre," for the purpose of institutionalizing OD work once funding for research was removed. Cadres consisted of district personnel representing various ranks and role groups (teachers, principals, central office administrators, counselors) who could provide organization training and consultation on an ongoing basis without having to rely on outside consultants. Cadre members received extensive training in theory and processes of organization development along with intervention and consultation skills. Members were organized into consulting teams who in turn contracted with various schools, teams, or other intact groups for the purpose of providing organization training and consultation. Cadre members also began working with student groups, teaching them interpersonal and group process skills and how to work together cooperatively.

Group Processes in the Classroom

While helping to develop strategies in organization development to enhance the capabilities of teachers and principals to work together more effectively, Richard Schmuck partnered with his wife, Patricia, to develop ways for teachers to work more effectively with students in their classrooms (Schmuck, R. and Schmuck, P., 1971). As with the organization development work, the Schmucks' work in group processes stemmed from ideas from social psychology, group dynamics, and small-group theory. This work was also a reflection of issues faced by the larger society and by educators in the 1950s and 1960s. The 1954 Supreme Court Brown v. Board of Education of Topeka striking down separate-but-equal policies and the 1964 Civil Rights Act provided impetus for educators to explore teaching processes that would reduce intergroup prejudice and foster higher regard for all students. Emerging issues promoting equal education opportunities for girls and special needs students added additional reasons for exploring the dynamics of classroom life. The reforms of the late 1950s and the 1960s that emphasized a curriculum with increased academic rigor were also starting to be questioned. Many educators joined with Carl Rogers, whose book *Freedom to Learn* was published in 1969 and Johnathan Kozol's *Death at an Early Age* (1967) in calling for more humanistic schools and classrooms.

During this time, the Schmucks joined with many other first-generation scholars (Sharan & Sharan, 1976; Johnson & Johnson, 1975; Robert Slavin, 1976) to explore how small-group teaching and CL environments might lead to more academic learning and better understanding and respect for all students including those from racially and ethnically different backgrounds, girls, and those with special needs.

As with the work in organization development, Richard and Patricia Schmuck drew on the social psychological perspective, particularly ideas and theories from group dynamics and group development as applied to classroom settings. The Schmucks highlighted the importance of interpersonal interactions and group processes in the classroom. They identified several important group processes that would produce a more positive and cooperative classroom environment.

Communication

Instruction proceeds in classrooms through verbal and non-verbal interactions. Positive classroom environments have communication patterns characterized by processes that are honest and open and with a high degree of full participation.

Friendship and Cohesiveness

This process involves the friendship patterns in classrooms and the degree to which participants have respect for one another. Positive classroom environments are free from cliques, with all students feeling a part of the friendship structure.

Shared Expectations and Norms

Classrooms with positive environments have expectations and norms in support of high academic achievement as well as in support of positive and cooperative interpersonal relationships.

Leadership

The Schmucks view leadership not from the perspective of individual traits but instead as a group property. They define it as an interpersonal influence process. Classrooms with positive learning and social environments are democratic and provide students and teachers opportunities to have shared influence within the classroom group.

Conflict

Conflict is inevitable in any group settings, including classrooms. Positive classroom environments recognize that conflicts exist and have processes for resolving them in productive ways.

In addition to defining critical group processes, the Schmucks drew on group development theories to describe how classrooms pass through discernible stages as they become more satisfying and productive learning communities. These stages include dealing with inclusion and membership, influence and collaboration, individual and academic goals, and self-renewal. Classroom processes are not fixed and can be influenced by teachers' actions, including assisting with the development of positive classroom groups.

Unlike some of the other early scholars included in this book, the Schmucks did not create specific CL strategies to be used by teachers in their classrooms. Their work, however, was important because it caused those who were developing various strategies to consider the dynamics of the classroom group, particularly when different goal, task, and reward structures were introduced. For example, in the early days (perhaps even today) when CL strategies were introduced in classrooms, developers found settings that were more or less teacher-centered and with task structures where teachers worked with the whole class and where students were expected to listen to transmitted academic content. Working in small groups required a different set of expectations and behaviors for both teachers and students. Teachers talked less and students more. Similarly, in traditional classrooms, goal structures were mainly individualistic, requiring little student interaction with others, and traditional reward structures were competitive. CL strategies, on the other hand, required students to work in teams with rewards oriented toward the team as well as individuals. These introduced a new set of group dynamics that were explained by the group processes described by the Schmucks.

Relationships Between Organization Development and Cooperative Learning

In 1998, Schmuck described the mutually sustaining relationships between OD and CL. His chapter, "Mutually Sustaining Relationships Between Organization Development and Cooperative Learning," in Brody and Davidson (1998) explored "how collegial relationships among the staff members of a school and teacher-student relationships in that school's classes can reciprocally affect one another . . . and become mutually enhancing and sustaining" (243). In this chapter, Schmuck presented data from four major case studies "on the bi-directional relationship between OD for school staffs and CL in the classroom." One case demonstrated "how OD can increase teachers' readiness to risk trying cooperative learning techniques in their classrooms" (247). Additional cases described the progression from CL to OD and how "schools in which a critical mass of teachers are employing cooperative learning in their classrooms can be ripe contexts for OD projects" (250). Schmuck concluded that

> "the relationship between cooperative learning and organization development is two way and reciprocal. The starting point for moving toward a cooperative school culture can be either through OD or through CL." He wrote, "I believe, for either OD or CL to be sustained effectively over the long run, both OD and CL must be going on" (252). He wrote further:
>
> When teachers collaborate with their principals and colleagues in setting school goals and in planning new instructional patterns, they begin to feel empowered as teachers, and their professional self-concepts and commitment to humane practices become increasingly stronger. Because they feel supported and respected, they can more easily give their support and respect to students. Moreover, when teachers become more interdependent with one another, they can more readily use the skill of constructive openness, thereby improving their teaching strategies through the giving and receiving of feedback. The prototype of

such an exchange of feedback, nowadays, is peer coaching and mentoring. . . . Some norms, roles, structures, and procedures, already common in cooperative learning, must become part of the school culture if cooperation is to be sustained as a system of values in education. The cooperative school culture has norms in support of respecting everyone's ideas and feelings, of equalitarian teamwork and collaborative effort, of openness, candor, and honesty, of warmth and friendliness, of caring for people of all ages, and of seeking self-esteem for everyone.

(253)

Schmuck believed that cooperative school cultures can be developed, that "we have the concepts, strategies, designs, and techniques to achieve that . . . [and that] the theory and technology of OD and CL are mature enough now to achieve that" (253–4).

Richard Schmuck's Leadership in the IASCE

In 1979, a local steering committee led by Shlomo Sharan invited Richard Schmuck to give the keynote speech at the First International Convention on Cooperation in Education to be held in Israel. Schmuck agreed and presented a scholarly description on how the theory and practice of organization development had been used in a high school he worked with in Oregon to bring students into an intervention with teachers and administrators for the purpose of creating a healthy social climate in the school. He called the project "Students as Participants in School-wide OD." During the question-and-answer period following the presentation, Neil Davidson (co-author of this chapter) asked: "What most excites you about OD?" He responded, "OD techniques can help students, teachers, and administrators use democratic cooperation to design a healthy social climate for all."

As the 1979 convention proceeded, a core group of the participants decided to create the IASCE, and as has been described in the introductory chapter, Richard Schmuck was elected the Association's first president. He continued to guide the infant organization during the next three years.

The third IASCE Conference was held in Saskatchewan in 1985. As that conference ended, the Board of Directors held an official meeting on the stage of the conference auditorium, inviting interested IASCE members to attend and sit in the chairs below the stage. Very soon, a hostile and tense climate developed between the Board seated on the stage and members seated below. Dick Schmuck, who had continued serving on the IASCE Board of Directors, along with others, spotted the tension immediately. They could see that although the physical distance between Board members and participants was small, the vertical social distance between them was considerable. Dick Schmuck changed the group dynamics of the session by announcing clearly, "I am very uncomfortable with the emotional tone of this meeting; let's change our seating arrangements!" The Board quickly descended from the stage and tool seats among the participants. That simple intervention changed the emotional tone of the meeting from hostile to cordial, and the Board had a productive session as it closed out the third IASCE Conference.

At the eighth IASCE Conference held in July 1994 at Lewis and Clark College in Portland, Oregon, Dick Schmuck was again asked to speak. He delivered a well-received presentation in which he used the metaphor of a 15-year-old adolescent to illuminate the current development of IASCE. During the latter part of his presentation, Dick called out all 54 conference presenters by name, and he identified each individual's contribution to IASCE, for example, theory, research, or practice in school-based CL. He also described their roles—school administrator, college teacher, researcher, and so on. His attention to this kind of detail about each presenter's contribution to IASCE was inspiring. It set a very positive tone for the remainder of the conference and helped develop a powerful sense of community where each participant could feel he or she had been worthy contributors to an international movement with shared values of cooperation.

From late 1994 through 1995 the IASCE Board experienced several internal conflicts and power struggles among various sub-groups. Disagreements existed over issues about the production of the IASCE professional magazine: Who should be involved in preparing the magazine? Where should it be printed? Even more severe, some members believed that the IASCE needed to identify new leadership and establish a renewed sense of purpose and direction. Further, the Board had become bogged down in debates regarding to what extent the IASCE should focus on "the study of cooperation in education" on the one hand or "interventions to make classroom and schools more cooperative" on the other.

In 1994, Neil Davidson asked Dick Schmuck if he would be willing to provide OD consultation with the Board and help members deal with some of the issues and conflicts they were facing. He said, "yes." His initial OD consultation occurred toward the end of the Portland Conference in 1994; the second consultation took place at the IASCE Conference in Brisbane, Australia, in 1995.

Schmuck had told the Board in Portland that he would employ an OD design "Process Observation and Feedback." He suggested interested board members could read about this design in *The Fourth Handbook of Organization Development in Schools*, which had been recently published with co-author Philip Runkel. Dick continued to use the same "Observation and Feedback" design. He carefully observed the Board as it conducted out a regular meeting, and he periodically provided feedback based on these observations. He then led the IASCE Board through an S-T-P problem-solving process. He asked members to identify what they perceived as the Board's current situation (S), the organizational targets (T) the Board would like to pursue, and the procedures (P) the Board might use to move toward desired targets. This process helped the board transform its internal conflicts and frustrations into productive problem-solving discussions. Both in Portland and Brisbane, Dick Schmuck's adept consultative skills, his caring, his commitment to the IASCE, and his experience as its first president were helpful in getting the board back on track as it began planning for the Association's next steps.

Finally, Dick Schmuck took an active role in two of the earliest IASCE publications He prepared a chapter on "Students as Organizational Co-Participants" (Schmuck, 1980), for the first volume, and he served as coeditor of IASCE's second volume, *Learning to Cooperate, Cooperating to Learn* (Slavin et al., 1985).

Reflections on Becoming an IASCE Pioneer, by Richard Allen Schmuck

When I declined Neil Davidson's request that I contribute to this volume, I was engaged day and night in creating my memoir, *Paths to Identity*. Neil proposed to ask an expert, versed in my career, to prepare with him a chapter about my pioneering work. I readily concurred, especially when Neil selected as his co-author Richard Arends, my student, colleague, and co-author. Richard and Neil have accurately described the academic ideas and events in my adult life that influenced my involvement and work in cooperative learning. They have astutely summarized my research in the social psychology of education and my efforts to develop strategies to make schools more productive and satisfying places to work and study, and they have highlighted my contributions to IASCE in its early days.

This, however, is not all of the story. Several personal paths I took between age 11 and age 18 had important influences on how I came to embrace a set of humanistic values that later guided all aspects of my life and career. Next, I draw on my refreshed reminiscences to add personal notes to Richard and Neil's information.

My career as student, teacher, researcher, developer, consultant, and administrator is rounded like a continuous never-ending cycle of circles. It loops back and forth and around my childhood, youth, and adult years in a series of bounding concentric circles, combining my adolescence, middle-age years, and current senior years into an integrated whole. That career was built on an under girth of humanistic values: I–thou as opposed to I–it interpersonal relationships, transactional communication, empathy and sympathy, poly-faceted influence and empowerment, and respect for the individual whatever might be that person's social or psychological attributes. The budding seeds of those values started to grow early inside me, and my formal schooling, intensive reading, and active collaborative partnerships have helped them to grow and expand.

In my recent memoir I describe eight personal paths I traveled in establishing my individuality. As I wrote, I marveled at how brightly my reveries shined about creating an identity during my teens. Perhaps, my colorful memories of becoming 18 appeared clear and distinct, because in the middle of that age 11–18 personal passage, my small nuclear family of four moved 325 miles east from Elmwood Park–Chicago to Dearborn–Detroit. That social class and cultural transition, entailing two contrasting neighborhoods, confronted me with anxiety-filled challenges and marvelously rich opportunities.

The first path opened when I became 11 in the summer of 1947 and Mrs. Lee, a neighbor four houses north, died in bed at home. After the funeral that my mother and I attended, Old Man Lee, as my peers called him, took several of his wife's Sunday dresses from their shared closet to spread them over their shared bed. He closed their bedroom door to live the rest of his life in a small back bedroom and the kitchen.

Old Man Lee lost his mind at Mrs. Lee's funeral. He stopped walking to the corner store. He stopped cleaning the house. He stopped bathing himself and washing his clothes. He stopped gardening and mowing the lawn. He locked the front door and would not open it again. He only went outside after dark. He turned down any offer of help.

During the next nearly two years, I walked by Lee's dirty house at least 20 times a week back and forth from school. In that time I might have looked directly at Old Man Lee's house well over 2,000 times. His Edgar Allen Poe-like dwelling worked like a magnet drawing my unwilling eyes toward it. I can close my eyes now at 83, and I still visualize it as though I were 11 and 12 years old again. Over my lifetime I have periodically dreamed about it in my sleep. In the sticky, hot summer of 1949, Old Man Lee died on the cot in the back bedroom. He and his horrible house became for me such an extraordinary memory, such a ghost-like dream, that I forever felt moved to search for answers in literary fiction and the study of abnormal and social psychology.

The second path was a potholed driveway of cinders leading in and out of an inglorious eyesore, the two-story wooden firetrap of our Elmwood Park junkyard. It stood next door to our city's primary softball field. I was 12, the batboy of our local young-adult softball team.

I never will forget when a crowded truckload of 12 standing Negro players arrived from Chicago's south side to play a double header at Junkyard Field. They were 14 in all, including their batboy, my age, and a manager, the driver of the truck, my father's age. Dressed neatly in the grays of a visiting team, they filed singly past our third base bench, where our white players sat, to sit on a long bench next to the first baseline with their backs to the junkyard.

I was the only white person to walk across the first baseline to them, where I handed two practice balls to their manager, who thanked me, and then told his batboy to shake my hand. The teams split the two games; we won the first, they took the second. During the games players avoided touching one another, even on close plays. No one shook hands with anyone, even after the two games were over. There was, I observed, a feeling of relief that the games were over without a nasty word spoken out loud. I knew down deep that I had just witnessed an extraordinary event, one I would never forget.

Chicago's junkyard, its cultural junkyard of 1948, was full of nasty ethnic and racial stereotypes, discrimination against more negative human categories than could be imagined, and prejudiced put-downs stacked up as high as the papers, magazines, and cardboard in the real junkyard. I often wished later that I had known about it sooner: Gordon Allport's masterpiece, *The Nature of Prejudice*. I did not read it until Dan Katz, my Michigan-based professor, urged me to when I was 23. There it was, all laid out before me, ways to understand the mental junkyards of my preteen years, ways of putting intergroup and interpersonal hatreds in perspective.

Taking the third path entailed meandering circuitously around the streets of Chicago in 1949 when I became 13. My brother had discovered a sandlot baseball team called "The Roamers" that traversed Chicago from north to south to west to play away games only, never having a home game because they did not have a home field.

The Roamers literally roamed or wandered about Chicago always competing as a visiting team on neighborhood diamonds, homes to the myriad of ethnic groups residing in one of America's most pluralistic urban centers. Because the Roamers often could muster only eight players as the summer progressed, my brother could arrange for me, some six years younger than most players, now and then, to play in the outfield and to bat last.

On one Sunday afternoon, when I was the ninth player, we played the Amundson Park Angels. I made no error. I caught two long fly balls, and although I made no hit, I walked twice, stole one base, and scored the run that won the game for us. I batted last, but felt as though I were the leadoff man as the nine-inning game progressed. The Roamer manager waved and winked at me when the teams left the field at the end of the game. It was the Roamers' first win in July.

My roaming around Chicago when I was only 13 taught me a good deal about urban sociology, although I didn't know what sociology was then. Roaming to play baseball gave me the gift of learning firsthand about the Chicago demographic crucible. Indeed, my baseball roaming became a metaphor for my later professional career as a worldwide traveling social psychologist. I roamed the academic world, always as part of the visiting team. I gathered around me international students from the far reaches of North and South America, Europe, Asia, Australia, Iceland, and New Zealand. Thank you Roamers, for making me an observant traveler and a participant observer of ethnic diversity. I shall never forget you.

The fourth path led me north up 73rd Avenue past Old Man Lee's empty lot across Belden and past Emily's house to the railroad tracks. Three days prior to my 14th birthday, the Saturday of my birthday party, our neighbor, Emily Swenson, knelt on one rail, her out-stretched arms reaching toward the other rail, before the silver Burlington Northern engine roared west from Union Station. Emily, just 21, home from Northern Illinois Normal, passed; her body was obliterated at 2:30 a.m., while I slept soundly.

One month before, in May 1950, my parents took me with them to see the movie of Tennessee Williams' *The Glass Managerie*, starring Jane Wyman as Laura, the shy daughter of Amanda played by Joanne Woodward. I was struck by similarities between Jane Wyman and Emily Swenson. Both presented a lurking visage of quiet desperation. Joanne Woodward expressed similarities to Hilda Swenson, Emily's cold and judgmental mother. After Emily's suicide, that film gripped me from head to toe for months. I thought about it during my birthday party and when I mowed lawns for wages in Oak Park that summer.

After my 14th birthday party, I got into bed at 10:30 p.m. My mother came to review highlights of the day. We chatted for a few minutes about the things I liked best about the day. Then, after a long pause of silence, I blurted longingly, "Why, Mommy, why did Emily do that? Why, Why, Why?" She looked down at me, a tear rolled off her cheek onto my covers. Shaking her head back and forth and with a lump in her throat, she uttered, "I don't know Dickie. I just don't understand. Emily had so much to live for; she was much too young to die." Emily's sad, tragic unraveling was much too much for me to fathom. I cried tears. As my mother reached toward me, I cried hot tears. Twelve years later, I would earn a doctorate in social psychology at the University of Michigan.

During the summer of 1951, when I became 15, my family moved from Elmwood Park–Chicago to Dearborn–Detroit. We moved so that my father could take on a much better job.

The fifth path entailed climbing a steep hill of upward social mobility. We moved from working-class Elmwood Park to upper-middle-class Dearborn. We sold our $12,000 small frame 30-year-old plain house; we bought a $20,000 redbrick brand new house. We moved into West Dearborn, where well-educated affluent automotive engineers, designers, and business executives resided. They lived in 8 and 9 rooms $45,000 fancy two- and three-story homes, with 2 and 1/2 bathrooms, and pool tables in the recreational rooms on nearby Long Boulevard.

When I reflected years later in a college American-literature class on the physical and cultural mobility that had happened to me, Long Boulevard with its grand row of large and expensive homes stood out like Long Island had shined brightly for F. Scott Fitzgerald. At Princeton, where he was out of place, Fitzgerald longed for the rich and well-off mansions lining Long Island Sound, after he had grown up in a much-more modest working-class St. Paul, Minnesota. Like Fitzgerald, I had climbed a fairy-tale ladder in one short summer.

Where my family settled in West Dearborn, my classmates did not wonder whether I would try to find work at the Rouge Steel Mill or the famous Ford assembly line, the technological wonder that made Frederick Taylor famous. No, they wondered instead whether I would go to Michigan or to Michigan State, or perhaps to Albion or Kalamazoo College. Perhaps, I might aspire to Princeton or Yale, or even do engineering at Purdue or business administration at Wharton. When we chose our new house around the corner from Long Boulevard, we had unwittingly placed ourselves in the heart of minor wealth and major formal education. We gradually realized that summer that our neighborhood was at the center of the 1950s technological prosperity.

In this affluent context I was fortunate indeed to make an intellectual transition from Mrs. Kessie, my ninth-grade Chicago-based English teacher to Mrs. Pugh, my upper secondary school English teacher at Dearborn High School. Early that summer before our move out of Chicago, Mrs. Kessie pulled me aside to say how much she appreciated my participation in her class. She said that I wrote well, that I read books carefully, and that I spoke up with good ideas in class. She went on to say,

> This wonderful book just came out in paperback. It is about a teenager nearly your age, and how he thinks about and understands his world of New York City. It is about his sister too that he protects. His name is Holden; her name if Phoebe.

She was talking about *The Catcher in the Rye*, which became the most important story of the initial 15 years of my life, a novel that still brings tears to my eyes, even as I reflect on it now. *Catcher* became one reason why I chose English Literature for my B.A. degree.

As I devoured that novel I cried in poetic awe over the image of Holden Caulfield patrolling the edge of a high field of rye grass to keep little children playing there from falling off the cliffs. I cried when he tells Phoebe in earnest about the sort of occupation he would like to take on as an adult, a catcher in the rye. When, during my early years at Dearborn High, I told Mrs. Pugh about how I felt awe when reading *Catcher*, she supplied me with a steady stream of important novels that shaped me into an English major in college and a social psychologist in graduate school.

Over the next few years, Mrs. Pugh made sure that I was fed: *Huckleberry Finn*, *The Heart Is a Lonely Hunter*, *The Grapes of Wrath*, *Native Son*, *Invisible Man*, *Gentleman's Agreement*, and *Razor's Edge*. Even when I was also preoccupied with competitive sports and dating a comely girlfriend, she understood that there was something else in my hungry heart that needed feeding. As I matured and got ready for higher education, the social ecology of Long Boulevard reminded me of what Theodore Dreiser revealed in *The American Tragedy*, or what F. Scott Fitzgerald, in *The Great Gatsby*, considered America's tragic romance with glamorous materialism. Like Sinclair Lewis, I imagined that Long Boulevard was replete with Babbits. From Mrs. Pugh I learned the importance of writing well to succeed in college, the beauty of Walt Whitman's *Leaves of Grass* and the poignancy of Robert Frost's *Birches*. Should I write well for the rest of my career, Mrs. Pugh deserves a credit.

The sixth path traveled to my church on a fateful racist Sunday and away from my membership on that same day. The never-to-be-forgotten events occurred in middle May when I was 17. My family hosted three Negro boys, each also 17, who came from Flint Northern High School to attend a statewide Hi-Y convention in West Dearborn. The mission of the Michigan Hi-Y was to create, maintain, and extend morally high standards of Christian life throughout its high schools. I was elected president of our Dearborn Hi-Y as a sophomore in fall 1952 when I was 16 to serve for two years to see that our statewide convention would come off well in spring 1954.

After breakfast at my house where the three black young men had slept the last two nights, the four of us drove my dad's company car to attend 11:00 a.m. services at my chosen church, St. Paul's Lutheran, the last obligatory scheduled requirement of our weekend Hi-Y conference. As we walked from the parked car to the church, I was impressed and moved by how the Michigan Spring had sprung alive all of a sudden. The Hi-Y conference had gone well, and I felt satisfied with how nicely the two nights and mornings had gone with my parents at my home.

The four of us constituted an especially colorful quartet for lily-white West Dearborn. We were three various shades-of-black Negros, and one pink Caucasian. We four stood out as the spring sun radiated down. We were athletic, handsome teenagers, confident and poised. I saw that the heavy front doors of the church had been propped open, so we strolled straight ahead toward the main center aisle.

Two ushers, both male and about 50, quickly moved alongside to accost us. One stretched his left leg in my path; the other stood in front blocking our progress forward. "Wait, wait boys!" one commanded, "We will find you a place to sit." We waited with surprised looks. The two ushers whispered to each other while covering their lips with church-service programs.

After a few seconds, one usher commanded, "Follow us!" directing us back toward the vestibule and motioning us to walk behind the back row of pews, toward the extreme right side of the sanctuary's far rear. They required that we sit in the back row as far right as we could be settled. I was embarrassed, feeling a hot flush of anger well up inside. I considered leaving then, but we stayed.

We stuck it out, staying for the whole 75 minutes, but for me all the time reluctantly. We left from the back right side to avoid the main exit. I never would return to the church. I had had my last "Last Supper." As we drove away from the church toward home, I choked out in a loud whisper simply, "I am sorry," all of us remembering how the ushers tried to hide us.

The seventh path ran up and down the football gridiron at Ford Field when I was 16 and 17 calling the plays to lead our Dearborn High Pioneers. In two unforgettable fall seasons, I lead our team in 18 staged presentations of high school football. Those days, players called the plays in Michigan high schools. By calling the plays I mean that I chose each new play from our team's playbook when we were on offense and that I described it to the other ten teammates in a huddle before every new play. I communicated by using our team's agreed-upon numbering system. During my senior year, I also called our defensive formations from the vantage point of my safety position in our defensive secondary. In my safety role, I stood as the last barrier to the other team's attempts to score points.

Those years of calling the plays will forever dwell in the library of my mind. As caller of the plays, I acted as a creator, designer, facilitator, and evaluator. Indeed, I was always mentally carrying out formative evaluation. I sought to encourage and to inspire my teammates to action. In fact, I sought to steer them toward constructive, cooperative action. I gently prodded, pushed, and nudged. As caller of the plays I was a certain kind of musician: concertmaster, orchestra conductor, and a band-leader. I was like the prompter for an opera, like a base-player to keep the beat, like a little drummer boy marching in a parade. I took on the roles of architect, shepherd, and a catcher in the rye. Indeed, I called our scripted plays decades before I would become expert in group dynamics and organization development.

The eighth path was walking through the dining room of Edison's Restaurant to the Butler's Pantry between the dining-room doors, the Ten Eyck Tavern, the Alexandria Ballroom, and the swinging doors back into the restaurant over and over again. I acted as a busboy in Edison's Fine Dining Restaurant in the northeast corner of the then 17-year-old Dearborn Inn, the New England–style red brick hotel that an inspired Henry

Ford had built in 1937. Now, 1954, when I became 18, freshly graduated from Dearborn High School, the Dearborn Inn was a well-known elegant hotel with 236 rooms, five guest cottages, and two large lodges for business meetings.

As a lowly busboy, I served in the servant's role of a waiter's assistant, nothing fancy, indeed a humbling set of functions. Co-workers and customers surrounding me could not have cared less that I had been on center stage, a graduating class salutatorian and recipient of the class's "highest honors in athletics" one night before when 367 received their diplomas. As second in my class, I had been charged with making the opening welcoming remarks. Even though I had received awards at nearby Dearborn High School, I was no more than a not-to-be-noticed secondary servant, performing menial, barely necessary tasks at the Dearborn Inn.

As was typical of my busboy job, I arrived in the kitchen one hour before Edison's opened. I retrieved table clothes and cotton napkins from the linen closet. I inspected them to insure they were clean, well pressed, and without spots, rips, or other imperfections. I covered eight tables for which I was responsible. I placed proper silverware and glassware in position on my tables. I went to the Butler's Pantry between the restaurant doors and the swinging door to the kitchen to fill glass pitchers with cold tap water and half fill silver buckets with ice cubes. I checked for cut butter squares to serve with Edison's Parker House rolls. I made certain that I was dressed correctly, and that my hands and fingernails were polished clean. A busboy's fingers are on display when serving.

Dearborn Inn waiters, all women, between 30 and 50, were far more important than its busboys. They directed what unfolded in the dining room. They controlled most of the busboys' actions. We did a few things without direction, but very few. In the cash economy of the day, busboys received only minor tips. My paycheck was a meager $50 every two weeks. For the rest of my eventful life whenever I dared to feel special, deserving, or privileged, I dug down deep trying to recall my busboy days.

Note

* The first three sections of this chapter, written by Richard Arends and Neil Davidson, deal with organization development, small-group processes, and the IASCE. Richard Schmuck added personal memoir excerpts, which occur in his section, "Reflections on becoming an IASCE pioneer."

References

Conant, J. (1959). *The American High School Today: A first report to interested citizens*. Boston, MA: McGraw Hill.

Johnson, D., & Johnson, R. (1975). *Learning together and alone, cooperation, competition, and individualization*. Englewood Cliffs, NJ: Prentice-Hall.

Kozol, J. (1967). *Death at an early age*. Boston, MA: Houghton Mifflin.

Lewin, K. (1944). Dynamics of group action. *Educational Leadership, 1*, 195–200.
Lewin, K. (1948). *Resolving social conflict.* New York, NY: Harpers.
Lewin, K. (1951). *Field theory in social science.* New York, NY: Harpers.
Lewin, K., Lippitt, R., & White, R. (1939). Patterns of aggressive behavior in experimentally created "social climates". *Journal of Social Psychology, 10*, 271–299.
Lippitt, R., Watson, J., & Westley, B. (1958). *The dynamics of planned change.* Under the editorship of Willard B. Spalding. New York, NY: Harcourt, Brace & Company.
Miles, M. (1959). *Learning to work in groups.* New York, NY: Teachers College Press.
Miles, M. (1963). *Organization development in schools: The effects of alternative strategies of change. Mimeographed research proposal.* New York, NY: Teachers College, Horace Mann-Lincoln Institute of School Experimentation.
Rogers, C. (1969). *Freedom to learn.* Columbus, OH: Charles E. Merrill.
Schmuck, R. (1980). Students as organizational coparticipants. In S. Sharan, P. Hare, C. Webb, & R. Hertz-Lazarowitz (Eds.), *Cooperation in education* (pp. 146–159). Provo, UT: Brigham Young University Press.
Schmuck, R. (1998). Mutually sustaining relationships between organization development and cooperative learning. In C. Brody & N. Davidson (Eds.), *Professional development for cooperative learning: Issues and approaches* (pp. 243–254). Albany NY: State University of New York Press.
Schmuck, R., Murray, D., Smith, M. A., Schwartz, M., & Runkel, M. (1975). *Consultation for innovative schools: OD for multiunit structures.* Eugene, OR: Center for Educational Policy and Management.
Schmuck, R., & Runkel, P. (1970). *Organizational training for a school faculty.* Eugene, OR: Center for Educational Policy and Management.
Schmuck, R., Runkel, P., Arends, R., & Arends, J. (1977). *The second handbook of organization development in schools.* Palo Alto, CA: Mayfield Publishing.
Schmuck, R., Runkel, P., Saturen, S., Martell, R., & Derr, B. (1972). *Handbook of organizational development in schools.* Palo Alto, CA: National Press Books.
Schmuck, R., & Schmuck, P. (1971). *Group processes in the classroom* (1st ed., Dubuque, IA: Wm C. Brown Publishers, 8th ed., 2000). Boston, MA: McGraw-Hill.
Sharan, S., & Sharan, Y. (1976). *Small group teaching.* Englewood Cliffs, NJ: Education Technology.
Slavin, R. (1976). *Using student team learning.* Baltimore, MD: The Johns Hopkins University.
Slavin, R., Sharan, S., Kagan, S., Hertz Lazarowitz, R., Webb, C., & Schmuck, R. (Eds.). (1985). *Learning to cooperate, cooperating to learn.* New York, NY: Plenum Press.
Thelen, H. (1954). *Dynamics of groups at work.* Chicago, IL: University of Chicago Press.
Trump, J. L. (1961). *Guide to better schools. Focus on change.* New York, NY: Rand McNally.

Chapter 10

Cooperative Learning in Mathematics and Beyond

Neil Davidson

My career in cooperative learning had two major aspects. The first was the development of cooperative learning in mathematics, and the second focused upon cooperative learning in general and beyond mathematics. This chapter is divided into two major sections addressing these two career aspects. Within this structure I provide personal retrospectives on professional and research experiences that informed my work in these two areas.

Section One: Genesis of Cooperative Small-Group Learning in Mathematics

In this first section, I offer some insights into the personal experiences leading to my work in cooperative learning. As a graduate student, preparing to become a mathematics professor, I had published one mathematical research paper (Davidson & Fabian, 1963). Then the University of Wisconsin hired John G. Harvey to create a new doctoral program in mathematics education within the Mathematics Department. Doctoral students would take all their coursework and comprehensive exams in mathematics and then go on to take additional courses in education (first taught by Tom Romberg) and write a dissertation in mathematics education. I jumped at the chance to join that program because of my love of teaching.

In the mid-1960s, I was looking for a dissertation topic. I had taken several graduate mathematics courses taught by Edward Fadell. Some of these employed the Moore method. This individualistic, competitive approach to math instruction, developed by R. L. Moore, led to spectacular successes in mathematical research for some (Moise, 1965) and discouragement for many others.

In contrast to the individualism of the Moore method, Dewey's (1916, 1938) philosophy of education, as taught by Donald Arnstine, emphasized learning through active personal experience; learning by doing non-routine, thought-provoking activities; learning as a social process; intrinsic motivation; and more. Dewey wrote, "The primary source of social control resides in the very nature of the work done as a social enterprise in which all individuals have an opportunity to contribute and to which all feel a responsibility" (1938, p. 56). I was fascinated by Dewey's philosophy but did not yet see how to apply it in teaching mathematics.

One day in the mid-1960s, on my way out of the psychology building, something riveted my attention: a class with small groups of students sitting and talking with one another. After watching in amazement for a few moments, I approached the professor, explained my status as a doctoral student, and asked permission to join the class, whatever it was. The teacher, a young social psychologist named David Bradford, generously agreed and asked me to try it out for three days to see if it was right for me. Thus, I enrolled as a student in theories of social change and later in in his course on group dynamics.

The use of small groups touched something deep within my spirit, in bringing the human community into the classroom. I became a "groupie," participating in T-groups, encounter groups, psychodrama, gestalt, Tavistock labs, and assorted marathon groups. These led to enormous personal growth for someone who had been a math nerd with poorly developed social skills. I became more aware of my thoughts and feelings and behavior, a bit more outgoing and expressive, less critical and judgmental of others, and less argumentative.

Bradford's two courses changed my view of what was possible in teaching and learning, by employing small-group processes supported by psychological research findings. Those courses in social psychology provided the third key for my dissertation. Incorporating Dewey's philosophy, I aimed to retain the intellectual discovery challenge of the Moore method of math instruction, bolstered by research-based social support in small groups to foster success for students. So the three key elements for my dissertation study were Dewey's philosophy of active engagement, intellectual challenge via discovery learning, and social support through small-group learning. This also became the beginning of a research and teaching career based on the combination of these three elements.

Rationale for Small-Group Learning in Mathematics

As my dissertation illustrated all those years ago, a rationale, showing that mathematics is well suited for cooperative group work, includes several main points.

1. Small groups provide a social support mechanism for the learning of mathematics.
2. Small-group learning offers opportunities for success for all students in mathematics.

3. Students in groups can help one another master basic facts, concepts, and computational procedures.
4. School mathematics problems can actually be solved in reasonable lengths of time, such as a class period.
5. Mathematics problems can often be solved by several different approaches, and groups can discuss the merits of different solutions.
6. Mathematics problems have solutions that can be demonstrated with logical reasoning, unlike many problems in real life.
7. The field of mathematics is filled with exciting and challenging ideas that merit discussion.
8. Mathematics offers many opportunities for creative thinking, exploring open-ended situations, and solving non-routine problems.

Genesis of the Small-Group Discovery Model

I conducted a pilot study in 1966–1967 and my dissertation study in 1967–1968 on small-group learning of calculus, for 12 brave students meeting five days per week for the academic year. Students working together cooperatively in small groups with four members discussed mathematical ideas, developed techniques for solving problems, made conjectures for investigation, proved theorems, and discovered many ideas and techniques which were new to them (Davidson, 1970, 1971a, b).

A class period typically began with a meeting of the entire class to provide an overall perspective. This can include presenting new material, holding class discussions, posing problems or questions for investigation, and clarifying directions for the group activities.

The class is then divided into small groups, typically with four members apiece. Each group has its own working space, which might include a flip chart or section of the chalkboard. Students work together cooperatively in each group on challenging activities. They actively exchange ideas with one another and help each other learn the material.

Varied leadership and management functions are handled by the teacher: initiate group work, form groups, and present guidelines to foster cooperation and mutual helpfulness. The teacher takes an active role, circulating from group to group, providing assistance and encouragement with learning and group process, and asking thought-provoking questions as needed.

Teachers furnish overall classroom management, tie ideas together, make assignments, and evaluate student performance.

The teacher presents to students the following guidelines for group problem-solving (Davidson, 1970, 1990a):

- Work together in groups of four.
- Cooperate with other group members.

- Achieve a group solution for each problem.
- Make sure that everyone understands the solution before the group goes on.
- Listen carefully to others and try, whenever possible, to build upon their ideas.
- Share the leadership of the group.
- Make sure that everyone participates and no one dominates.
- Take turns writing problem solutions on the board.
- Proceed at a pace that is comfortable for your own group.

The course design was based on the educational philosophy of Dewey (1916, 1938). Learning by doing includes personal experiences and reflection on those active learning experiences. Students are engaged in nonroutine, thought-provoking activities. Learning is a social process, "a social enterprise in which all individuals have an opportunity to contribute and to which all feel a responsibility."

Motivation is intended to be intrinsic, whenever possible. Interest in the mathematical ideas and activities is intended to be the main source of motivation. The motivational goal is for students to view each mathematical topic as being intrinsically interesting, valuable, or useful.

The course design incorporated several research findings from social psychology. Cooperation was superior to competition in groups (Deutsch, 1960). Democratic leadership was more effective than authoritarian or laissez-faire leadership (White & Lippitt, 1960). Conformity pressure was a risk in groups, and it could be reduced by setting norms for independent judgment (Asch, 1960).

Group size affects discussions (Bales & Borgatta, 1961). In mathematics, I found that groups of four are large enough to generate ideas for discussion and solution of challenging problems, and large enough to keep functioning if one member is absent. Groups of four are small enough to permit active participation, and not to require a leader or elaborate organizational structure. Groups of four can also split into pairs for computational practice or simple application problems.

Results of the Study

In the original study, students in the experimental group scored slightly higher but not significantly higher on a standard final exam than students in a lecture control group. Perhaps more importantly, student attitudes toward learning, the course structure, and its impacts were overwhelmingly positive. This is clearly illustrated by some sample statements made in relation to this original course "Other students, no matter who, force you to learn more." "Most classes stress being able to use formulas while this stresses total understanding." "It is my most interesting and liked class. I enjoy coming to it." "I think I learned a lot more this year than in all three years of high school math." "It showed me that I can do things that before looked impossible. All it takes is a little understanding. Math doesn't scare me as much now."

Early Publications on Small-Group Learning in Mathematics

My dissertation study (1970), published in 1971, was later condensed into a first journal article on the small-group discovery method (Davidson, 1971b). The dissertation became the basis and the launching pad for my entire professional career in small-group learning in mathematics and beyond.

Discovery learning was a central notion in my dissertation. Discovery learning in mathematics can occur in three different approaches: whole-class discovery (Polya, 1962, 1965), individual discovery as in the Moore method, or small-group discovery. Development of cooperative small-group discovery occurred over many years. For example, one paper was a theoretical comparison of the Moore method and the small-group discovery method (Dancis & Davidson, 1970). In the Moore method, students work individually to solve difficult problems outside of class, without talking to other students and without reading pertinent texts. They present their results to the class, for critique or approval. A number of fine research mathematicians in point-set topology were students in the Moore method, yet many students cannot handle this approach.

In contrast, in the small-group approach students work together to solve challenging problems, mainly during class but sometimes in small groups outside of class. The same sequence of content topics could be approached through discovery learning, either via isolated individual work in the Moore method or via social support for learning in the small-group approach, throughout the full range of undergraduate courses.

Beyond Research: Challenging Personal Career Experiences

A digression from my academic work occurred at the University of Wisconsin, which was a hotbed for social change movements in the 1960s. During the Vietnam War, I devoted a couple of years to the peace movement and the civil rights movement. These activities were deeply meaningful to me and, I hope, socially beneficial to these causes. Yet they also cost me a two-year delay with my dissertation, which I finally managed to complete in 1970.

Alongside research, my experiences as an educator undoubtedly shaped my insights into teaching and learning. I was implementing my research in my teaching, and the two were intimately connected and informed one another. This is not a typical mode of research in an academic subject area.

I must confess having a rough beginning with the Mathematics Department at the University of Maryland, where I also had a joint appointment in Education. I arrived in 1968 with all but dissertation completed, as a mathematics educator in a research-oriented Mathematics Department. And I was practicing active learning with small groups in the late 1960s and 1970s, way before anyone had heard of such a radical approach. Moreover, I was not a very skillful change agent in that early stage of my career.

Two factors helped to gain more acceptance of small-group learning. A Mathematics Department committee, chaired by Professor Stanley Jackson, conducted a study of student attitudes toward instruction in the Department. They found that students had favorable attitudes toward learning in small groups and they would like to see that approach implemented in more mathematics courses.

In this context, one of the world's greatest mathematicians, Alexander Grothendieck, visited the University of Maryland. He appeared one day in my abstract algebra class and stayed for the entire period. He quickly became engaged as a co-teacher with me, observing the student groups, noting their progress or struggles, asking them questions, and giving hints as needed.

In Grothendieck's colloquium, someone asked about his recommendations for teaching mathematics. He immediately made complimentary remarks about my teaching with small groups. This helped a bit in my standing in the Department—perhaps my ideas about small-group learning were not as crazy as they first seemed. (On reflection, this event could be viewed as a striking example of a status treatment, described in Chapter 4 on Complex Instruction).

In later years, Chancellor Brit Kirwan of the University of Maryland System, who had earlier been Chair of the Mathematics Department, presented me with an Award for Outstanding Service to the Schools in 1992. He commented as follows: "Neil was way ahead of his time. He showed us how to do active learning and small group learning long before we were prepared to accept those approaches. Now we are."

Support Through Professional Associations in Mathematics

During the 1970s, small-group learning began to attain recognition in the mathematics education community through publications by major professional associations. The Mathematical Association of America has published a number of journal articles (e.g., Davidson, 1971b; Weissglass, 1976; McKeen & Davidson, 1975; Davidson & McKeen, 1979). The latter two addressed educational objectives and gave a theoretical comparison of small groups versus individual instruction, as described next.

The movement toward self-paced individual instruction in the 1970s was often linked to the precise specification of behavioral objectives for learning. Davidson and McKeen (1979) addressed the advantages and limitations of behavioral objectives. Such objectives can be useful for learning facts or skills but are too limited for inquiry or discovery learning. We suggested a range of "higher order" objectives such as these. The student will explore a situation and state a set of conjectures, prove a theorem, derive a formula, develop a technique for solving a class of problems, and locate fallacies in an argument.

We note that such objectives are suitable for small-group discovery learning but are far beyond the bounds of typical individual instruction programs. Moreover, individual self-paced instruction programs, where students work alone, do not make any use of the social motivation that is present in small-group learning (McKeen & Davidson, 1975).

Motivation

Motivational factors in small-group learning of mathematics were described by Davidson (1976), applying a framework presented by Sears and Hilgard in the *National Society for the Study of Education Yearbook* (1964). Three types of motives were identified.

Cognitive motives have to do with knowing and understanding one's environment. Examples are interest, curiosity, exploration, manipulation, creative thinking, and understanding.

Ego-integrative motives serve to build and maintain self-confidence and self-esteem. Examples are achievement, competence, mastery, meeting a standard of excellence, and striving toward full intellectual functioning.

Social motives are based on the powerful human need for affiliation with others. Examples include affiliation with peers, building a relationship between student and teacher, and the effects of cooperation.

My chapter shows how each of these motives comes into play in a mathematical environment rich in active learning, pursued through challenging academic tasks, and with students engaged in small-group interaction for social support and intellectual stimulation.

Cooperative Learning in Junior High (Middle School)

Middle school or junior high can be a difficult assignment for teachers, because students' hormonal changes can strongly affect their behavior.

Small-group learning offers a way out of the battle to quiet down the noisy students and wake up the sleepy ones. Talking and moving around, which are viewed as discipline problems in traditional classrooms, are now permitted. A paper co-authored with two teachers offers a number of practical suggestions for implementing small groups in middle school mathematics. Guidelines for cooperative behavior are stated in simple language. For example: Everyone is to help. No person is to be the boss. Stay in your group. Don't race with other groups to be the first one finished (Davidson, Agreen, & Davis, 1978). (This paper was published by a different professional association, the School Science and Mathematics Association.)

NCTM

Additional publications on small-group learning in mathematics occurred through another major professional association, the National Council of Teachers of Mathematics (NCTM). Examples are those by Artzt and Newman (1990), Leikin and Zaslavsky (1999), an *NCTM Yearbook* chapter by Davidson (1990b), and an article on curriculum construction, described immediately here.

Curriculum Development for CL

The NCTM published an article by Davidson, McKeen, and Eisenberg (1973), creating a model for developing curriculum materials with student input. The main idea is that a curriculum should reflect the interests and aptitudes of the students for whom it is intended. In the model a teacher observes one small group at a time, grappling with a challenging concept or problem, which might not be stated initially in the most clear and comprehensible form. The students receive minimal teacher guidance and have maximal opportunity for exploration, trial, and error. Observations and input from one group lead to a refined activity for the next group. After the model is applied several times in succession with three or four different groups, the activity is polished into an effective final form. This curriculum design process is a form of qualitative research on students learning.

This curriculum design process was used repeatedly, one lesson topic at a time, to develop a small-group discovery course in abstract algebra (Davidson & Gulick, 1976). This course had previously been considered impervious to discovery learning (although point-set topology had been taught for many years through individual discovery via the Moore method). This course demonstrated that every topic, even in a very abstract mathematics course, can be learned mainly through a small-group discovery process.

I had the good fortune to work in a congenial and collegial mathematics education group at the University of Maryland. One of our major projects with faculty and graduate students was developing a course in mathematics for elementary teachers (UMMaP: Cole, Davidson, Fey, Henkelman et al., 1978). The course was based on a framework of unifying concepts and processes in elementary mathematics, and it was taught mainly through small-group discovery learning. Several of our doctoral students wrote dissertations related to this course, including the curriculum development model described previously.

Small-group learning gradually began to gain acceptance in the Mathematics Department. In addition to our courses using small-group learning in abstract algebra and mathematics for elementary teaching, two others were developed. Jerome Dancis designed a course in linear algebra using small groups. And Denny Gulick and Scott Wolpert created a "close contact calculus" course with small groups.

NCTM Standards

The NCTM Curriculum and Evaluation Standards for School Mathematics (1989) emphasized thinking, reasoning, problem-solving, and communication in mathematics.

Bassarear and Davidson (1992) showed how these standards can be met through cooperative learning. This theme was developed further by Robertson, Davidson, and Dees (1999).

Cooperative learning plays a major role in Reform Mathematics, an approach to mathematics teaching and learning, primarily in North America, based on the principles of the NCTM Standards.

> Reform mathematics curricula challenge students to make sense of new mathematical ideas through explorations and projects, often in real contexts. Reform texts emphasize written and verbal communication, working in cooperative groups, making connections between concepts, and connections between representations. By contrast, 'traditional' textbooks emphasize procedural mathematics and provide step-by-step examples with skill exercises.
> (Wikipedia, 2019 version)

Major Projects on Cooperative Learning in Mathematics

In the late 1980s, Laurel Robertson and the Developmental Studies Center in California convened a conference on cooperative learning in mathematics. The small group of invited participants were all leading figures in that field. We decided to publish a handbook to help mathematics teachers implement cooperative learning throughout the grade levels. That volume became my first edited book, entitled *Cooperative Learning in Mathematics: A Handbook for Teachers* (Davidson, 1990a).

My colleagues and I had developed multiple perspectives on cooperative learning ranging through the elementary, middle school, high school, and college/university levels, and these were detailed in the volume. Chapters are included on several major models of cooperative learning. Mathematical approaches range from skill development, concept development, mathematical explorations, laboratory activities with manipulative materials, problem-solving and problem posing, guided inquiry and guided discovery, real-world problem situations, use of computers, and implementation issues for teachers and administrators.

By the 1990s, mathematics faculty at the college and university levels were becoming interested in cooperative learning. The Mathematical Association of America (MAA) published three major books related to cooperative learning in mathematics. Initial volumes by Hagelgans, Reynolds et al. (1995) and by Dubinsky, Mathews, and Reynolds (1997) incorporated aspects of Davidson's work.

The final book in this series, an edited volume by Rogers, Reynolds, Davidson, and Thomas (2002), arose through national summer workshops for mathematics faculty via Project CLUME: Cooperative Learning in Undergraduate Mathematics Education. A team of us joined together to create this book. The volume provides a historical overview of cooperative learning; practical ways to develop a social climate conducive to cooperative learning; many cooperative strategies with mathematical examples; several recommendations concerning evaluation, assessment, and grading; varied approaches to designing activities based on how people learn mathematics; stories about how different beliefs in teaching and learning helped to shape teaching practices; and practical ideas for conducting introductory faculty development workshops for undergraduate mathematics faculty.

Tales of Faculty Resistance to CL

My journey of developing CL wasn't always as straightforward as this chapter might lead you to believe. Here are two true tales of initial faculty resistance to cooperative learning. At one university, I was having a pleasant lunch with the chair of the mathematics department and several colleagues interested in teaching. A professor strode up, pointed a finger at me, and asked, "Are you Davidson?" Upon my assent, he pounded the table and shouted: "I have read some of your papers and you are wrong: WRONG, WRONG, WRONG! That is not the way to teach mathematics." Not knowing what to do, I simply listened while he gave a long tirade about how he learned mathematics through lectures and extensive study, and how the lecture method was the only way to teach. When he finally identified himself, I recognized his name as a well-known mathematician, one of whose papers I had read as a doctoral student. How intimidating this was for me.

He indicated that he was going to come to my colloquium later that day, and I thought, "my goose is cooked." Much to my surprise he participated cooperatively in the group activities. Afterward he came up, shook hands with me, and said, "well, perhaps an old dog can sometimes learn new tricks."

In a colloquium in the Mathematics Department at another major research university, I demonstrated several cooperative learning techniques, including think-pair-share. One of the senior professors erupted about the name for that technique, saying, "I can't stand all this educational jargon." I responded by quoting a complicated theorem in abstract algebra, loaded with numerous terms. I asked him how he felt about that mathematical terminology and how it compared with the educational terminology for think-pair-share. He said the math terminology was perfectly clear and everyone knows that theorem.

At that point, one of the mathematics faculty asked him: "Do you know what it means to think? Do you know what it means to pair up and talk with another person? Do you know what it means to share ideas with the class?" That seemed to end the argument.

A different type of challenge occurred at that same university. I had been asked to act as a consultant to help improve their calculus courses. They had an impressive program using small-group learning in calculus, but it wasn't working as well as they wished. After observing a number of classes and talking with course instructors, the nature of the problem became clear. They were expecting students to do extensive group projects outside of class, without first teaching them how to work together cooperatively within class. I pointed out that group projects outside of class are the most difficult type of small-group learning. There are issues of finding a time to meet and of accountability; one person might do most of the work, and others take little responsibility. Hence, it is best to conduct small-group activities regularly and frequently during class time so that students can learn to work together cooperatively to solve challenging mathematical problems. With that basis, students would then be better prepared to do a limited number of group projects outside of class.

Faculty and Staff Development for CL in Mathematics

In contrast to these challenges, most presentations proceeded without dramatic confrontations. For example, the Mathematical Association of America sponsored Project NExT, New Experiences in Teaching, a professional development program designed for new Ph.Ds in the mathematical sciences. I was privileged to co-present a session on cooperative learning for an exciting group of about 80 such faculty members in 2013. These new Ph.Ds mostly had no formal training in teaching, and they were bright, receptive, and eager to learn.

I have presented over 200 staff development workshops for mathematics teachers, and have developed some ideas about making such workshops effective. In a paper by Davidson, Weissglass, and Roberston (1990), we described four models of staff development for CL in mathematics. These are the workshop model, extended school-based staff development model, project model, and the graduate seminar model.

In using a workshop model with mathematics teachers, some commented that they had previously attended general cooperative learning workshops but couldn't see how to apply them in mathematics. Then, throughout the workshop, we demonstrated a number of cooperative procedures using specific mathematics content topics. For each procedure, we had a group experience with one topic, and then listed half a dozen others. Many math teachers commented that this was exactly what was needed to "get them up and running."

Research on CL in Mathematics

In this section we address the question: "How does small-group learning in mathematics affect student achievement?" To provide a perspective on this question, a synthesis of ten years of studies with small-group discovery was given by Davidson (1979). A brief, conceptual overview of research on small-group learning of mathematics was provided by Davidson and Kroll (1991). Results from these and other studies are described next.

A selective review of research on cooperative small-group learning in mathematics was presented by Davidson (1985) and expanded upon later (Davidson, 1990b; Urion & Davidson, 1992). About 80 studies in mathematics compared student achievement in cooperative learning versus whole-class traditional instruction. In over 40% of these studies, students in the small-group approaches significantly outscored the control students on individual mathematical performance measures. In only two studies did the control students perform better, and both of these studies had design irregularities. In a smaller subset of cooperative discovery studies, about a third favored the discovery treatment and none favored traditional instruction.

If the term "achievement" refers to computational skills, simple concepts, and straightforward application problems, these studies support Slavin's (1983) conclusion: "Cooperative learning methods that use group rewards (goals) and individual accountability consistently increase student achievement more than control methods . . . in elementary and secondary classrooms."

Discussion: Cooperative learning in mathematics can be done with or without discovery learning. There is a challenge involved in designing studies of cooperative discovery learning. In a discovery treatment, the emphasis is on non-routine problem-solving where the students develop a creative solution, rather than simply applying a given rule or procedure (what Polya calls "one rule under your nose"). As creative problem-solving is not in the curriculum for the control group, it is usually not deemed fair to include such difficult problems on a comparison test.

A small-group discovery treatment typically does not place much emphasis on learning facts, simple concepts, and straightforward skills. But these are usually the basis of experimental comparisons. So if one expects students in small-group discovery to be highly effective in basic facts and skills, the teacher would need to provide opportunities for students to practice and master the discovered facts and skills. This can be done by incorporating some practice structures such as Pairs Check or STAD. (One of my professional misconceptions was in believing that because students would gain practice of skills while making discoveries, the need for additional skill practice would be greatly reduced.)

If this were a literature review, not a personal retrospective, I would include major works by many other authors. But one particular work must be cited here, the meta-analysis by Springer et al. (1999) on the effects of small-group learning in STEM courses: Science, Technology, Engineering, and Mathematics. It shows that small-group learning, in contrast to lecturing, produced significantly higher results in student achievement, attitudes, and persistence in STEM courses or programs.

Conclusion and Current Projects

In my 50-year career with cooperative small groups, I have found that the entire mathematics curriculum at the school or college/university level can be taught using substantial small-group interaction—perhaps with some lecture/discussion. With cooperative small-group learning in mathematics, the classroom blossoms into a vital intellectual learning community of engaged, communicative, supportive, thoughtful learners. And in a cooperative discovery approach, students often demonstrate impressive creative thinking and logical reasoning while developing their own group approaches to solving challenging problems.

My current project on cooperative learning in mathematics, with Hope Gerson and Charlene Beckmann, is well under way. It is a mathematics curriculum book ranging from pre-algebra through calculus. In this work we demonstrate through curriculum examples and classroom-tested lessons that every major mathematical topic at the school level can be approached through cooperative discovery learning.

Fifty-plus years after beginning my journey with cooperative small-group learning in mathematics, I am gratified to see statements from three major professional associations. The Mathematical Association of America *Instructional Practices Guide* (2020) recommends use of small-group learning and collaborative learning.

A leading editorial entitled "Drop the Chalk" in the influential journal *Science* (January 24, 2020) advocates "active learning that is heavy in group work and discussion."

An article by Braun et al. entitled "What does active learning mean to mathematicians" gives examples of active learning, small-group learning, and think-pair-share. It appears in the *Notices of the American Mathematical Society* (February 2017, 64(2), 124–128).

Section Two: CL in General and Beyond Mathematics

In the first 20 years or so of my career, I focused on teaching and learning in mathematics; in the later years, I continued this focus but expanded it to include teaching and learning in general. This portion of the chapter is divided into seven sections: cooperative learning and the IASCE, theoretical issues and edited books, presentations (sometimes leading to publications), graduate education with doctoral programs and dissertations, teacher education and staff development, university faculty development, and personal reflection on my role in the IASCE.

Cooperative Learning and the IASCE

In 1979, Shlomo Sharan, after hearing of my work in small-group learning in math, invited me to participate in the first international convention on cooperation in education, held in Israel. Some participants were surprised to learn that small groups could be used in mathematics because, in their view, there was nothing to discuss in math. At the convention, some people who had been instrumental in developing small-group approaches for learning met one another for the first time, and some of us became long-term colleagues and professional friends. I was fortunate to be in the right place at the right time with the right people. Several of these scholars, who became the first-generation leaders of the cooperative learning movement, have written chapters for this volume.

The first major book published by the IASCE included two of my papers (Davidson, 1980a, 1980b), the first on introducing small-group learning in mathematics to non-mathematicians, and the second on using Re-evaluation Counseling to change education.

Re-evaluation Counseling is a peer counseling approach developed by Harvey Jackins (1972, 1973). In this co-counseling approach, partners take turns in pairs in the roles of client and counselor. The client "discharges" distressed feelings, while the counselor listens deeply and attentively. Release of the feelings of distress leads to more clear thinking about the issues involved. For many years I taught co-counseling and led a community program in it.

Later conferences of the IASCE led to a paper reviewing CL research in math (Davidson, 1985) and one by Robertson et al. (1999) in the *Handbook* by S. Sharan—previously mentioned in the math portion of this paper.

For me, the IASCE has been a wonderful source of stimulation, new learning, keeping up with the field, and collegial support. Association members get to meet and work with varied contributors to CL, which stimulates fruitful dialogues and further scholarship.

At the IASCE conference in 1985, we founded three regional associations to support teachers, staff developers, and administrators with professional development for cooperative learning. These were CACIE, GLACIE, and MAACIE (see the introductory chapter). Bob Slavin and I co-founded the Mid-Atlantic Association for Cooperation in Education (MAACIE), which Frank Lyman and I led for many years. Three remarkable staff developers soon joined our leadership team: Pat Jones, Thelma DeLagrange, and Ellen Miller. The five of us were the leaders and officers for many years.

Our leadership team expanded into an active, cross-functional board consisting of faculty, teachers, staff developers, and principals. MAACIE published a newsletter and offered a variety of CL workshops for thousands of teachers, as did its sister organizations CACIE and GLACIE. The first large conference held by MAACIE drew a couple of hundred participants in 1988. Then, MAACIE organized and hosted the 1990 international conference of the IASCE in Baltimore, with over 900 participants—200 in the pre-conference and 700 in the main conference. MAACIE received an Award for Excellence in Staff Development from the Maryland Council of Staff Developers.

Theoretical Issues and Edited Books

Through the IASCE, I developed respect for all the major approaches to CL, taught them in graduate courses for teachers, and demonstrated them selectively in presentations. This led to the questions: How are these approaches similar and how are they different? Are there common elements (critical attributes) common to all the approaches?

These questions stimulated careful analysis, resulting in formulation of five attributes common to all cooperative learning approaches and a dozen others that vary according to the approach (Davidson, 1994, 2002; Davidson & Worsham, 1992; Davidson & Major, 2014). These elements are presented in the introduction to this volume.

I like to illustrate the common elements of CL by an example in music. In school and in the university, I played brass instruments: trumpet and cornet, and later French horn and valve trombone. I aspired to play in a major symphony orchestra but did not quite have the talent to do so. So I became a professor instead and have loved the teaching and scholarship in that profession.

In explaining the essentials of cooperative learning, I often use the analogy of the trumpet trios in which I played and performed. (This analysis could apply to any musical ensemble.)

- We shared a common goal, to perform the music as perfectly and beautifully as possible.
- Our task was to practice and rehearse until we got it right in all respects: tone quality, harmony, volume, cadence and rhythm, synchronization.
- We were interdependent; all of us were essential and had to play our parts well.
- We had to play cooperatively in tune and in harmony with one another. To do so, we had to listen carefully to our partners. If there were differences of opinion or performance style, we had to discuss and resolve them and smooth them out.
- We could not compete with one another by trying to play faster or louder or more dramatically than the others. That would ruin the performance, which had to be fully cooperative.
- We were accountable both individually and as a group for our performance. Whether in a concert or in a contest, we would be rated by our performance as a whole.
- We had role assignments: high, middle, and low parts.

To summarize, playing a trumpet trio exemplified the following major aspects of cooperative learning. A common goal, a group task, working together to accomplish the goal, positive interdependence, cooperative rather than competitive behavior, and individual and group accountability for performance.

The aspect of assigned roles might or might not occur, depending on the cooperative approach and the task. This same comment also applies to group accountability.

Collaborative Learning

At an IASCE conference in 1985, Mark Brubacher and colleagues were talking about collaborative learning (Barnes & Todd, 1977; Britton,

1973; Bruffee, 1993), which was new to me. They edited a book with broad perspectives, including both cooperative and collaborative learning (Brubacher et al., 1990). The book included a chapter on applying Perry's nine-stage intellectual development scheme to small-group cooperative learning (Davidson & Shearn, 1990).

For many years, a puzzling theoretical issue in the field was the relationship between cooperative and collaborative learning. A set of publications addressed this question (Brubacher et al., 1990; Davidson, 1994, 2002; Matthews, Cooper, Davidson, & Hawkes, 1995; Davidson & Major, 2014). Details of the relationships between the two CLs are presented in the introductory chapter. That chapter includes references to books on collaborative learning by Barnes and Todd (1977), Britton (1973), Bruffee (1993), Goodsell, Maher, and Tinto (1992), and Barkley, Major, and Cross (2014).

The key finding is that cooperative and collaborative learning are both types of small-group learning and have certain elements in common. But cooperative learning is not a particular form of collaborative learning and vice versa. The two approaches are different even though related by five common elements.

Four Approaches to Small-Group Learning in Higher Education

This line of inquiry about relationships between two different forms of small-group learning was expanded to include two additional forms. This culminated in a volume describing, analyzing, and comparing the four main forms of small-group learning in higher education: cooperative, collaborative, problem-based (PBL), and team-based learning (TBL) (Davidson, Major, & Michaelsen, 2014). Although these four active learning approaches are different, and are usually presented in different publications and conferences, they have much more in common with each other than with passive modes such as listening to lectures.

This volume, based on the scholarship of integration, arose in part from the annual Lilly Conferences on College Teaching, where all four of these approaches were presented separately. Two of the comparisons, between cooperative and collaborative learning, are presented in the introduction to this current book. And the other two approaches, PBL and TBL are also briefly described here.

Problem-Based Learning

In PBL, complex, real-world problems are used to motivate students to identify and research the concepts and principles needed to work through and solve the problems. Students work in learning teams (each of which typically has a trained facilitator), bringing together collective skill in acquiring, communicating, and integrating information. In PBL students are expected to think critically and be able to analyze and solve complex, real-world problems; find, evaluate, and use appropriate learning resources; work cooperatively in teams and small groups; and demonstrate versatile and effective communication skills, both verbal and written (Barrows, 1986).

Team-Based Learning

TBL places the focus on students actively engaging in activities that require them to *use* concepts to solve problems. Every aspect of a TBL course is specifically designed to foster the development of self-managed learning teams. Four foundational practices are essential for implementing TBL. These are (1) strategically forming permanent teams, (2) ensuring student familiarity with course content by utilizing a Readiness Assurance Process, (3) developing students' critical thinking skills by using carefully designed, *in-class* activities and assignments, and (4) creating and administering a peer assessment and feedback system (Michaelsen, Knight, & Fink, 2004).

Remarks on the Four Approaches to Small-Group Learning

Three of the four approaches have developed a strong research base through quantitative studies. These three are cooperative learning, PBL, and TBL. Studies of collaborative learning are typically more qualitative in nature.

The four approaches to small-group learning came from different origins and developed separately. Initially, advocates of the different approaches were unaware of each other. Each movement had its own territory, including conferences and publication venues.

The four major forms of group learning share important elements. All four stand against passive modalities and lengthy lectures, and they use small-group work as the means to achieve active learning. In addition, they have similar goals for teaching and learning, to encourage development of content knowledge and related intellectual skills, and the ability to work with others.

It is illuminating to step back and consider the relationships among these approaches. Doing so enables us to learn from one another, and perhaps consider opportunities for working together. For a detailed development along these lines, see the volume by Davidson et al. (2014) plus several points in the concluding chapter.

This current volume is devoted to cooperative learning—its historical development, foundational theories, varied approaches of pioneering scholars, current research and classroom practices, and predictions about its long-term future. No doubt, similar volumes could be created for collaborative learning, PBL, and TBL, and I hope they will be.

Professional Development for CL

At an IASCE conference in the 1990s, some of us were talking about the need for professional development for cooperative learning; most faculty cannot learn these techniques simply by reading. We found that approaches to faculty development for CL varied considerably. Celeste Brody and I decided to create a volume on this theme, including multiple viewpoints on professional development for CL. The result was the edited book by Brody and Davidson (1998).

Very briefly, here are a few key points from that volume. An introductory workshop is necessary but not usually sufficient for teachers to become skilled implementers of cooperative learning. The worst mistake in staff development is to give lengthy lectures about active learning and cooperative learning; this is bad modeling. Teachers need to experience cooperative learning as participants in workshops or classes and reflect on their experiences. They need to see example applications in their own subject areas and think about further applications in their classes.

Workshops include some information about the rationale, theory, and research about CL, but they must provide cooperative learning experiences with reflection afterward and address practical implementation questions such as group formation, role of the teacher, assessment and evaluation, and so on. Strong implementation is facilitated when a team of teachers from a school participate in an ongoing program over time, and they then form a collaborative learning community, a support system for one another.

Teachers' beliefs interact with instructional innovations such as CL, and teachers can reconstruct their assumptions and practices through reflective professional development. Professional development program leaders need to create training programs that promote teachers' effective decision-making and that support transfer of learning for classroom and school use.

Fostering Thinking Through CL

In the late 1980s I became interested in the connection between higher-order thinking skills (HOTS) and cooperative learning. For decades, two powerful movements in education had evolved separately—the movement to improve thinking and the cooperative learning movement. The main idea of this project was to link them together consciously.

An acronym suddenly popped into mind: HOTSICLE—Higher-Order Thinking Skills in Cooperative Learning Environments. With that acronym,

I conceived the idea of a book on this topic and formed a partnership with Toni Worsham, an expert on thinking studies. The result was an edited book on enhancing thinking through cooperative learning (Davidson & Worsham, 1992). It brought together multiple perspectives on thinking and learning, and it was far beyond the capabilities of any single author. The chapter authors were experts in one of the two movements being linked, and some were adept in both. Here are a few of the intriguing chapter titles:

> The many faces of cooperation across the dimensions of learning
> Cooperation: worldview as methodology
> Co-cognition: the cooperative development of the intellect
> Cooperative metacognition
> Cooperating for concept development
> Thinking skills and social skills that facilitate cooperative learning
> Encouraging thinking through constructive controversy
> Think-pair-share, Thinktrix, Thinklinks, and weird facts.

Public Presentations, Sometimes Leading to Publications

I have had the opportunity to give hundreds of presentations on CL, ranging from keynote addresses and plenary sessions to research papers to workshops for teachers.

More than 200 of these were on CL in math, and another 200-plus on general CL. Venues included professional conferences, colleges and universities, and school districts.

Some years ago, I was invited to be the keynote presenter for several hundred teachers at the Maryland Middle School Association, and I wrote up my talk in advance. In driving up to the site, I realized that this presentation would be all teacher-talk, and not suitable modeling for middle school teachers. So in the car, I re-designed the presentation with an active learning design, utilizing six different simple cooperative structures. These included the two- or three-step interview, round robin and roundtable, numbered heads together, pairs check (Kagan & Kagan, 2009), and think-pair-share (Lyman, 1992). Some key questions were: What are typical behavior patterns displayed by middle school students in grades 6–8? What are their developmental needs, and how can these be best addressed with varied procedures for learning?

With this approach, the energy and participation level were high throughout and evaluations were "off the charts." Here is a key point: When a teacher is experienced with varied cooperative structures, he or she can often quickly design activities by choosing suitable structures to address the content. This can sometimes be done in more than one way. (I am not advocating last-second, risky redesigns of major presentations.)

Faculty Development in Lilly Pre-conferences

The Original Lilly Conference on College and University Teaching is a major annual event for faculty from diverse institutions to gather together. The conference always includes a strand on small-group learning in its varied forms. Every November, my colleague Barbara Millis and I have offered an annual full-day preconference on cooperative learning, 2015–2019. The presentation involves theory and research on cooperative learning, theoretical distinctions between approaches, a variety of practical techniques, active engagement, reflection on experience, and the connection between cooperative learning and deep learning.

Introverts in CL

Among my dozens of presentations at Lilly Conferences, a recent one deals with helping introverts to thrive in structured cooperative groups—unlike unstructured group work where they can be intimidated by fast talkers and dominators (Davidson, 2015).

This presentation later turned into an article by Millis and Davidson (2018a). We responded to Susan Cain (2012), who argues against group work for introverts in her excellent book, *Quiet*. . . . She has a point for unstructured group work.

Yet well-structured cooperative learning is good for both introverts and extraverts. The structured procedures provide equal time for everyone. Introverts have their turn to talk without interruption, and extraverts cannot take over the conversation. Think-time gives introverts a chance to reflect before they speak. Having taught thousands of introverts for more than 30 years, the two authors, who are introverts ourselves, attest that introverts can indeed thrive during cooperative group work.

Motivation Re-visited

Forty years after my publication on motivation in math (1976), I took another look at this issue with a colleague (Millis & Davidson, 2018b). Cognitive psychologists currently agree that four factors influence motivation: environment, goals, values, and expectations. Among the environmental factors in cooperative learning, most prominent is positive interdependence. The paper describes its role in creating a positive environment for motivation and learning through goals, design of the task, rewards, limited or jigsaw resources, assigned roles, or group structures.

CL and Technology

In my presentation at the Lilly Conference in 2017, a question arose about the possibility of doing cooperative learning online. A participant suggested a particular platform, Adobe Connect, for doing so. This led to the creation of a paper on the promise and challenge of synchronous online cooperative learning (Davidson, Kuthy, Kuthy, & Solomon, 2018). Here are some of the main ideas.

Online learning often occurs asynchronously, with students signing on at different times. In contrast, cooperative learning in the classroom is a synchronous event, where all members are present at the same time in the same space. A synchronous form of online CL simulates face-to-face interaction in a live classroom, via screen-to-screen interaction that allows the participants and instructor to see and hear each other and work on a common document. Hence, it appears that the powerful body of classroom CL research results may transfer from the synchronous classroom environment to the synchronous online environment—but not necessarily to an asynchronous online environment. More details about this are presented in the concluding chapter.

Lecturing and CL

In my beginning days of presenting cooperative learning workshops for faculty, I almost always encountered a point of resistance. Participants balked when hearing the research that cooperative learning is superior to lectures in promoting student achievement. Viewing that research as a "putdown" of the lecture method, they argued in defense of lecturing.

In a humorous conversation about this resistance, Emily Jensen and I created a "twelve step recovery program for lectureholics (teachers addicted to lecturing)." The key idea of our program, which is based on the life-changing Alcoholics Anonymous steps, is to respect the importance of lecturing but to get it under control by alternating brief lectures (lecturettes) with short pair or group activities (groupettes). That approach keeps participants awake and engaged. I have presented this program numerous times with high levels of participant satisfaction and no resistance (Jensen & Davidson, 1997; Davidson, Jensen, & Solomon, 2018).

Week-Long CL Programs

When Richard Solomon and I were invited to present week-long programs in Texas on cooperative learning for enhancing student thinking, the 300 or so participants were teachers in all different grade levels and subject areas. The setting for each year was a large cafeteria with some obstructed views, and the program for each of the five days lasted for six hours. We were fortunate enough to have a cadre of "teaching assistants," who were highly capable and respected teachers. They helped keep their team members focused and engaged. Our constant use of cooperative structures with community-building and team-building activities and classroom management techniques kept the energy level high and the atmosphere lively and enthusiastic. This demonstrated to the participants that cooperative learning can work even in very large classes (which has also been shown repeatedly by several other authors in this volume).

Graduate Teaching, Doctoral Programs, and Dissertations

I was invited by the Regional Training Center (RTC) to design a graduate course for teachers in three states, dealing with enhancing thinking through cooperative learning. My teacher education partner Richard Solomon and I designed the course, created a handbook for participants and an instructors' manual, and trained a cadre of instructors to teach the course. The course demonstrates how varied cooperative procedures can be used to stimulate students' skillful, critical, and creative thinking and metacognition. The first edition of the course used a framework of teaching for, of, and about thinking. The second edition, in use for the past 12 years, is entitled *Encouraging Skillful, Critical, and Creative Thinking*. The handbook is by Solomon and Davidson (2009b) and the instructors' manual by Davidson and Solomon (2009).

Another handbook dealt with relationship activities for cooperative and collegial learning (Solomon, Davidson, & Solomon, 1993). Related papers on varied topics were published by Solomon and Davidson (1990, 1992, 1993, 1996, 2009a) and by Solomon, Davidson, and Solomon (1992). A third handbook by Carroll and Davidson (2004) presented classroom assessment techniques (CATS) applicable with cooperative learning.

Graduate Courses on CL

I offered graduate courses on cooperative learning for teachers at the University of Maryland for many years, and also for one semester apiece at Arizona State University and Salisbury State University. For several years at the University of Maryland, the graduate seminars focused on CL in mathematics. Then I extended the scope of the seminars to include teachers in all subject areas.

The course was wide-ranging in content. It addressed all the major topics and issues in CL rationale, theory, research, curriculum design, and practical classroom implementation.

The seminar was highly experiential in nature. Every cooperative procedure/structure was modeled and demonstrated with the participants as group members. For each procedure/structure, participants brainstormed curriculum activities, implemented that procedure in their own classes, and reflected on how well it worked and what improvements were needed. Support for teachers implementing CL during the practicum was provided through peer observation and coaching, and through reflection sessions during the seminar periods.

Doctoral Courses and Programs

Graduate teaching includes mentoring the next generation of scholars by fostering and advising doctoral students research. I served as major advisor (or co-advisor in a few cases) for 75 doctoral graduates. In leading the doctoral research proposal seminar for many years, my colleagues and I learned to balance challenge and support: setting high standards and supporting students to meet them. The structure for this included cooperative peer editing, where students read and critiqued each other's research proposals, which were exchanged by email. To set a constructive tone of supporting the person while critiquing the document to improve it, students and faculty followed these steps in the critique session: (1) positive aspects of this proposal, (2) questions for clarification, and (3) suggestions for improvement. This structure led to a dramatic increase in the number of doctoral students who were able to complete their proposals for research in a timely manner.

Doctoral Cohort Program

Colleagues Arends, Henkelman, Nash, and I offered a doctoral program in professional development based on learning communities in cohort groups. Each of the three cohort groups took all their courses together in a learning community emphasizing mutual support, active learning, reflection on experience, interpersonal and small-group communication, organization development and culture, training and consulting skills, varied internship settings, and more. Cooperative learning was a major instructional method demonstrated and applied throughout the program. (My experience in Re-evaluation Counseling plus a second master's degree, in counseling, helped enable me to teach these courses.)

The doctoral completion rate for the first cohort group was over 60%, which was much higher than the 25% rate for the College of Education overall. However, we were disappointed by this result and aimed to increase it in the second cohort group. We hypothesized that the problem was this: intense community support during the coursework program was followed by isolated individual effort during the dissertation phase. We countered that by establishing a doctoral dissertation cooperative support group that met regularly to offer encouragement, sharing and presentations of work, and constructive peer critique in cooperative peer editing. That intervention boosted the completion rate to 92% in the second cohort group (Henkelman & Davidson, 2014). (The results for a third cohort group were mixed, because an administrative structural issue forced the group in midstream to split into two separate cohorts.)

Teacher Education and Professional Development

How can cooperative learning be incorporated into teacher education preparation programs? One research-based approach is a combination of theory, clear modeling, and practice opportunities with feedback. In applying this notion, my colleagues and I repeatedly demonstrated varied methods of cooperative learning in courses on methods of teaching in secondary schools. Students design lessons for CL, and practice by presenting short lessons to small groups of peers in videotaped microteaching sessions. Constructive feedback with clear criteria is provided by students and by the instructor. This is also done with other models of teaching such as the lecture, concept attainment model, and behavioral skill mastery model. (Arends, 1998; Lyman & Davidson, 2004).

Combining Student Teaching With Professional Development for Teachers

In addition to my regular faculty role, I was invited by my colleague Jim Greenberg to serve as coordinator of an innovative campus/field program, combining student teaching and professional development for teachers, and did so for 17 years through the University of Maryland Office of Laboratory Experiences. We worked closely with Maurice Erly, Coordinating Supervisor of Staff Development in Prince George's County, MD, who identified several middle and senior high schools with innovative principals. These schools became professional development centers for the preparation of student teachers. Each school had a small, interdisciplinary school-based supervision team of outstanding teachers who took responsibility for the student teaching program at their school. They learned to function as a cooperative team of field-based teacher educators and staff developers with unusually high levels of professional responsibility.

My co-coordinator Richard Solomon and I offered a series of graduate courses providing intensive staff development for the teams. Cooperative learning was a central theme throughout the course program. The teams of teachers in turn provided staff development for their school colleagues, as well as for the student teachers. This program won an Award for Excellence in Staff Development from the Maryland Council of Staff Developers. Professional conference presentations about the program sometimes included several of our supervising teachers. One example of this, presented at a national conference, was by Solomon, Davidson et al. (1990).

The Clinical Classroom Project, developed by Richard Arends and Joyce Murphy of the Maryland State Department of Education, brought together teacher educators from several colleges and universities. For three years, we functioned as demonstration teachers, who opened up our own university classrooms to observers and conferred with them about our lessons, which employed active learning and cooperative learning techniques. At the request of teachers, we also gave demonstration lessons in schools to provide modeling of active learning and cooperative learning for teachers in their own classrooms with their own students. This helped teachers to see how to apply cooperative learning in their own classroom situations (Winitzki & Arends, 1991).

Mastery Teaching and CL

Through the Clinical Classroom Project, I had the opportunity to participate in two stimulating workshops with Madeline Hunter, founder of the prominent seven-step Mastery Teaching model, which had been adopted by multiple school districts. This led me to see how to enhance her model by incorporating research-based cooperative learning practices in several of its phases: input, modeling, checking for understanding, and guided practice (Davidson & O'Leary, 1990). We found that this combination helped teachers who had been confined by administrators to rigidly follow the steps of Hunter's model, and who wanted a stronger research base for their teaching.

University Faculty Development

For several years at the University of Maryland, I worked closely with Jim Greenberg in the Center for Teaching Excellence, providing workshops for faculty, department consultations on teaching, and developing a faculty consultation program for individual faculty who wanted to improve their teaching. One outgrowth of my work with CTE was a publication reflecting on practical implementation of cooperative small-group learning (Davidson, 1998).

A second outgrowth was co-creating (with colleagues Alt, Assad, and Varner) an Academy of Excellence in Teaching and Learning (AETL), an ongoing community of faculty who have shown outstanding devotion to teaching and learning and who strive to enhance its quality and status in this research university. One of its goals is to stimulate faculty participation in the scholarship of teaching and learning (SoTL).

Personal Reflections on the IASCE and My Roles in It

I became the fourth president of the IASCE in 1990, following in the footsteps of three distinguished leaders: Richard Schmuck, Shlomo Sharan, and Robert Slavin. It was a favorable time to be president of the Association. Cooperative learning was riding on an ascending wave of popularity globally, due to its solid research base, well-developed theory, and cadres of strong faculty/staff developers in different models of CL.

Our long-term newsletter editors, Ted and Nancy Graves (later known as Liana Forrest), expanded their publication into the *Cooperative Learning Magazine*, which was colorful and appealing to teachers, not just to researchers.

For the first time, we held regular Board meetings of the IASCE, via telephone conference calls. The format with multiple people on the phone was somewhat difficult to manage, but Liz Cohen's "meeting tamer" approach was helpful in keeping the lines of communication more clear. (Video conferencing did not exist at that time.)

Membership in the IASCE was growing, largely due to the growth of the regional CL associations. And we held IASCE conferences almost every year from 1990 to 1995 in four different countries.

By 1992, I was ready to turn over the leadership of the Association over to the next person, but there was no next person. Elizabeth Cohen would have been the logical choice in terms of stature in the field, but she was much too busy to take on that job. Everyone else on the Board refused to take on the role of president, and I agreed reluctantly to stay on for a second term—which was not as good as the first one because the Board was facing some difficult decisions. At my request, Richard Schmuck provided a skillful organization development consultation with the Board, which helped us to establish a new direction. Finally, in 1995, I happily retired as president, and Mara Sapon-Shevin agreed to take on that role. Soon thereafter, she and Bette Chambers shared the role jointly. Thus began a system of co-presidents, which was a fine idea compatible with cooperative values and which persisted for many years. Lynda Baloche, Celeste Brody, and Maureen Breeze took turns serving effectively as co-presidents for years.

The IASCE was active for a period of 40 years. Then it finally closed, and the last newsletter was published in the summer of 2020 during the coronavirus pandemic. Several past or present Board members felt there was still a need for communication about cooperative learning among the members, and Laurie Stevahn and I formulated a proposal to establish a CL network.

Its purpose is to cultivate ongoing communication among educators worldwide who are passionate about fostering continued growth and development of CL. With the closing of the IASCE, the CL movement can benefit from an energizing international presence to keep alive theory, research, and practice relevant to CL, curriculum development, professional development, and effective leadership in educational organizations.

Our proposal to establish a network was co-sponsored by several prominent IASCE leaders, and the formation of the network was announced in the final newsletter. At that time, to provide ongoing communication opportunities for people interested in CL, the IASCE morphed into a network: Network of International Cooperative Learning Educators and Enthusiasts (NICLEE)—pronounced "nicely," which can be accessed at http://www.2020niclee.com.

Concluding Remarks

It has been a privilege to take part in the development of cooperative learning in and beyond mathematics for the past half century. I honor, respect, and value the contributions of my cooperative friends and colleagues in bringing to fruition their diverse approaches to CL

Cooperative learning is now well established in the educational landscape and will have a bright future, for all the following reasons. It is firmly based on a combination of active learning and social learning; it mobilizes student energy for learning and builds upon basic human needs for affiliation.

CL has a strong rationale, a solid theory of social interdependence, and an impressive research base with varied types of positive outcomes. There are several approaches to CL with well-honed instructional practices and effective methods for staff development.

CL can be applied with any age group of students and any curriculum area. Instructional materials have been created for CL across a wide range of academic disciplines. And CL can be used effectively in conjunction with other instructional approaches such as the lecture, class discussion, projects, and online learning.

CL has been widely recognized through presentations and publications of varied major professional associations. And CL has become linked with several other educational movements including intercultural and multicultural education, thinking studies, multiple intelligences and abilities, win-win discipline, conflict resolution, and peace education.

The discussion of the future of cooperative learning is continued and elaborated upon in the concluding chapter.

References

Arends, R. (1998). *Learning to teach*. Boston, MA: McGraw Hill.
Asch, S. E. (1960). Effects of group pressure upon the modification and distortion of judgments. In D. Cartwright & A. Zander (Eds.), *Group dynamics*. Evanston, IL: Row & Peterson.

Bales, R. F., & Borgatta, E. F. (1961). Size of group as a factor in the interaction profile. In A. P. Hare, E. F. Borgatta, & R. F. Bales (Eds.), *Small groups, studies in social interaction*. New York, NY: Alfred A. Knopf.

Barkley, E., Major, C., & Cross, K. P. (2005, 2014). *Collaborative learning techniques: A handbook for college faculty*. San Francisco, CA: Jossey-Bass.

Barnes, D., & Todd, F. (1977). *Communicating and learning in small groups*. London: Routledge, Kegan Paul.

Barrows, H. S. (1986). A taxonomy of problem-based learning methods. *Medical Education, 20*, 481–486.

Bassarear, T., & Davidson, N. (1992). The use of small group learning situations in mathematics instruction as a tool to develop thinking. In N. Davidson & T. Worsham (Eds.), *Enhancing thinking through cooperative learning*. New York, NY: Teachers College Press.

Britton, J. (1973). *Language and learning*. Baltimore, MD: Penguin.

Brody, C., & Davidson, N. (Eds.). (1998). *Professional development for cooperative learning: Issues and approaches*. Albany, NY: SUNY Press.

Brubacher, M., Payne, R., & Rickett, K. (Eds.). (1990). *Perspectives on small group learning: Theory and practice*. Oakville, ON: Rubicon.

Bruffee, K. (1993). *Collaborative learning: Higher education, interdependence, and the authority of knowledge*. Baltimore, MD: The Johns Hopkins University.

Cain, S. (2012). *Quiet: The power of introverts in a world that can't stop talking*. New York, NY: Broadway Paperbacks.

Carroll, K., & Davidson, N. (2004). *Classroom assessment techniques (CATS)*. Randolph NJ: Regional Training Center.

Dancis, J., & Davidson, N. (1970). The Texas method and the small group discovery method. In *The Legacy of R. L. Moore* (online and on CD).

Davidson, N. (1970, 1971a). *The small discovery method of mathematics instruction as applied in calculus*. Doctoral Dissertation, University of Wisconsin, Madison. Published in 1971 by the Wisconsin Research and Development Center for Cognitive Learning.

Davidson, N. (1971b, August–September). The small group discovery method as applied in calculus instruction. *American Mathematical Monthly*, 789–791.

Davidson, N. (1976). Motivation of students in small-group learning of mathematics. *Frostburg State College Journal of Mathematics Education, 11*, 1–18.

Davidson, N. (1979). The small-group discovery method: 1976–77. In J. Harvey & T. Romberg (Eds.), *Problem solving studies in mathematics*. Madison, WI. The Wisconsin Research and Development Center for Individualized Schooling.

Davidson, N. (1980a). Small-group learning and teaching in mathematics: An introduction for non-mathematicians. In S. Sharan, P. Hare, C. Webb, & R. Hertz-Lazarowitz (Eds.), *Cooperation in education* (pp. 136–145). Provo, UT: Brigham Young University Press.

Davidson, N. (1980b). Using reevaluation counseling to change education. In S. Sharan, P. Hare, C. Webb, & R. Hertz-Lazarowitz (Eds.), *Cooperation in education* (pp. 182–194). Provo, UT: Brigham Young University Press.

Davidson, N. (1985). Small-group learning in mathematics: A selective review of the research. In R. Slavin, et al. (Eds.), *Learning to cooperate, cooperating to learn*. New York, NY: Plenum Press.

Davidson, N. (Ed.). (1990a). *Cooperative learning in mathematics: A handbook for teachers*. Menlo Park, CA: Addison-Wesley (available through Dale Seymour).

Davidson, N. (1990b). Small group cooperative learning in mathematics. In T. Cooney (Ed.), *Teaching and learning mathematics in the 1990s*. Reston, VA: National Council of Teachers of Mathematics. NCTM Yearbook.

Davidson, N. (1994, 2nd ed., 2002). Cooperative and collaborative learning: An integrative perspective. In J. Thousand, R. Villa, & A. Nevin (Eds.), *Creativity and collaborative learning: A practical guide for empowering teachers and students* (pp. 13–30). Baltimore, MD: Brookes Publishing.

Davidson, N. (1998). Small-group cooperative learning: What I have learned in the past thirty years. In S. Selden et al. (Eds.), *Essays on quality learning* (pp. 169–178). College Park, MD: University of Maryland. IBM Total Quality Project.

Davidson, N. (2015). *How to help introverts thrive in cooperative groups*. Presentation at the International Lilly Conference on College Teaching. Miami University, Ohio.

Davidson, N., Agreen, L., & Davis, C. (1978). Small group learning in junior high school mathematics. *School Science and Mathematics, 1*, 23–20.

Davidson, N., & Fabian, R. (1963). Some cardinal equivalences with explicit formulas. *American Mathematical Monthly, 20*(6), 647–649.

Davidson, N., & Gulick, F. (1976). *Abstract algebra: An active learning approach*. Boston, MA: Houghton Mifflin.

Davidson, N., Jensen, E., & Solomon, R. D. (2018). 12 step recovery program for lectureholics: Workshop summary. In C. Sweet, H. Blythe, & R. Carpenter (Eds.), *It works for me with high impact practices* (pp. 32–39). Stillwater, OK: New Forums.

Davidson, N., & Kroll, D. L. (1991). An overview of research on cooperative learning related to mathematics. *Journal for Research in Mathematics Education, 22*(5), 362–365.

Davidson, N., Kuthy, A., Kuthy, D., & Solomon, R. D. (2018). The promise and challenge of synchronous online cooperative learning. In C. Sweet, H. Blythe, & R. Carpenter (Eds.), *It works for me with high impact practices* (pp. 44–47). Stillwater, OK: New Forums.

Davidson, N., & Major, C. (2014). Boundary crossings: Cooperative learning, collaborative learning, and problem-based learning. In Davidson, N., Major, C., and Michaelsen, L. (Eds). (2014). Small group learning in higher education—cooperative, collaborative, problem-based and team-based learning. *Journal on Excellence in College Teaching, 25*(3&4).

Davidson, N., Major, C., & Michaelsen, L. (Eds.). (2014). Small group learning in higher education—cooperative, collaborative, problem-based and team-based learning. *Journal on Excellence in College Teaching, 25*(3&4).

Davidson, N., Major, C., & Michaelsen, L. (2016). Understanding cooperative, collaborative, problem-based and team-based learning through the scholarship of integration. In H. Blythe, C. Sweet, & R. Carpenter (Eds.), *It works for me with SOTL*. Stillwater, OK: New Forums Press.

Davidson, N., & McKeen, R. (1979, December). An expanded domain for objectives in mathematics education. *American Mathematical Monthly, 86*(10), 858–862.

Davidson, N., McKeen, R., & Eisenberg, T. (1973, March). Curriculum construction with student input. *The Mathematics Teacher*, 271–275.

Davidson, N., & O'Leary, P. (1990, February). How cooperative learning can enhance mastery teaching. *Educational Leadership*, 30–34.

Davidson, N., & Shearn, E. (1990). Use of small group teaching and cognitive developmental instruction in a mathematical course for prospective elementary school teachers. In M. Brubacher, R. Payne, & K. Rickett (Eds.), *Perspectives on small group learning: Theory and practice* (pp. 309–327). Oakville, Ontario: Rubicon.

Davidson, N., & Solomon, R. D. (2009). Instructors manual. In R. D. Solomon, & N. Davidson (Eds.), *Encouraging skillful, critical, and creative thinking*. Graduate course handbook. Randolph, NJ: Regional Training Center.

Davidson, N., Weissglass, J., & Roberston, L. (1990). Staff development for cooperative learning in mathematics. *Journal of Staff Development, 11*(3), 12–17.

Davidson, N., & Worsham, T. (Eds). (1992). *Enhancing thinking through cooperative learning*. New York, NY: Teachers College Press.

Deutsch, M. (1960). The effects of cooperation and competition upon group process. In D. Cartwright & A. Zander (Eds.), *Group dynamics*. Evanston, IL: Row & Peterson.

Dewey, J. (1916). *Democracy and education*. New York, NY: Macmillan. (Republished by Collier, 1966).

Dewey, J. (1938). *Experience and education*. New York, NY: Kappa Delta Pi. (Republished by Collier, 1966).

Dubinsky, E., Mathews, D., & Reynolds, B. (Eds). (1997). *Readings in cooperative learning for undergraduate mathematics*. Mathematical Association of America. MAA Notes Series #44. Washington, DC: Mathematical Association of America.

Goodsell, A., Maher, M., & Tinto, V. (Eds.). (1992). *Collaborative learning: A sourcebook for higher education*. University Park, PA: National Center on Post-Secondary Teaching, Learning, and Assessment.

Hagelgans, N., Reynolds, B., et al (1995). *Practical guide to cooperative learning in collegiate mathematics*. Mathematical Association of America. MAA Notes Series #37.

Henkelman, J., & Davidson, N. (2014). Building a learning community in a doctoral programme in professional development. In B. Cocklin, K. Coombe, & J. Retallick (Eds.), *Learning communities in education* (pp. 230–246). London: Routledge.

Jackins, H. (1972). *Fundamentals of co-counseling manual*. Seattle: Rational Island Publishers.

Jackins, H. (1973). The nature of the learning process. In *The human situation*. Seattle: Rational Island Publishers.

Jensen, E., & Davidson, N. (1997). 12-step recovery program for lectureholics. *College Teaching. 45*(3), 102–103.

Kagan, S., & Kagan, M. (2009). *Kagan cooperative learning*. San Clemente, CA: Kagan.

Lyman, F. (1992). Think-Pair-Share, Thinktrix, Thinklinks, and weird facts: An interactive system for cooperative thinking. In N. Davidson, & T. Worsham (Eds.), *Enhancing thinking through cooperative learning*. New York, NY: Teachers College Press.

Lyman, F., & Davidson, N. (2004). Cooperative learning in preservice teacher education at the University of Maryland. In E. Cohen, C. Brody, & M.

Sapon-Shevin (Eds.), *Teaching cooperative learning: The challenge for teacher education* (pp. 83–95). Albany, NY: State University of New York Press.

Matthews, R. S., Cooper, J. L., Davidson, N., & and Hawkes, P. (1995). Building bridges between cooperative and collaborative learning. *Change, 27*(4), 34–37.

McKeen, R., & Davidson, N. (1975). An alternative to individual instruction in mathematics. *American Mathematical Monthly, 82*(10), 1006–1009.

Michaelsen, L. K., Knight, A. B., & Fink, L. D. (2004). *Team-based learning: A transformative use of small groups in higher education.* Sterling, VA: Stylus.

Millis, B., & Davidson, N. (2018a). Helping introverts thrive during cooperative group work. In C. Sweet, H. Blythe, & R. Carpenter (Eds.), *It works for me with high impact practices* (pp. 29–32). Stillwater, OK: New Forums.

Millis, B., & Davidson, N. (2018b). How structured small groups (cooperative learning) can motivate students. In C. Sweet, H. Blythe, & R. Carpenter (Eds.), *It works for me with high impact practices* (pp. 26–28). Stillwater, OK: New Forums.

Moise, E. E. (1965). Activity and motivation in mathematics. *American Mathematical Monthly, 72*(4), 407–412.

National Council of Teachers of Mathematics. (1989). *Curriculum and evaluation standards for school mathematics.* Reston, VA: NCTM.

Polya, G. (1962, 1965). *Mathematical discovery* (Vols. 1 & 2). New York, NY: Wiley.

Robertson, L., Davidson, N., & Dees, R. (1999). Cooperative learning to support thinking, reasoning, and communicating in mathematics. In S. Sharan (Ed.), *Handbook of cooperative learning methods.* Westport, CT: Greenwood.

Rogers, B., Reynolds, B., Davidson, N., & Thomas, A. (2002). *Cooperative learning in undergraduate mathematics: Issues that matter and strategies that work.* Mathematical Association of America. MAA Notes Series #55.

Sears, P., & Hilgard, E. (1964). The teacher's role in the motivation of the learner. In E. Hilgard & H. Richey (Eds.), *Theories of learning and instruction.* Sixty-third Yearbook of the National Society for the Study of Education (pp. 182–209). Chicago, IL: University of Chicago Press.

Slavin, R. E. (1983). When does cooperative learning improve student achievement? *Psychological Bulletin, 94,* 429–445.

Solomon, R. D., & Davidson, N. (1990). *Collaborating with schools from a campus-based perspective.* Presentation at the American Association for Higher Education Conference on School/College Collaboration. Chicago, IL. 6/19/90.

Solomon, R., & Davidson, N. (1992). Cooperative learning and the relationship skills: Tools for positive social development. *Cooperative Learning, 11*(2), 25–27.

Solomon, R., & Davidson, N. (1993). Cooperative dimensions of learning. *Cooperative Learning, 13*(2), 37–43.

Solomon, R., & Davidson, N. (1996). Staff development in cooperative learning using cooperative structures and relationship skills. In H. Rimmerman (Ed.), *Resources in cooperative learning.* San Juan Capistrano, CA: Kagan Cooperative Learning.

Solomon, R., & Davidson, N. (2009a). Cooperative learning: Research and implementation for Jewish education. *Jewish Educational Leadership, 7*(3).

Solomon, R. D., & Davidson, N. (2009b). *Encouraging skillful, critical, and creative thinking.* Graduate course handbook. Randolph, NJ: Regional Training Center.

Solomon, R., Davidson, N., & Solomon, E. (1992). Some thinking skills and social skills that facilitate cooperative learning. In N. Davidson & T. Worsham (Eds.), *Enhancing thinking through cooperative learning* (pp. 101–119). New York, NY: Teacher's College Press.

Solomon, R., Davidson, N., & Solomon, E. (1993). *The handbook for the fourth r: Relationship activities for cooperative and collegial learning, Vol. III*. Columbia, MD: National Institute for Relationship Training, Inc.

Springer, L., Stanne, M. E., & Donovan, S. (1999). Effects of small group learning on undergraduates in science, mathematics, engineering, and technology: A meta-analysis. *Review of Educational Research. 69*, 21–51.

University of Maryland Mathematics Project. (Cole, M., Davidson, N., Fey, J., & Henkelman, J. et al). (1978). *Unifying concepts and processes in elementary mathematics*. Boston, MA: Allyn and Bacon.

Urion, D., & Davidson, N. (1992). Student achievement in small-group instruction versus teacher-centered instruction. *Primus, 2*(3), 257–264.

Weissglass, J. (1976). Small groups: An alternative to the lecture method. *The Two-Year College Mathematics Journal, VII*, 15–20.

White, R., & Lippitt, R. (1960). Leader behavior and member reaction in three "social climates". In D. Cartwright & A. Zander (Eds.), *Group dynamics*. Evanston, IL: Row & Peterson.

Winitzki, N., & Arends, R. (1991). Translating research into practice: The effects of various forms of training and clinical experience on preservice students' knowledge, skill, and reflectiveness. *Journal of Teacher Education, 42*(1), 52–65.

Chapter 11

Synthesis of CL Approaches and a Multifaceted Rationale for CL—Past, Present, and Future

Neil Davidson

This chapter is divided into four sections. The first section provides a synthesis of the varied approaches to cooperative learning (CL). The second presents a multifaceted rationale for using CL in the classroom environment—past, present, and future. The third section presents a number of questions for future research with CL. The fourth section is a discussion of the development of CL in online environments.

Synthesis of CL Approaches

The field of CL can be viewed as a big tent (or as a large umbrella) covering multiple approaches to small-group learning. In this section, we pull together all the major approaches to CL. The authors speak for themselves, mostly through direct quotations.

> *In each small section here, an author's name is given at the start with italics. Every statement or quotation in that section comes from the chapter by that author.*

Sharan and Sharan: "A sweeping movement to break the mold and actively engage students of all ages in learning emerged in the 1960s and 1970s. Many educational researchers and educational psychologists, some of whom are represented in this volume, perceived that a change was crucially needed. They came from different theoretical and cultural backgrounds, and developed a variety of interactive methods and models, many of which were eventually grouped under the 'umbrella' term 'cooperative learning'. Their efforts heralded a fundamental change in educational practice that has since spread worldwide."

Deutsch via Stevahn: Deutsch's original research on the effects of cooperation or competition in discussion groups became foundational for the CL movement.

  Deutsch's (1949a, 1949b) theory, supported by his doctoral dissertation research, predicts that people in cooperative relations (defined by positive goal interdependence) compared to competitive relations (defined by negative goal interdependence) display a consistent set of characteristics. . . . Specifically, cooperators (versus competitors) tend to:

- Communicate effectively (versus ineffectively).
- Interact in friendly, helpful, and trusting ways (versus unfriendly, unhelpful, and untrusting ways).
- Coordinate effort productively (versus disjointedly or ineffectively).
- Experience feelings of agreement and similar beliefs and values that increase self-confidence (versus repeated disagreement and rejection that diminish self-confidence).
- Recognize, respect, and respond to the needs of others (versus disregarding or disrespecting others).
- Enhance the power of others (versus one's own to diminish the power of others).
- View interpersonal conflicts as mutual problems to solve (versus contests to win).

"Because cooperative learning induces, cultivates, and nurtures the very characteristics conducive to constructive conflict resolution, it becomes more than solely an instructional strategy to promote student achievement. It also helps establish the types of supportive relationships, respectful norms, and democratic values in schools and classrooms that underpin constructive conflict."

"There are many kinds of research, all with merit. They have differing purposes and often require varying types of skill. . . . Mort would encourage us to recognize and uphold the value of each other's contributions toward collectively furthering understanding of effective cooperation, conflict, and justice."

Johnson and Johnson. "We developed our [Learning Together] method following four principles: (a) practical procedures should be derived from theory, (b) the theory must be validated by research, (c) operational procedures should be formulated from the validated theory, and (d) the implementation of the operational procedures will reveal shortcomings and "holes" in the theory, which results in revisions in the theory."

"We now have over 1,200 research studies from which we can calculate effect sizes and hundreds more that have been conducted but do not report enough data to calculate effect sizes."

For Johnson and Johnson, CL has five key elements: "positive interdependence, face-to-face promotive interaction, individual and group accountability, development of teamwork skills, and group processing."

"It is only when teachers carefully structure five basic elements into a lesson that students truly cooperate with each other and the full potential of the group will be reached. Through the use of the five basic elements, teachers become instructional engineers/designers who can take their existing lessons, curricula, subject areas, courses, and students and structure any lesson cooperatively."

"It should be recognized that the use of cooperative learning groups creates certain opportunities that do not exist when students work competitively or individually. In cooperative groups discussions can take place in which students can construct and extend conceptual understanding of what is being learned and develop shared mental models of complex phenomena. Group members can hold each other accountable to learn, provide feedback on how well groupmates are doing, and give support and encouragement for further attempts to learn. . . . It is through discussions in small groups that students acquire attitudes and values. Finally, it is within cooperative groups that students establish a shared identity as members of the school or university."

"We developed four types of cooperative learning: formal, informal, base groups, and constructive controversy," all described in their chapter.

"Constructive controversy is a form of cooperation when ideas and opinions clash but must be reconciled. The teacher's role consists of assigning students to groups of four, dividing the groups into pro and con pairs, having each pair prepare the best case possible for their assigned position, present their position as persuasively as they can, engage in an open discussion in which they critically analyze each other's positions and give it a 'trial by fire,' reverse perspectives and present the opposing position as best they can, and, dropping all advocacy, come to an agreement reflecting their best reasoned judgment about the issue."

Slavin and Madden: The methods of Student Team Learning include STAD, TGT, TAI, and CIRC, all described in their chapter. Each of these employs two key conditions, group goals/rewards and individual accountability, found to be necessary for CL to improve student achievement.

"Group goals mean that the team is working together to achieve success, and they can earn recognition or small rewards for doing so. Individual accountability means that in achieving their group goals, teams have to ensure that every member of the team is mastering the material the group is studying. The purpose of the combination of group goals and individual accountability is to try to make sure that team members are teaching each other, explaining difficult ideas, helping each other study, and encouraging each other's success."

Slavin identified motivationalist, social cohesion, and cognitive theoretical perspectives on the achievement effects of CL. The cognitive view includes both developmental and elaboration issues.

"Motivationalist-oriented scholars focus more on the reward or goal structure under which students operate. . . . Methods derived from this perspective emphasize the use of group goals and individual accountability, meaning that group success depends on the individual learning of all group members."

"The social cohesion perspective (also called social interdependence theory) suggests that the effects of cooperative learning are largely dependent on the cohesiveness of the group. This perspective holds that students help each other learn because they care about the group and its members."

"The cognitive perspective holds that interactions among students will in themselves increase student achievement for reasons which have to do with mental processing of information rather than with motivation."

Cohen via Lotan and Holthuis: Complex Instruction is "designed to create equitable learning opportunities and outcomes for all students by supporting equitable interactions in academically, racially, ethnically, and linguistically diverse classrooms." It employs multiple-ability tasks, task cards, assigned roles, random assignment to groups, and an intervention for students of low status by "assigning competence."

"Many different intellectual abilities are needed to complete the task successfully. Intellectual abilities such as analyzing, asking good questions, explaining, interpreting complex texts, diagrams and graphs, making plans, designing an experiment with multiple variables, synthesizing information, organizing a group, facilitating adeptly, and many more kinds of 'smarts' are demonstrated by members of the group."

"Teachers emphasize that while no one person is good at all these intellectual abilities and is able to demonstrate them all convincingly and consistently, everyone is good at some of these abilities and can demonstrate intellectual strengths."

"Unlike tightly defined, recipe-like tasks with predictable outcomes, groupworthy tasks are open-ended, productively uncertain, and require authentic problem solving and critical thinking."

Kagan: "We work with a basic formula: *Structure + Content = Activity*. Because structures are content-free, any one structure can generate an infinite number of activities. Structures can be thought of as activity generators. Given any one structure, we can insert different content every day to create a new activity."

Four basic principles of the structural approach to CL (with the acronym PIES) are Positive interdependence, Individual accountability, Equal participation, and Simultaneous interaction.

Seven keys to success in the structural approach are identified as structures, teams, management, classbuilding, teambuilding, social skills, and basic principles (PIES)—all described in Kagan's chapter.

"In the cooperative learning classroom which includes integrated student teams, teambuilding, and cooperative projects and learning tasks, students come to know each other as individuals, not merely as members of a racial group. Through teambuilding activities students get to know each other and appreciate individual differences. Cooperative projects and cooperative learning include mutual support activities, tutoring, coaching, praising, and celebrating. Students experience themselves as on the same side, working together to reach common goals. Through this process students get to know the humor, intellect, feelings, thoughts, and perspectives of their classmates. When then asked who they want to sit next to or invite home, they can decide based on knowing their classmates as individuals, not just as members of a racial group. In essence, cooperative learning makes possible the vision of Martin Luther King Jr., who dreamed of a time when students would relate to each other by the quality of their character not the color of their skin."

"When students are on the same side and a gain for one produces a gain for another, they are motivated to encourage, tutor, coach, and praise each other, which in turn leads to greater academic achievement. It also produces a 'same-side' cooperative social orientation that improves social relations. Students develop positive social skills, social relations, and character virtues like caring, compassion, and responsibility to others."

Sharan and Sharan: "Group Investigation (GI). As part of the 'umbrella' of CL procedures, GI incorporates the essential principle of positive interdependence. Although cooperative learning methods and models vary in their goals and emphasize different skills, they all structure group members' interaction so that each member's efforts are required and indispensable for reaching the group's goal. A firm base in fundamental cooperative social and learning behaviors is an essential prerequisite for carrying out a GI project."

"As a cooperative learning model Group Investigation integrates interaction and communication among learners with the process of academic inquiry. In the course of a GI project learners take an active part in the investigation of a multifaceted problem that is, generally, part of the curriculum. The classroom becomes a social system built on cooperation in learning *within* groups and on coordination of learning *among* groups. Organizing learning in this way creates conditions that allow students, in collaboration with their classmates, to identify questions for inquiry, plan together the procedures needed to understand and research these questions, collect relevant information, and cooperatively (though not necessarily *collectively*) prepare a presentation of the results of their investigation, usually in some creative and interesting way."

"Teaching and learning through CL and GI systematically develop habits of active participation, social interaction, inquiry, and reflection. These learning and social skills are essential to productive group processes, whether at work or in school. They are becoming increasingly important wherever there is genuine concern about initiating and managing productive teamwork, problem-solving, and continuous learning in schools and workplaces."

Aronson: "The Austin public schools were finally desegregated and all hell broke loose. African-American, Anglo, and Mexican-American youngsters were in open conflict; fistfights were breaking out among these groups in corridors and schoolyards."

"There was residential segregation, and the schools in the black and Latino neighborhoods were substandard; as a result, the reading skills of the minority kids were approximately one full grade level behind those of the Anglo kids."

"We invented a technique that created small interdependent groups, designed to place students of different racial and ethnic backgrounds in a situation where they needed to cooperate with one another in order to understand the material. We called it the jigsaw classroom, because the process was like assembling a jigsaw puzzle, with each student contributing a vital piece to the total picture." "The formal data confirmed our casual observations: Compared to students in traditional classrooms, students of all ethnicities liked school more (absenteeism significantly declined) and liked each other more—across and within ethnic and racial groups. For white students, self-esteem and test performance remained constant. But the minority students in jigsaw classrooms showed a significant increase in self-esteem and their test performance averaged nine percentage points higher than those of minority students in traditional classrooms. This difference was highly significant both statistically and meaningfully."

"My students and I had shown that prejudice *can* be overcome, and that children of different ethnic backgrounds can learn to like one another. What it takes is not simply *increased* contact but the right *kind* of contact."

"Diane Bridgeman [doctoral student with Aronson] speculated that working in jigsaw groups would lead to the sharpening of a youngster's general empathic ability. The fact that the children, who learned to work cooperatively, developed the ability to put themselves in another person's shoes is a crucial precursor to compassion and prejudice reduction."

"Not only did our experiments demonstrate that, by changing the structure of the classroom from competitive to cooperative, desegregation could work.... In one experiment after another, my students and I had shown over and over again that jigsaw was an effective, simple way to reduce prejudice and bullying, improve performance, and raise the self-esteem of minority students. We also succeeded in increasing children's liking for school and their ability to empathize with their classmates."

Schmuck via Arends and Davidson: Organization development (OD) in schools is aimed at helping teachers and school principals to develop skills in interpersonal communication, procedures to work more effectively in groups, and new ways of setting goals, solving problems, and making decisions. "OD techniques can help students, teachers, and administrators use democratic cooperation to design a healthy social climate for all."

The OD approach was designed to improve the capabilities and functioning of schools' intact subsystems. The following capabilities become the targets of their interventions: clarifying communication, establishing goals, working with conflict, improving meetings, solving problems, and making decisions.

As with the organization development work, the Schmucks' work in group processes stemmed from ideas from social psychology, group dynamics, and small-group theory. The Schmucks highlighted the importance of interpersonal interactions and group processes in the classroom. They identified several important group processes that would produce a more positive and cooperative classroom environment: communication, friendship and cohesiveness, shared expectations and norms, leadership, and conflict resolution.

They drew on group development theories to describe how classrooms pass through discernible stages as they become more satisfying and productive learning communities. These stages include dealing with inclusion and membership, influence and collaboration, setting individual and academic goals, and self-renewal.

Unlike some of the other early scholars included in this book, the Schmucks did not create specific CL strategies to be used by teachers in their classrooms.

Schmuck described the mutually sustaining relationships between organization development and CL. He explored "how collegial relationships among the staff members of a school and teacher-student relationships in that school's classes can reciprocally affect one another . . . and become mutually enhancing and sustaining."

"The relationship between cooperative learning and organization development is two way and reciprocal. The starting point for moving toward a cooperative school culture can be either through OD or through CL. . . . I believe, for either OD or CL to be sustained effectively over the long run, both OD and CL must be going on."

"When teachers collaborate with their principals and colleagues in setting school goals and in planning new instructional patterns, they begin to feel empowered as teachers, and their professional self-concepts and commitment to humane practices become increasingly stronger. Because they feel supported and respected, they can more easily give their support and respect to students. Moreover, when teachers become more interdependent with one another, they can more readily use the skill of constructive openness, thereby improving their teaching strategies through the giving and receiving of feedback. The prototype of such an exchange of feedback, nowadays, is peer coaching and mentoring. . . . Some norms, roles, structures, and procedures, already common in cooperative learning, must become part of the school culture if cooperation is to be sustained as a system of values in education. The cooperative school culture has norms in support of respecting everyone's ideas and feelings, of equalitarian teamwork and collaborative effort, of openness, candor, and honesty, of warmth and friendliness, of caring for people of all ages, and of seeking self-esteem for everyone."

Davidson part 1: Davidson developed the "small group discovery method" of learning mathematics, an early form of CL. Three key elements in the design were Dewey's philosophy of active engagement, intellectual challenge via discovery learning, and social support through small-group learning. A strong rationale showed that mathematics is well suited, even ideally suited, for small-group learning. This method was first implemented in a university course in calculus for an entire academic year.

The course design was based on the educational philosophy of Dewey (1916, 1938). Learning by doing includes personal experiences and reflection on those active learning experiences. Students are engaged in non-routine, thought-provoking activities. Learning is a social process, "a social enterprise in which all individuals have an opportunity to contribute and to which all feel a responsibility."

Motivation is intended to be intrinsic, whenever possible. Interest in the mathematical ideas and activities is intended to be the main source of motivation. The motivational goal is for students to view each mathematical topic as being intrinsically interesting, valuable, or useful.

The course design incorporated several research findings from social psychology. Cooperation was superior to competition in groups. Democratic leadership was more effective than authoritarian or laissez-faire leadership. Group size affected discussions. Conformity pressure, a risk in groups, could be reduced by setting norms for independent judgment.

Students work together in small groups, typically with four members apiece, in a working space with a flip chart or section of the chalkboard. Students work together cooperatively in each group on challenging activities. They actively exchange ideas with one another and help each other learn the material.

The teacher presents guidelines for cooperative group problem-solving, including the following: achieve a group solution for each problem, make sure that everyone understands, listen carefully to others and build on their ideas, make sure that everyone participates and no one dominates, and take turns writing problem solutions on the board.

Students working together cooperatively in small group discuss mathematical ideas, develop techniques for solving problems, make conjectures for investigation, prove theorems, and discover many ideas and techniques that were new to them.

Davidson part 2: Expanding his scope from CL in mathematics to general CL, Davidson has identified five attributes that are common to all the approaches to CL.

1. A common task or learning activity suitable for group work.
2. Small-group interaction focused on the learning activity.
3. Norms for cooperative, mutually helpful behavior among students as they strive together to accomplish the learning task.
4. Individual accountability and responsibility for what students have learned and/or contributed toward the learning goal. (Some approaches also include group accountability.)
5. Positive interdependence in working together—also known as interdependence or mutual interdependence.

In addition to the common attributes, there are also a dozen attributes that vary among the approaches to CL. These varying attributes are helpful in analyzing similarities and differences among CL approaches (and also among collaborative learning, problem-based learning, and team-based learning).

The four major forms of small-group learning share the common elements of CL. Moreover, they share some common educational goals and values. All four stand against passive modalities and lengthy lectures, and they use small-group work as the means to achieve active learning. In addition, they have similar goals for teaching and learning: to encourage development of content knowledge and related intellectual skills, and the ability to work with others. Proponents of these four approaches have much more in common with each other than with advocates of the lecture method. We are among friends with similar values yet different approaches to small-group learning.

A Multifaceted Rationale for CL—Past, Present, and Future

It has been a labor of love for the first-generation pioneers to lead the development of CL for the past half century. CL is now well established in the educational landscape, occurring regularly in thousands of classrooms around our planet.

The future of CL will vary according to global conditions of health and safety, affecting the ability to learn with others in classrooms. Let us begin with the "normal" pre-pandemic conditions, where learning together can take place in physical classrooms. I will present a multifaceted rationale for CL in the classroom, followed by a set of questions for research with CL. After that will follow a brief discussion of CL online, which has become an area of research and development in recent years. Doing CL online has also become a widespread need during conditions of widespread infectious disease.

Multifaceted Rationale for Classroom CL

1. CL is firmly based on a combination of active learning and social learning. It mobilizes student energy via active learning and builds upon basic human needs for affiliation, through small-group interaction.
2. There are ancient historical roots of cooperative small-group learning. People have taken turns speaking in discussion circles throughout the ages. An ancient Jewish tradition is having a partner with whom to study the Talmud through discussion and disputation.
3. From an evolutionary biological perspective, Samples (1992, p. 38) concludes:

   "Cooperation is not a new idea. . . . Rather it is an ancient legacy. It lives in residence in our biological make up—forming the basis for our earliest socialization and represents a powerful expression of human spirituality."

4. CL has a strong foundation through the educational philosophy of John Dewey. That philosophy emphasizes learning by doing through personal experience, reflection on experience, non-routine, thought-provoking activities, intrinsic motivation, and learning as a social process: "A social enterprise in which all individuals have an opportunity to contribute and to which all feel a responsibility."
5. The philosophy of constructivism asserts that students find or make their own meaning, in contrast to having it supplied by the teacher or text. A constructivist psychological foundation for CL is provided by the Russian psychologist Lev Vygotsky. He found that knowledge is a social product, that social interaction plays a fundamental role in the development of cognition. "Every function in the child's cultural development appears twice: first on the social level, and later, on the individual level" (1934, p. 57). Whether or not one accepts this order of development in all cases, Vygotsky's findings and theory establish a clear connection between individual and social cognitive functions.

Several approaches to CL have roots in the theory of constructivism. Constructivist authors include Vygotsky, Dewey, and Piaget (1950), who established a theory of four main stages in child development through adolescence. (The stages are sensorimotor, preoperational, concrete operational, and formal operational.)

6. The theory of multiple intelligences (Gardner, 1983) encompasses nine "intelligences," which some scholars regard as abilities (as in Complex Instruction). The intelligences are as follows: verbal-linguistic, visual-spatial, interpersonal, intrapersonal, logical-mathematical, bodily kinesthetic, musical, naturalist, and existential. The first three of these come into play in all CL activities. Intrapersonal intelligence is

activated by reflection on group process and individual learning. The last five occur depending on the task.
7. In Complex Instruction, "many different intellectual abilities are needed to complete the task successfully." These multiple abilities were described in the first section. "Teachers emphasize that while no one person is good at all these intellectual abilities and is able to demonstrate them all convincingly and consistently, everyone is good at some of these abilities and can demonstrate intellectual strengths" (Lotan and Holthuis, for Cohen).
8. Based on brain research, Caine et al. (2009) set forth several foundational brain/mind principles. Each brain/mind learns in a unique way, and it requires social interaction. The brain/mind is influenced by emotions, and searches for patterns and seeks meaning. These principles are put into action in CL environments.
9. PET scans of the brain (Carter, 1998) show the following: Widespread brain activity occurs when explaining to a partner—much more so than in listening, reading, or thinking about words. The latter three stimulate only the auditory cortex, visual cortex, and Broca's area, respectively (Figure 11.1).
10. Students' attention span is a major issue in learning. How long can students pay attention to a lecture before their mind wanders? Teachers often respond to this question by saying 4 minutes, 8 minutes, 12 minutes or even as long as 20 minutes. Several studies show that as a lecture gets longer, students' pulse rate, respiration rate, and alertness decrease significantly. Based on an analysis of working memory and cognitive overload, Felder and Brent conclude: "There is no possible way that a student can absorb even a small fraction of the information that routinely bombards their senses during your class" (2016, p. 93). A student who is overloaded or comatose or asleep is not going to learn from the presentation, whereas a student who is awake has a chance to learn. CL keeps students wide awake and engaged during the class time.
11. There are several views of student motivation in CL. An intrinsic motivation perspective (Dewey, 1938; Deci & Ryan, 1985) makes use of internal motivators such as interest, curiosity, task accomplishment, and enjoying group discussion. An external motivation perspective employs rewards such as bonus points and team recognition in team competitions (Slavin, 1995).

Slavin (1995) identified motivationalist, social cohesion, and cognitive theoretical perspectives on the achievement effects of CL. These perspectives were described earlier. They emphasize, respectively, the reward or goal structure, or cohesiveness of the group, or interactions related to mental processing of information.

An additional perspective by Sears and Hilgard (1964) and by Davidson looks at a combination of cognitive, ego-integrative, and social

PET Scans

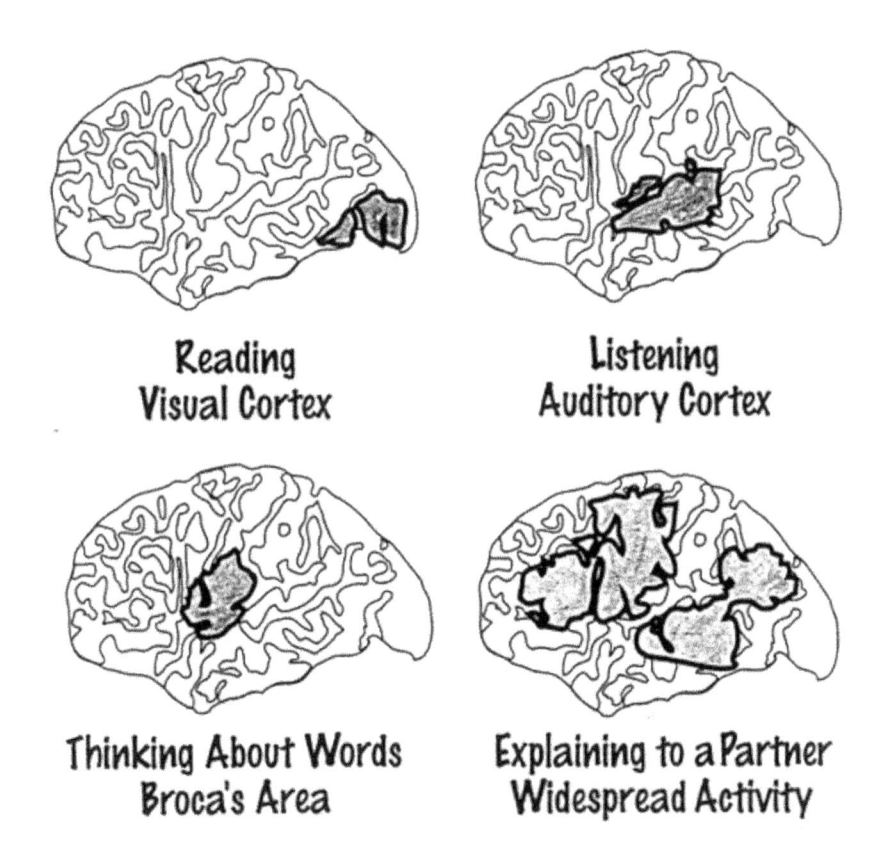

Reading
Visual Cortex

Listening
Auditory Cortex

Thinking About Words
Broca's Area

Explaining to a Partner
Widespread Activity

Figure 11.1 PET scans of the brain
Source: Rita Carter (1998). *Mapping the mind*, p. 150. Berkeley: University of California Press.

motives for learning. A strength of cooperative learning is having several different sources of motivation for students, leading to several explanations for the achievement effects of CL.

12. CL has a strong rationale and a solid, empirically validated theory of social interdependence, which focuses on cooperative, competitive, or individualistic efforts. Positive interdependence leads to promotive, mutually beneficial interaction. Negative interdependence leads to oppositional interaction. And no interdependence leads to working alone

with no interaction. These three types of interdependence lead to different psychological processes and outcomes (Deutsch and the Johnsons).

The theory of positive social interdependence is illustrated by several slogans:

> We sink or swim together. We're all in this together. None of us is as smart as all of us.
> Two heads are better than one. All for one and one for all.
> TEAM: Together Everyone Accomplishes More

13. CL has a strong foundation in years of research in social psychology. A central finding is that cooperation is more effective than competition in discussion groups. Democratic leadership or friendly directive leadership are more effective than laissez-faire leadership styles by the teacher. Conformity pressure can be an issue in groups, and there are ways to reduce conformity and to foster independent thinking. Size of the group can affect the quality of interaction. Techniques exist to build trust and cohesiveness in groups. (References for all these are given in Chapters 1 and 10 by Davidson.)
14. The combination of affiliative needs and student energy, and the resulting research outcomes, is displayed in Figure 11.2.

CL has an impressive research base with several types of positive outcomes—cognitive, affective, and related to diversity and inclusion—as shown in Figure 11.2. Much of this research base was contributed by Slavin, the Johnsons, the Sharans, Aronson, and Cohen.

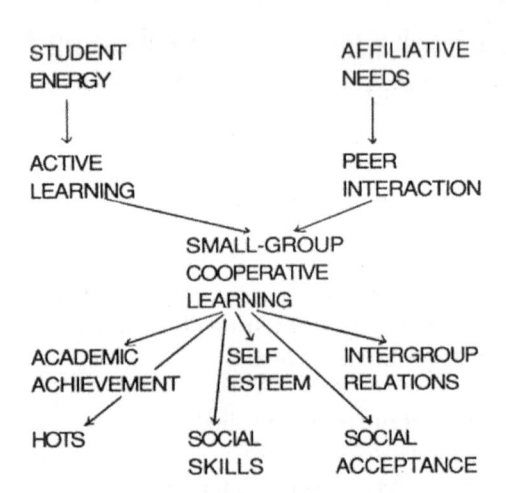

Figure 11.2 Research outcomes from using student energy and affiliative needs

15. More recent research by Kagan and colleagues on the structural approach contributes several positive outcomes. Some of these confirm previous research results, specifically with the structural approach, and some of these are new. The outcomes include increased achievement both individually and school-wide, reduced achievement gaps (high-low gap and racial gap), and progressive reduction of the achievement gap with longer duration of CL. Disruptive behaviors decreased and prosocial behaviors increased, leading to improved race relations and positive school integration.
16. From a sociological perspective, Complex Instruction is "designed to create equitable learning opportunities and outcomes for all students by supporting equitable interactions in academically, racially, ethnically, and linguistically diverse classrooms" (Lotan and Holthuis, for Cohen).
17. "There are many kinds of research, all with merit. They have differing purposes and often require varying types of skill" (Deutsch via Stevahn). In their reviews and meta-analyses of cooperative learning, the Johnsons have included all the available studies from which they can calculate effect sizes. In contrast, Slavin has selected studies that met "best-evidence" inclusion criteria such as use of control groups with minimum duration of 12 weeks, measures not made by researchers, and random assignment, if possible. Although the selection criteria for studies varied in these two approaches, the positive outcomes of cooperative learning turned out to be the same, even if the effect sizes were different. This is a striking confirmation for the empirical research results of cooperative learning.
18. How do students feel about cooperative learning? Attitude surveys by a number of researchers and teachers generally show student liking for and satisfaction with CL (which is not the same as unstructured group work). Students often make comments such as: "CL is fun. It keeps you awake. Other students help you understand. My team-mates explain in their own language; I understand it better than the teacher's. It's so interesting that the class period goes by quickly. It's exciting to talk about these ideas. I never expected to like this subject, but I do because we get to talk it over. I make friends in this class at the same time as I am learning."
19. Effects of cooperative learning on teachers who use it include renewed enthusiasm for teaching and learning, and enjoying the freshness and creative ingenuity of their students' thinking. Teachers experience a sense of intellectual companionship with their students, and come to know them as individuals, while leading and participating in a vibrant community of learners.

Teachers who employ cooperative learning for several years often develop a personal vision and philosophy for teaching and learning such as this:

- Student engagement and energy in active learning.
- Social learning with lively intellectual discussions.
- Peer interaction in small groups and the whole class.
- Skills in communication, cooperation, and teamwork.
- Critical and creative thinking.
- Hands-on, minds-on classroom.
- Everyone awake and involved, no one asleep.
- Academic success for all learners.
- Enjoyment of learning and developing friendships.
- Including everyone with respect for diversity.

20. Seven principles of good practice in undergraduate education (Chickering & Gamson, 1987) include the following:

    - Encourages contact between students and faculty.
    - Develops reciprocity and cooperation among students.
    - Encourages active learning.
    - Gives prompt feedback.
    - Emphasizes time on task.
    - Communicates high expectations.
    - Respects diverse talents and ways of learning.

Virtually all of these occur in CL.

21. Studies of student retention versus dropping out of higher education by Astin (1977, 1993) and others addressed multiple variables. They found that the most important influences on the quality of university life and retention of students are relationships with teachers and relationships with peers. CL in small groups provides for both of these.
22. In business, industry, and government, the use of small groups and teams has become common practice. A number of major reports address the question: What do business and industry want from employees? Consistent findings across the reports include communication skills, being a team player, critical and creative thinking, initiative and persistence. Cooperative learning helps to develop all these abilities, thereby giving students skills needed for success in the "real world" of work.
23. There are now several approaches to CL with well-honed instructional practices and effective methods for staff development, as shown by the authors in this volume.
24. There are several models for developing entire cooperative schools or for promoting and supporting CL throughout an entire school district

25. CL can be applied with any age group of students and any curriculum area. Instructional materials have been created for CL across a wide range of academic disciplines.
26. CL can be used effectively in conjunction with other instructional approaches such as the lecture, class discussion, project development, and online learning.
27. CL has been recognized through presentations and publications of varied major professional associations.
28. CL has become linked with several other educational movements, including intercultural and multicultural education, thinking studies, multiple intelligences and abilities, win-win discipline, conflict resolution, and peace education.

Conclusion About the Future of Classroom CL

CL has a strong multifaceted rationale with well-developed theoretical foundations, an impressive body of research results, well-honed classroom practices and procedures for professional development, applicability with varied age groups and curriculum areas, acceptance by major professional organizations, and much more. For all these reasons, cooperative learning has staying power; it will not go away. All these points, which are valid in the past and present, will also be valid in the future. The best predictor of the future success of CL is its success in the past and present, which is already well established. Hence, CL will have a bright future in classroom learning wherever it is safe for people to gather together in groups.

Selected Research or Inquiry Questions

With a strong multifaceted rationale for CL and an impressive body of positive research results, one would expect CL to be widely implemented. To what extent is this actually the case? While thousands of teachers are implementing CL, many others are not doing so.

The first set of questions for inquiry deals with the extent and type of implementation of CL. In these following questions, the term "schools" also refers to colleges and universities and "teachers" also refer to professors.

- What are the main concerns of teachers in deciding whether or not to implement CL?
- How many teachers implement any form of small-group learning?
- How many of them implement cooperative learning?
- In what age groups and curriculum areas do they use CL?
- In what percentage of their class time do they implement CL?
- What, if any, professional development have they received in CL?
- Does their school or district have a professional development program for CL?

- How successful is the CL program in one's school or district?
- Are teachers who become "stars" of CL assisting other teachers to succeed?
- Are teachers designing special CL lessons or are they using CL in part of every lesson?
- Are teachers using CL in conjunction with other instructional approaches? If so, which?
- What approaches to classroom management are being employed with CL?"

The following questions deal with cognition or development with CL.

- What are the effects on student cognition when CL is combined with a system for classifying types of questions such as Think Trix (Lyman), the Question Matrix (Wiederhold), Six Types of Data (Solomon), or Bloom's Taxonomy? (see Davidson & Worsham, 1992).
- In terms of Piaget's development stages, does long-term CL help students to progress from a pre-operational stage to concrete operational, or from concrete operational to the formal operations stage?
- In terms of Perry's scheme of intellectual development, does long-term CL help students to progress from dualism to multiplicity, or from multiplicity to contextual relativism?
- What are the ramifications of Vygotsky's "zone of proximal development" in cooperative learning groups?
- How well does CL, which is different from unstructured group activities, work with introverts? (Many of us already "know" the answer from experience—introverts do very well in CL—but this has not yet been formally studied.)

The following three questions deal with the relationship of CL to the other major forms of small-group learning: collaborative learning, PBL, and TBL

- What can practitioners of collaborative learning, as described in the Introduction, learn from CL and vice versa? For example, collaborative teachers might benefit from using a few specific techniques from CL and by developing students' social skills as needed. Cooperative teachers might benefit from eventually loosening their structure a bit, somewhat akin to collaborative learning, after students are well-versed in working together cooperatively.
- What can TBL practitioners gain from CL and vice versa? TBL teachers could benefit from the CL use of teambuilding and some specific cooperative techniques to develop effective team functioning. CL teachers could benefit from an assessment system, perhaps modified

from the one in TBL but less bureaucratic, that motivates students to study outside of class
- What might PBL teachers learn from cooperative learning and vice versa? CL teachers might incorporate more real-world problems as a basis for meaningful and productive group work, as in PBL. (This already takes place in the group investigation model of CL.) PBL teachers could benefit from the CL use of teambuilding and some specific cooperative techniques to develop effective team functioning. PBL teachers might also benefit from the occasional use of assignments other than real-world problems to provide more variety in tasks.

"There remains a need for development and evaluation of cooperative learning programs that solve key problems of teaching and learning in all subjects and grade levels, and for continued research to identify the conditions under which cooperative learning is most likely to be effective. The greatest need at this point, however, is to develop and evaluate forms of cooperative learning that can be readily and successfully adopted by schools on a large scale, and to study the impediments to successful adoption of cooperative strategies. There is also a continued need to combine cooperative learning with other elements to create whole-school approaches capable of making a substantial long-term impact on the achievement of disadvantaged students. After 50 years of research and application, cooperative learning still has much more to contribute to students' learning" (Slavin and Madden).

CL and Technology via CL Online

The founders of CL have focused for decades on CL in the classroom. In recent years, some scholars have begun to focus on the possibilities of doing CL online. There is now considerable interest in developing CL online, which is still in its early stages.

One of the greatest challenges to cooperative learning in the year 2020 and after is the coronavirus pandemic. Educational institutions all around the globe have been forced to shut down physically and to provide online learning for students. The tendency in this situation will be to resort to traditional presentation formats with skills practice via individual worksheets or online individual practice assignments.

How can CL survive in such an environment? A presentation at the Lilly Conference in 2017 led to creation of a conceptual paper on the promise and challenge of synchronous online CL (Davidson et al., 2018). Here are some of the main ideas adapted and expanded from that paper.

The traditional paradigm for online learning, prior to the pandemic, involves asynchronous learning, where participants are working in their own time frames and not necessarily simultaneously Now, however, numerous teachers around the world have suddenly become online teachers. Their default mode is often synchronous, as in: I record myself giving lectures and I broadcast the videos on scheduled days at the same class times.

Let us distinguish between the presentation phase and the student activity phase of online learning. During an online presentation, students can watch and listen either synchronously, all at once, or asynchronously, at varying individual times. Similarly, students can engage in activities either simultaneously or at varying times. We propose to expand the earlier traditional paradigm of asynchronous group activity to include synchronous cooperative learning, where group members are working together online simultaneously.

Cooperative learning in the classroom is a synchronous event, where all members are present at the same time in the same space. A synchronous form of online CL simulates face-to-face interaction in a live classroom, via screen-to-screen interaction that allows the participants and instructor to see and hear each other and work on a common document. Each small group meets together at one time in its own separate "breakout room." Hence, it appears that the powerful body of classroom CL research results might transfer from the synchronous classroom environment to the synchronous online environment—but not necessarily to an asynchronous online environment. While asynchronous learning in small groups is a legitimate educational activity, it is different from cooperative learning.

In terms of platforms, video conferencing via ZOOM offers promise for cooperative learning in the online classroom. Adobe Connect, Webex, Go to Meeting, Google Meet, or other platforms that offer similar features and reliability with breakout rooms might also facilitate comparable interactions.

CL has never been simple for teachers. The implementation issues arising in online CL are complex, even more than in classroom CL. The technological issues, for example in getting the breakout rooms to function, add an extra layer of complexity. Basic problems need to be resolved, such as being able to log in online and stay online, with unstable internet connectivity resulting in frozen images or distorted sound or dropping offline. Considerable development and research need to be done rapidly to manage all the implementation issues arising in online CL. The future of CL online will depend on the ability of educators and technologists to work together to resolve these issues rapidly.

There are many examples of development work for online CL. The final issue of the IASCE Newsletter in the summer of 2020 is accompanied by abstracts of articles over a period of many years; some of these deal with CL and technology. One can access this information by going to the site for the Network of International Cooperative Learning Educators and Enthusiasts (NICLEE): http://www.2020niclee.com.

One recent example of a study of online CL is by Ferenc Arato (personal communication). It is entitled "A shift to the future—the cooperative paradigm online." "This chapter presents how to transfer the cooperative paradigm into the online world. It explains how to follow the basic elements or principles of cooperative learning online, how to structure the online learning process in a cooperative way, how to preserve the interpersonal space and time in the virtual world, and gain more offline time for the students and teachers. This chapter explains through practical examples how one can quickly build the cooperative principles into their online learning and teaching process from primary level to university level."

A major review of active engagement in learning online in STEM subjects is currently underway by Prince, Felder, and Brent (personal communication). A portion of that review deals with online CL. It is organized into sections according to the Johnsons' model with studies pertinent to positive interdependence, individual accountability, promotive interaction, appropriate use of collaborative skills, and regular self-assessment of team functioning. The review demonstrates that substantial efforts are being made in the development and research of online CL.

In the larger picture, humanity has shown resilience in meeting some major crises in the past. There has been noteworthy progress in the last few years in developing platforms for online presentations, meetings, and classes. With an optimistic outlook, we can look forward to technological progress in online learning capabilities, so that CL can function smoothly and effectively online with minimal technology glitches. This is a case where technological progress can benefit both social and educational well-being. With such progress, if teachers understand and can implement the basic elements of CL, cooperative learning can have a bright future online as well as in the physical classroom setting.

Concluding This Story

Let us conclude this volume in the same way as it began, with two quotations from anthropologist Margaret Mead.

> *Never doubt that a small group of thoughtful, committed citizens can change the world; indeed, it's the only thing that ever has. Never believe that a few caring people can't change the world. For, indeed, that's all who ever have.*

These quotations truly apply to the group of pioneering authors of cooperative learning, whose work has changed the educational world in significant ways.

To recap, we each began our work in a time period of growing interest in the social sciences. We aimed to apply the concepts and practices of social psychology or sociology and group dynamics to foster cooperation in the classroom and to enhance active learning in small groups. To this end, we each developed our own independent line of inquiry.

Many of us met each other for the first time in Israel in 1979. We collectively formed a professional association, the IASCE, for scholarship supporting the growth and development of cooperation in education. We also formed several regional associations to reach large numbers of teachers and staff developers. We met together periodically in conferences of the IASCE, its regionals, and other scholarly associations such as the AERA. We shared our ideas with our colleagues, and we learned from and were stimulated by their ideas. We worked individually at times, but often with a partner or a small team, so we were both independent and interdependent.

While all of us agreed on the goal of fostering cooperation in the classroom, some of us were also working toward a larger goal of fostering cooperation and peace in the wider world. Naturally, we each preferred our own approach and values, and we sometimes disagreed with one another. But even when we disagreed, we usually did so respectfully and with true appreciation for our colleague—in the spirit of the advice of Shimon Peres: "When a friend makes a mistake, the friend remains a friend, and the mistake remains a mistake."

Collectively and individually, we produced an extensive and powerful body of theory, research, classroom practice, professional development, and curriculum development. Emerging from all this scholarship, there came into being the "big tent" of cooperative learning, covering many different approaches and perspectives for CL. Each approach inspired many teachers to adopt it and put it into practice, and every day, thousands of teachers are implementing the diverse approaches to CL. This is our legacy to the world of education.

Second Volume Planned

The living pioneers of cooperative learning are all now in their seventies or eighties, and the torch is being passed or has been passed to the next generation. A number of second-generation scholars have made important contributions to cooperation in education. We anticipate and are planning another edited volume with second-generation CL leaders from around the world, whose published works began in the mid-to-late 1970s or later. It will be interesting and exciting to see how their work builds upon and extends ours in the first generation. The second volume will be edited mainly by a team from the second generation of CL, with Robyn Gillies taking the lead, Barbara Millis, and Neil Davidson (helping out from the first generation).

References

Astin, A. W. (1977). *What matters most in college: Four critical years*. San Francisco, CA: Jossey-Bass.

Astin, A. W. (1993). *What matters most in college: Four critical years revisited*. San Francisco, CA: Jossey-Bass.

Caine, R., Caine, G., McClintic, G. C., & Klimek, K. (2009). *12 brain/mind principles in action: Developing executive functions of the human brain* (2nd ed.). Thousand Oaks, CA: Corwin Press.

Carter, R. (1998). *Mapping the mind*. Berkeley, CA: University of California Press.

Chickering, A. W., & Gamson, Z. F. (1987). Seven principles of good practice in undergraduate education. *Washington Center News*.

Davidson, N., Kuthy, A., Kuthy, D., & Solomon, R. D. (2018). The promise and challenge of synchronous online cooperative learning. In C. Sweet, H. Blythe, & R. Carpenter (Eds.), *It works for me with high impact practices* (pp. 44–47). Stillwater, OK: New Forums.

Deci, E. L., & Ryan, R. M. (1985). *Intrinsic motivation and self-determination in human behavior*. New York, NY: Plenum.

Deutsch, M. (1949a). A theory of cooperation and competition. *Human Relations, 2*, 129–151.

Deutsch, M. (1949b). An experimental study of the effects of cooperation and competition upon group process. *Human Relations, 2*, 199–231.

Dewey, J. (1916). *Democracy and education*. New York, NY: Macmillan. (Republished by Collier, 1966).

Dewey, J. (1938). *Experience and education*. New York, NY: Kappa Delta Pi. (Republished by Collier, 1966).

Felder, R. M., & Brent, R. (2016). *Teaching and learning STEM: A practical guide*. San Francisco, CA. Jossey-Bass.

Gardner, H. (1983). *Frames of mind: The theory of multiple intelligences*. New York, NY: Basic Books.

Piaget, J. (1950). *The psychology of intelligence*. London: Routledge.

Samples, R. (1992). Cooperation: Worldview as methodology. In N. Davidson & T. Worsham (Eds.), *Enhancing thinking through cooperative learning* (pp. 29–40). New York, NY: Teachers College Press.

Sears, P., & Hilgard, E. (1964). The teacher's role in the motivation of the learner. In E. Hilgard & H. Richey (Eds.), *Theories of learning and instruction*. Sixty-third Yearbook of the National Society for the Study of Education (pp. 182–209). Chicago, IL: University of Chicago Press.

Slavin, R. E. (1995). *Cooperative learning: Theory, research, and practice* (2nd ed.). Boston, MA: Allyn and Bacon.

Vygotsky, L. (1934, 2012). *Thought and language* (revised ed.). Cambridge, MA: The MIT Press.

Index

Note: Page numbers in *italics* indicate a figure and page numbers in **bold** indicate a table on the corresponding page.

ABCD Tally Chart 113
academic achievement: cooperative, competitive, and individualistic learning 50; in jigsaw classrooms 6, 153–154; and social relations in GI classroom 176
academic achievement gains, with Kagan Structures 104–107, *105*; across content and grade levels 106–107; high school algebra 105–106; high school chemistry 104–105; school-wide achievement 106
academic learning 5, 184, 187
Academy of Excellence in Teaching and Learning 226
achievement effects of cooperative learning 132, 244; cognitive perspective on 134, 236, 237; integration of theoretical perspectives on 134–135, *135*; motivationalist perspective on 133, 236; social cohesion perspective on 133–134, 237
achievement gap 95, 104, 124, 247; reduction with Kagan Structures 107–108; in TSQA 95; *see also* academic achievement
Acme-Bolt Trucking Game 24–25
active learning 3, 204, 206, 214, 218, 219, 224, 226, 228, 242, 248
active listening 91
Adolescent Society, The (Coleman) 129
AERA *see* American Educational Research Association

AETL *see* Academy of Excellence in Teaching and Learning
African-American adolescents 64
Allport, Gordon 154
American Educational Research Association 25
Arnstine, Donald 201
Aronson, Elliot 3; as change agent 157, 159; classroom structure analysis 150–151; communication strategies to increase condom usage 159–160; doctoral pursuit at Stanford 147–148; under Festinger's guidance 148; on human cognition and motivation 148–149; jigsaw classroom 151–152; letter received from student 160–161; love with art of experimentation 149; personal journey with prejudice 146–147; sophomore at Brandeis University 147; on US Supreme Court decision 149–150
asynchronous learning 251–252
attention span of students 244
attitude 27, 28, 34, 108, 109, 247
Austin public schools, desegregation of 149, 150–151, 157, 239

Baltimore schools 132
Black history classes 45
blackline masters 131
black–white achievement gap reduction, with Kagan Structures 107–108
Bradford, David 202

brain/mind principles 244
Brown v. Board of Education 63
bungling actions 28

"Cadres of OD specialists," district-based 186
"Cadres of Organization Specialists" 186
California Association for Cooperation in Education (CACIE) 15, 215
cathexis 27, 28
Center for Interracial Cooperation 64
Center for Teaching Excellence 226
child development, stages in 243
CI *see* Complex Instruction
CIRC *see* Cooperative Integrated Reading and Composition
Civil Rights Act of 1964 187
Civil Rights Commission 157, 158
civil rights movement of early 1960s 44–46
CL *see* cooperative learning
classbuilding 90, 105
classroom 237; CL strategies in 188–189; competitive structure of 150–151; ethnically heterogeneous 176–177; management options 11; processes 188; *see also* cooperative learning; desegregated classrooms, equal-status interactions in; GI classroom, students' language in; groups, processes in classroom; jigsaw classroom
classroom CL 243–249
classroom, ways of structuring: group work 96–98; Kagan Structures 98–100; traditional instructional strategies 93–96
Clinical Classroom Project 225–226
closure pair discussion 54
CLUME (Cooperative Learning in Undergraduate Mathematics Education) Project 210
coaching, in Structural Approach 102–103, *103*, 107
cognitive dissonance theory 147, 160
cognitive motives 207
Cohen, Elizabeth 3, 63, 237; experimental tests of Status Characteristics Theory 64; tribute to 73–74; *see also* Complex Instruction

Coleman, James 129
collaborative learning 3, 216, 250; online 178; philosophy of 12; qualitative nature of 218; versus cooperative learning 12–13, 217
Common Core State Standards 71
communication effectiveness 185
community-building 11, 13, 223
competition: and conflict 32; destructive and constructive variation of 33; social orientation towards 117–118
competitive learning: competitive efforts 57; competitive orientations and conflict processes 34; research reviews of 49–52
competitive social comparison 96
competitive social orientation 118
Complex Instruction 63–64, 237, 247; attributes of 11; case study of 65–66; conceptual framework of 66–67; factors contributed to growth of 71–72; outcome measures 67; programmatic precursor of 65; promoting equitable learning 66; student interactions in 67; theoretical and practical aspects of 73
Complex Instruction implementation: collegial interactions 67; conditions necessary for successful 69–70; exploring aspects of 70–72; intellectual heterogeneity promotion 68; investments in 72; in multilingual classrooms 67–68; observations and data in 72–73; positive outcomes of 67–68, 72; status interventions 68–69, 73
Conant, James 184
condom usage, communication strategies to increase 159–160
conflict 32–33, 37, 185
conflict resolution 18, 32, 33
constructive competition 33
constructive conflict resolution: core aspects of 32; Deutsch's theory 33–35; role in justice orientation 37
constructive controversy 54–55, 236
constructivism 243
contact theory 45, 49
Continuous Simultaneous RoundTable 99–100

cooperation 4; basic elements of 55–57; from evolutionary biological perspective 243; versus competition in discussion groups 246
cooperation and competition, theory of 27–30; bungling actions of cooperators 28; characteristics of cooperators 29–30; competitive conditions 28; cooperative conditions 27; effective actions of cooperators 27–28; goal interdependence and actions 27–29, 28, 49; validating research of 49–52
cooperative base groups, teacher's role in 54
cooperative behavior 8, 177, 178, 208
Cooperative Elementary School 131
cooperative goals: achievement 28; and conflict 32–33
cooperative groups: discussions 52, 236; experience of being member of 172; introverts in CL 221; problem-solving guidelines 241; student behavior within 137
Cooperative Integrated Reading and Composition 128, 131, 139–140
cooperative interaction 45
cooperative learning 1–2, 165; challenges to 251; critical attributes of 6–10, 235–236; definitions and descriptions of 4–5; effectiveness of 6; future of 59–60; groups 4, 18, 52, 56, 236; implementation in United States 167; institutionalization of 47, 50; multifaceted rationale for 242–249; and OD, relationships between 189–190; origins 3–4; research 6; research reviews of 49–52; sample procedures and techniques 5; structural approach to 4, 7; success of 59; support resources 103–104; types of 53–54; varying attributes of 10–12; versus collaborative learning 12–13; worldwide implementation of 59; see also Complex Instruction; jigsaw classroom; Kagan Cooperative Learning; organization development; small-group learning, in mathematics; Student Team Learning; Success for All; teacher education project for CL

Cooperative Learning Center 46
cooperative learning teaching procedures 52; importance of 59; Parker's and Dewey's approach 53; principal guiding development of 53; teacher's role in 53–55
cooperative methods 134
cooperative orientations and conflict processes 34
cooperative small-group discovery see small-group learning, in mathematics
cooperative versus competitive behavior, situations determining 78–80
cooperators 235; bungling actions of 28; characteristics of 29–30; effective actions of 27–28
Co-op Meetings 103
curriculum development for CL 208–209

Davidson, Neil 3, 241–242; as advisor for doctoral graduates 224; designed graduate course 223; doctoral pursuit of 201–206; faculty development for CL 219; fascinated by Dewey's philosophy 201–202; graduate courses on CL 223–224; on HOTS and CL 219–220; insights into teaching and learning 206; launching pad for professional career 205; on lecturing versus CL 221; personal reflections on IASCE 226–228; publication on motivation in math 221; public presentations on CL 220–223; social change movements 205–206; views on Moore method 201; see also small-group learning, in mathematics
DeAvila, Ed 65
decision making 185
delayed feedback 96
democratic leadership 246
desegregated classrooms, equal-status interactions in: conditions supporting 71; cooperative learning methods for 64–65; educational interventions for 63–64; status interventions 68–69; see also school desegregation

desegregation *see* school desegregation
Designing groupwork: Strategies for the heterogeneous classroom (Cohen & Lotan) 72, 73
destructive conflict 37
Deutsch, Morton 3, 17, 234–235; at 1996 AERA 25–26; achievements of 17; childhood and adolescence of 19; clinical internships 20; concern for sustained peace 35–37; death of 38; defined social situations 17; definition of conflict 32; doctoral pursuits of 20–21, 26, 234; early influences on 18; enduring personal qualities of 41; exposure to theorists 19; focus on distributive justice 36; focus on injustice 19, 20, 35; framework for considering injustice/oppression 36–37; game theory as rigorous methodology 23–25; graduate studies of 19–20; initial grandiose theory 23; interracial housing study 35; lessons learned from 38–40; Lewin as mentor of 21; living legacy of 37–41; as navigator in World War II 20; private practice of psychoanalysis 19; scientific research on social issues 21–23; social interdependence theory of 30–31; as social psychologist 21, 31; theory of constructive conflict resolution 33–35; theory of cooperation and competition 27–30; as tough-minded theorist 21, 22; transitioned to civilian life 26; on wartime devastation 20
Deutsch's Crude Law of Social Relations 34–35
DeVries, David 45–46, 129
Dewey, John 53; philosophy of active engagement 241; philosophy of education 167, 201–202, 204, 243
diffuse status characteristics 64
discipline referrals decline, with Kagan Structures 110–111
discovery learning 205
discovery-oriented science activities 134
discussion groups, cooperation versus competition in 234, 246
dispositional attributions 154–155
disruptive behavior decline, with Kagan Structures 110–111
dissonance theory 148
distributive justice, social psychology of 36
divided resources 56
doctoral courses and programs 224–225

educational interventions for equitable interactions 63, 64; *see also* Complex Instruction
Edwards, Keith 45–46
effective actions, of cooperators 27–28
ego-integrative motives 207
Eisenhower, Dwight 46
elementary schools: cooperative procedures implementation in 167; discipline referrals, drop in 110–111
Elementary Science Study (ESS) science curriculum 46
Elementary Secondary Education Act (1965) 184
equality principle 36
equal participation 11, 80, 81; in group problem-solving 97; reasons for gains produced by *119*, 120; in Solo Worksheet Work 95; in TSQA 94; in Turn-N-Talk group work 97
ethnically heterogeneous classrooms, group investigation in 176–177
Eugene OD project 186
Expectation States Theory *see* Status Characteristics Theory, experimental tests of
"expectation training" 64
experiential learning 45
experiential learning workshop 170–175; CL or GI related activity 172–173; conceptualization component of 172; design of 170; directions for cooperative task 174–175; experience component of 170–171; group formation variation in 170; planning component of 172; questions and students' answers 173–174; reflection component of 171–172
experimental schools 165–166
external motivation perspective 244

faculty development: for CL 219; in Lilly Pre-conferences 221; university 226
Fadell, Edward 201
FCAT *see* Florida Comprehensive Assessment Test
Festinger, Leon 147–149
Finding Out/Descubrimiento 65, 134
Find-My-Rule 86
Flashcard Game 87
Florida Comprehensive Assessment Test 107
formal cooperative learning 53–54, 236
"free rider" problem of group work 130
friendly directive leadership 246
friendship 6

game theory, as rigorous methodology 23–25
GI *see* Group Investigation
GI classroom, students' language in 175–176
GLACIE *see* Great Lakes Association for Cooperation in Education
goal interdependence 26; and actions 27–29, *28*, 33; influence on social interaction *30*, 30–31, 33; negative *28*, 30–31; positive 27, 30–31, 49; types of 49
goals in schools, establishing 185
graduate course for teachers 225–226; designing 223; offered at University of Maryland 223–224
graduate teaching 223–224
Great Lakes Association for Cooperation in Education 15
grouping 10
Group Investigation 134, 167, 238; attributes of 12; CL procedures 169; effects of CL in 175–178; experiential learning 169; interaction among learners 168; prerequisite for carrying 168; stages of 168, **168**; workshops for teachers of 169–175
groups: accountability 56; cohesion 133; development theories 188; discussion 8, 236; goals/rewards 8, 11, 130, 133, 136–137, 236; oral responses 96–97; problem-solving, guidelines for 203–204; processes in classroom 183, 187, 188; processing 57; work 6–7, 96–98; written responses 97–98
groupworthy tasks 69–70
Guide to Better Schools: Focus on Change (Trump) 184

Herrold, Kenneth 45
Hertz-Lazarowitz, Rachel 3
heterogeneous teams 88, 92
Hettleman, Buzzy 131
higher education, small-group learning in *see* small-group learning, in higher education
higher-order thinking skills 6, 219
Higher-Order Thinking Skills in Cooperative Learning Environments 219–220
high-low achievement gap reduction, with Kagan Structures 107
high school discipline referrals, drop in 111
homogeneous teams 88
HOTS *see* higher-order thinking skills
HOTSICLE *see* Higher-Order Thinking Skills in Cooperative Learning Environments
human cognition and motivation 148–149
Hunter, Madeline 226
hypocrisy paradigm 160

IASCE *see* International Association for the Study of Cooperation in Education
independent line of inquiry 254
individual accountability 8, 10, 54, 56, 80, 81, 130, 133, 136–137, 236, 242; in group problem-solving 97; reasons for gains produced by *119*, 119–120; in Solo Worksheet Work 95; in TSQA 94; in Turn-N-Talk group work 97
individual discovery 205
individualism: of Moore method 201; social orientation towards 117–118
individualistic learning 53, 57; individualistic social orientation 117–118; research reviews of 49–52
individualization with cooperative learning 131

inducibility 26
informal cooperative learning 54, 236
injustice/oppression, framework for considering 36–37
inner-city schools, successful approach for 131–132
inquiry learning 46–47
inquiry questions for CL: cognition development 250; implementation extent and type 249–250; and small-group learning connection 250–251
instructional material 12
Instructional Practices Guide (Mathematical Association of America) 214
instructor, role of 11
intellectual abilities 237, 244
intellectual challenge 241
intellectual heterogeneity, appreciating 68
intelligences 243–244
interactive methods of teaching 166
intergroup relations 6
intermittent pair discussion 54
International Association for the Study of Cooperation in Education 13–14, 254; books published by 14, 214–215; closing of 15; collaborative learning 216–217; conferences 14–15, 214–215; cooperative learning and 214–215; Davidson's personal reflections on 226–228; formation of 13; goals of 13–14; members, publications by 14; professional development for CL 219; regional associations 14–15, 215; Schmuck as Pioneer of 192–199; Schmuck's leadership in 190–192; theoretical issues and edited books 215–217
interpersonal and small group skills 56–57
interpersonal attraction and achievement, relationship between 50
interpersonal interdependence 26
Interpersonal Relations Assessment Technique 113
interpersonal relationships 50–51
interpersonal skills 6
interracial housing 35

intrinsic motivation perspective 244
IRAT *see* Interpersonal Relations Assessment Technique
Israel 166
Israel Educational Television 169
Israeli school supervisors 166, 167
"It's Academic!" tournaments 129

jigsaw classroom 134, 239; assembling jigsaw puzzle 152; attributes of 12; events popularizing 157–158; "expert" group 152; fifth-grade groups 152; impact on attributions 154–155; impact on scientific research 158; invention of 151–152; objectives of 151; positive change with 152–154, 156–157; resistance to adopt 156, 157; sharpening empathic ability 155–156; teacher-proof feature of 153–154; versus competitive classroom 155
Johnson, David W. 3, 18, 130, 235–236; efforts to reduce racism 49; focus on education 45; internship at NTL 45; involvement in civil rights movement 44–46; on Miles' findings 45; partnership with Roger 47; position at University of Minnesota 45; research reviews of cooperative learning 49–52; Russell Bull Scholarship awarded to 44; studies on Black history classes 45; teaching procedures for cooperative learning 53–57; theory-based approach to cooperative learning 48; training program for cooperative learning 58–59
Johnson, Roger T. 3, 18, 130, 235–236; involvement in cooperative learning 46–47; partnership with David Johnson 47; position at University of Minnesota 46; research reviews of cooperative learning 49–52; teaching procedures for cooperative learning 53–57; training program for cooperative learning 58–59
joint rewards 56
junior high, small-group learning in 207; cooperative behavior guidelines 207, 241; curriculum development 208–209; NCTM 208
justice, relationship with conflict 37

Kagan Associate Trainer Program 101–102
"Kagan Boot Camp" 101
Kagan Coaching 102–103, *103*, 107
Kagan Cooperative Learning 123, 237–238; applied situationism as 78–79; attributes of 12; classbuilding 90; definition of 78; management techniques 89; PIES principles 80–81, *82*, 92; promoting cooperation 80; social skills 91; supporting 121–122; teacher resources 103–104; teacher training 100–104; teambuilding 89–90; teams 88–89; workshop 105; *see also* Kagan Structures
Kagan Professional Development 101–102
Kagan Publishing 103
Kagan Publishing and Professional Development 86
Kagan School Trainer Program 101
Kagan, Spencer 3, 237; *see also* Kagan Cooperative Learning
Kagan Structures 81, 83–88, 98–100; academic achievement gains with 104–107; as activity generators 85; adoption at Mills Hill School 106; basic formula 85; benefits for students with disabilities 108–109; benefits for teacher 85–86; Continuous Simultaneous RoundTable 99–100; decline in disruptive behaviors with 110–111; decline in school violence with 116–117; definition of 84–85; Find-My-Rule 86; Flashcard Game 87; functions of 86–87, *87*, 92; importance of contextual elements for 91–93, *92*; improved race relations with 113–116; learning to drive analogous to 86; Logic Line-Ups 86, 87; Numbered Heads Together 81, 83, *84*; oral responses 98–99; Paired Heads Together 83; Paraphrase Passport 86–87; prosocial behaviors with 111–113; RallyRobin 85, 86, 98–99; reasons for gains produced by 118–121; reduced achievement gaps with 107–108; repeatable and content-free 85–86; revisions 81, 83; RoundRobin 86, 90, 91; Sage-N-Scribe 99; selection of 87; simultaneous response modes 83; Spend-A-Buck 109; as stand-alone instructional strategies 91; StandUp—HandUp—PairUp 89, 92; Stir-the-Class 83; student satisfaction with 109; Talking Chips 87; Team Statements 90; Timed Pair Share 81, 86, 91, 92, 98–99; time on task of students using 109–110; Traveling Heads Together 83; written responses 99–100
Kent OD project 186
knowledge 167

language arts achievement 108–109
language, in GI classroom 175–176
learning activity 9
learning tasks 4, 66; design of 69–71; directions for 174
"Learning Together and Alone" method 47–48
Learning Together approach 8, 235; attributes of 11; origin of 44
lecturing 59
Lewin, Kurt 21, 26
Lichtenberg, Georg C. 165
Lilly Conferences on College Teaching 217; faculty development in 221; presentations at 221–222
Logic Line-Ups 86, 87
low-status students, assigning competence to 68

MAA *see* Mathematical Association of America
MAACIE *see* Mid-Atlantic Association for Cooperation in Education
Madden, Nancy A. 3, 236; *see also* Student Team Learning
Madison Camelview Elementary School 111–112
"make and take" teacher training procedures 53
ManageMats 103
Maryland Middle School Association 220
Maslow, Abraham 147, 150
mastery teaching and CL 226

Mathematical Association of America 207, 210, 214
mathematics education community 206–207
mathematics faculty: resistance to CL 210–211; and staff development for CL 211–212
math instruction: individualism of Moore method of 201; mathematical approaches 210; mathematics curriculum book 213–214; *see also* small-group learning, in mathematics
MD-ICCCR *see* Morton Deutsch International Center for Cooperation and Conflict Resolution
Mead, Margaret 253
meetings 185
meta-analyses of cooperative learning 50, 247
Mexican-American adolescents 64
Mid-Atlantic Association for Cooperation in Education 15, 215
Miel, Alice 167
Miles, Matthew 45
Mills Hill School, adoption of Kagan Structures at 106
mirror neurons 121
Moore method 201, 205
Morton Deutsch International Center for Cooperation and Conflict Resolution 38
motivation 133; and achievement, relationship between 50; in CL 244; external 244; human cognition and 148–149; intrinsic 244
motivational factors, in small-group learning 207, 241
motives 207
Multicultural Improvement of Cognitive Abilities (MICA) project 65
multiple-abilities intervention 68
multiple intelligences, theory of 243–244
"Multiunit Elementary School Project" 186
"mutual adaptation" 72
mutual gain 23
mutual interdependence *see* positive interdependence
mutual loss 23
myelination 121–122

National Council of Teachers of Mathematics 72, 207; Curriculum and Evaluation Standards for School Mathematics 209; curriculum design process 208; publications 208
National Defense Educational Act (1958) 184
National Training Laboratory 45
Navarrete, Cecilia 65
NCTM *see* National Council of Teachers of Mathematics
need principle 36
negative attitudes 27, 29
negative interdependence 245–246
Network of International Cooperative Learning Educators and Enthusiasts 253
NExT (New Experiences in Teaching) Project 211–212
NICLEE *see* Network of International Cooperative Learning Educators and Enthusiasts
non-CL students, STEM courses for 6
non-representative sample 94–95
Numbered Heads Together 81, 83, 84, 104–105, 107

OD *see* organization development
Oliver Brown v. the Board of Education of Topeka Kansas decision 63, 149, 187
online learning 222, 251–253; active engagement in 253; adoption after coronavirus pandemic 251; asynchronous 251–252; development work for 252–253; implementation issues 252; platforms 252; presentation phase of 252; student activity phase of 252; study of 253; synchronous 252; traditional paradigm for 251–252
oppression *see* injustice/oppression, framework for considering
Oregon OD group intervention 184; effectiveness testing of 186–187; subsystem capabilities aimed by 185
organization development 239; books and research reports on 183–184; and CL, relationships between 189–190; intervention strategies

184–187; reasons for introducing 184; reforms initiating 184
Original Lilly Conference on College and University Teaching 221
other-gain/self-loss 23

Paired Heads Together 83
Paraphrase Passport 86–87
Parker, Francis 53
PBL *see* problem-based learning
peace psychology and social justice 35–37
peer cooperation and communication 5
personal support system 56
perspective-taking 11
PET scans of brain 244, *245*
PIES analysis: of Continuous Simultaneous RoundTable 99–100; of group problem-solving 97–98; of RoundRobin 98–99; of Solo Worksheet Work 95–96; of Teacher-Student Question-Answer 94; of Turn-N-Talk 96–97
PIES principles 80–81, 82, 92, 237; critical questions for 80–81, 82; reasons for gains from 118–121; structures modified to implement 81, 83; Timed Pair Share 92, 92
positive attitudes 27, 29, 52
positive interdependence 8, 18, 54, 55–56, 80, 81, 242, 245–246; alternative techniques to foster 10; in cooperative learning 12–13; in group problem-solving 97; reasons for gains produced by 118–119, *119*; in Solo Worksheet Work 95; in TSQA 94; in Turn-N-Talk group work 96–97
positive outcomes 120–121, 246–247
positive referrals 112, 113
postsecondary students, STEM courses for 6
preinstructional decisions 53–54
preinstructional pair discussion 54
prejudice: Aronson's personal journey with 146–147; assumptions 150; conditions needed to reduce 45, 49
Prisoner's Dilemma game 23–24
problem-based learning 3
problem solving 205
procedural justice 36
procedural memory, social skills in 91

professional associations 206–207
professional development: for CL 219; teacher education and 225; training program 211–212
Program for Complex Instruction at Stanford 71, 72
project-based learning 130
promotive interaction 56
prosocial behaviors with Kagan Structures: decline in disruptive behavior 112–113; inverse relation with disruptive behaviors 111–112; progressive improvement 113
psychological health 50–51

race: achievement gap reduction 107–108; impact on participation and influence 64
race relations improvement, with Kagan Structures 113–116; friendship choices 114–115; Gutman analysis 114; IRAT administration 114; social relations 115–116; versus instruction produced racial self-segregation 114–115
racism and conflict 45, 63
racist attitudes 63, 64
RallyRobin 85, 86, 98–99
random teams 88, 89
RCGD *see* Research Center for Group Dynamics
Reagan, Ronald 59
reasoning 6
re-evaluation counseling 215
reform mathematics 209
regional associations 14–15, 254
Regional Training Center 223
Research Center for Group Dynamics 20
retributive and reparative justice 37
retrograde memory enhancement 83
Riverside Cooperative Learning Project 113
Rogers, Carl 187
role: assignments 8; modeling 64
RoundRobin 86, 90, 91
RTC *see* Regional Training Center

Sage-N-Scribe 99
San Francisco Unified School District 72
satisfaction with CL 247

Schmuck, Richard Allen 3, 13, 239–241; on becoming IASCE Pioneer 192–199; books published by 183; leadership in IASCE 190–192; on link between OD and CL 187–189; OD work in schools 183–187; partnered with wife 187; specialties of 183; work in group processes 187–189
scholarship of teaching and learning 226
school desegregation 150–151, 156; benefits of 63; challenges 150–151; conditions to be met for 63; effect on minority kids 150
school districts, OD project in 186–187
school violence 116–117
science teaching, revolution in 46
segregation, US Supreme Court decision on 63, 149
self-confidence 6
"self-contained" classroom 184
self-esteem 6
self-gain/other-loss 23
self-paced individual instruction, movement toward 207
semantic memory 91
sense of justice 36
separate-but-equal policies 187
SFA *see* Success for All
Sharan, Shlomo 3, 166–169, 167, 170, 234
Sharan, Yael 3, 166–169, 170, 234
simultaneous interaction 11, 80, 88; in group problem-solving 98; reasons for gains produced by *119*, 120; in Solo Worksheet Work 96; in TSQA 94; in Turn-N-Talk group work 97
situationism 78–79
Slavin, Robert E. 3, 236; *see also* Student Team Learning
small-group learning, in higher education 217–218
small-group learning, in mathematics 3, 241–242; ancient historical roots of 243; common elements of 242; conference on 209–210; course design 241; effect on student achievement 212–213; elements in design of 241; faculty and staff development for 211–212; faculty resistance to 210–211; genesis of 201–202; in junior high/middle school 207–209; leadership and management functions 7; motivational factors for 207; NCTM standards 209; projects on 209–210, 213–214; publications on 205, 210; rationale for 202–203; research on 212–213; small-group discovery model 203–205; support through professional associations 206–207
small groups discovery learning 12, 134, 207; interaction 9, 242; processes 12; skills 56–57; work methods 64
Small Group Teaching (Sharan & Sharan) 166
social acceptance 6
social change movements 205
social cohesiveness theories 133–134
social control, primary source of 201–202
social interdependence theory *30*, 30–31, 52, **52**, 57, 237, 245–246
social issues, scientific research on 21–23
social justice and peace psychology 35–37
social motives 207
social orientations, one-sided training program in 117–118
social pain 73
social-psychological processes 26, 27, 33
Social Psychology Network 157, 158
social science theory 48
social skills 56–57, 91
Solo Worksheet Work 95–96
SoTL *see* scholarship of teaching and learning
SPN *see* Social Psychology Network
sporting contests 33
STAD *see* Student Teams Academic Divisions
staff development for CL 211–212
StandUp—HandUp—PairUp 89, 92
Status Characteristics Theory, experimental tests of 64
status treatments 11
STEM courses 6, 213
stereotypes 151
Stir-the-Class 83

STL *see* Student Team Learning
Structural Approach to cooperative learning *see* Kagan Cooperative Learning
structured boredom, in TSQA 95
student achievement 236; in lecturing versus CL 221; small-group learning in mathematics affecting 212–213; *see also* academic achievement
students: attitude 109, 204, 206; energy and affiliative needs 246; retention versus dropping out of higher education 248; satisfaction measures and Kagan Structures 109; with disabilities, Kagan Structures benefits for 108–109
student-selected teams 88
student–student interaction: cooperative social orientation 117; effect on achievement 134; and learning goals, link between 49; promotive 56
student teaching and professional development for teachers 225–226
Student Team Learning 8, 142, 236; attributes of 11; definition of 128; group rewards and individual accountability 136–137; personal history of 128–132; programs 137–140
Student Teams Academic Divisions 128, 137, 176, 177; characteristics of 129, 138; creation of 129; implementation support to teachers 131
Student Team Writing 128
STW *see* Student Team Writing
substitutability 26
Success for All 128, 131–132; attributes of 12; program components 141; research on 141; theory of action for 140–141
synchronous online cooperative learning 222, 252

TAI *see* Team-Assisted Individualization
Talking Chips 87
"task specialization" methods 134
TBL *see* team-based learning
teacher education: on functions of structures 86; and organizational support 70; and professional development 225; team 167 teacher education project for CL 234; duration 169; to effect change in teaching 167; experiential learning 169; interaction among learners 168; prerequisite for carrying 168; rationale for 167; stages of 168, **168**; workshops 169–175
teachers: attitudes toward CL 175, 177; CL effects on 247–248; CL strategies use in classrooms 188–189; leadership and management functions 203; professional development, prevailing model of 166; status interventions 68–69; training program for cooperative learning 58–59
teacher's role 7, 12–13, 236; basic elements of cooperation 55–57; in constructive controversy 54–55; in cooperative base groups 54; in formal cooperative learning 53–54; in informal cooperative learning 54
Teacher-Student Question-Answer: Numbered Heads Together for 104–105; PIES analysis of 94; problems with structuring using 94–95; steps of 93–94; ubiquitous, brain processes of 121–122
teacher training, in Structural Approach: coaching 102–103, *103*; Kagan School Trainer 100–102; versus cooperative learning 100; workshops 102
Team-Assisted Individualization 128, 131, 139
team-based learning 3
team-building 11, 89–90, 105, 116
Teams-Games-Tournament 128, 129, 138–139
Team Statements 90
team teaching 184
team types and Structural Approach 88–89
TGT *see* Teams-Games-Tournament
theory-based approach to cooperative learning 48–49
thinking 6
Timed Pair Share 81, 86, 91, 92, 98–99
time on task, using Kagan Structures 109–110
traditional instructional strategies 93–96; oral responses 93–95; written responses 95–96

Traditional Q&A versus Kagan Structures: high-low achievement gap with 107; time on task of students using 109–110
transaction model of CL 166
transformation model of CL 166
Traveling Heads Together 83
true cooperative learning 80–81
Trump, J. Lloyd 184
TSQA *see* Teacher-Student Question-Answer
Turn-N-Talk 81, 96–97
turn-taking 91

undergraduate education, principles of good practice in 248
United Nations 26
United States Civil Rights Commission 157
university faculty development 226
University of Maryland 209, 226
US Supreme Court decisions 63, 149, 189

video conferencing 252
violence in schools *see* school violence
Vygotsky, Lev 243

Warren, Earl 149
Watson, Goodwin 44
W-C instruction *see* Whole-Class instruction
WestEd's regional laboratory 71
whole-class discovery 205
Whole-Class instruction 176, 177
whole-school participation, workshops for 170
workshops 169; for experiential learning 170–175; faculty development 219; staff development 212; for whole-school participation 170
WorldLab 129
World War II 26
writing-based learning 130

ZOOM 252